West's Law School
Advisory Board

2005 SUPPLEMENT
TO
CRIMINAL LAW
CASES, MATERIALS AND PROBLEMS

By

Russell L. Weaver
Professor of Law & Distinguished University Scholar
University of Louisville
Louis D. Brandeis School of Law

Leslie W. Abramson
Frost Brown Todd Professor of Law
University of Louisville
Louis D. Brandeis School of Law

John M. Burkoff
Professor of Law
University of Pittsburgh
School of Law

Catherine Hancock
Professor of Law
Tulane University
School of Law

AMERICAN CASEBOOK SERIES®

Mat #40383722

© West, a Thomson business, 2001–2004
© 2005 Thomson/West
       610 Opperman Drive
       P.O. Box 64526
       St. Paul, MN 55164–0526
       1–800–328–9352

Printed in the United States of America

ISBN 0–314–16223–2

 *TEXT IS PRINTED ON 10% POST CONSUMER RECYCLED PAPER*

Table of Contents

*

Table of Cases

The principal cases are in bold type. Cases cited or discussed in the text are in roman type. References are to pages. Cases cited in principal cases and within other quoted materials are not included.

2005 SUPPLEMENT
TO
CRIMINAL LAW
CASES, MATERIALS AND PROBLEMS

*

Chapter 2

THE REQUIREMENT OF A "VOLUNTARY ACT"

A. THE ACT REQUIREMENT

On p. 29, add a new problem at the end of the problems:

10. In 2003, New Jersey adopted a new law which prohibits drivers from operating automobiles while drowsy. The law authorizes a conviction of vehicular homicide, punishable by up to 10 years in jail and a $100,000 fine, for anyone who causes a deadly car accident due to sleepiness. Was the new law needed? In other words, would it have been possible to convict a motorist who grew drowsy and fell asleep of homicide without the law?

B. OMISSIONS

On p. 46, at the end of the problems, add the following new problem:

11. A stay-at-home mother called 911 just after midnight and stated that "I've just killed my boys." She also stated that God ordered her to do it. When they arrived at the scene, police found a 6 year-old and 8 year-old boy in the front yard with their skulls smashed. They also found an alive 14 month old baby in his crib with a fractured skull. The evidence revealed that the mother had suffered from delusional psychotic disorder and had been through three major psychotic episodes over the prior three years.

The evidence reveals that the father was aware of the psychotic episodes, but nonetheless left the children with the mother. On the night of the murders, the father was asleep and heard nothing. Did the father have a duty to protect the children against the mother? Did he breach that duty?

Chapter 4

CAUSATION

On p. 130, add a new problem at the end of the problems:

8. In 2003, in Connecticut, a child committed suicide and his single mother was charged with contributing to his death. The evidence reveals that the mother kept a filthy home. The house had a foul odor, it was filled with so much debris that it was virtually impossible to move around the home, and the kitchen was full of dirty dishes and evidenced stains and spills. The evidence also revealed that the mother failed to wash the child's clothes and failed to work with the child on his hygiene. As a result, the child had bad breath and body odor. He was constantly teased and sometimes attacked by other children in his school, but the mother failed to get him medical or psychological help. The boy eventually killed himself by hanging himself with a necktie in a closet. Was the mother a "cause" of the death?

Chapter 6

ATTEMPT

B. ACTUS REUS

On p. 199, add a new problem at the end of the problems:

2.   The police observed defendant acting suspiciously in front of a bank. Police questioned him. Following a consensual search, police found a note in defendant's backpack which stated: "I want $10,000 in $100 bills. Don't push no buttons, or I'll shot (sic) you." Did defendant commit the actus reus of attempt?

Chapter 8

HOMICIDE

On p. 287, at the end of the problems, please add the following new problem:

7. During the Summer of 2005, a former Klu Klux Klan member, Edgar Ray Killen, was convicted of killing three civil rights workers in 1964. The evidence shows that the victims were brutally beaten and shot, and that their bodies were buried in an earthen dam. The case was complicated by the age of the evidence and fading witness recollections. It was also complicated by the fact that no witness was able to positively place Killen at the scene of the crime. The trial ended with a conviction of manslaughter rather than murder. Given the brutal nature of the killings, how do you explain a conviction for manslaughter?

Chapter 11

JUSTIFICATION DEFENSES

On p. 479, at the end, add the following new section:

G. CONSTITUTIONAL DEFENSES

In recent years, there have been constitutional challenges to various sexual offense statutes. In *Lawrence v. Texas*, 539 U.S. 588 (2003), the Court struck down a Texas statute prohibiting "deviate sexual intercourse" that made it a crime for two persons of the same sex to engage in certain intimate sexual conduct. In doing so, the Court stated that:

> [This case involves] two adults who, with full and mutual consent from each other, engaged in sexual practices common to a homosexual lifestyle. The petitioners are entitled to respect for their private lives. The State cannot demean their existence or control their destiny by making their private sexual conduct a crime. Their right to liberty under the Due Process Clause gives them the full right to engage in their conduct without intervention of the government. "It is a promise of the Constitution that there is a realm of personal liberty which the government may not enter." *Casey, supra,* at 847. The Texas statute furthers no legitimate state interest which can justify its intrusion into the personal and private life of the individual.

Justice Scalia dissented:

> Our opinions applying the doctrine known as "substantive due process" hold that the Due Process Clause prohibits States from infringing *fundamental* liberty interests, unless the infringement is narrowly tailored to serve a compelling state interest. *Washington v. Glucksberg,* 521 U.S., at 721. We have held repeatedly, in cases the Court today does not overrule, that *only* fundamental rights qualify for this so-called "heightened scrutiny" protection—that is, rights which are " 'deeply rooted in this Nation's history and tradition,' "See *Reno v. Flores,* 507 U.S. 292 (1993). All other liberty interests may be abridged or abrogated pursuant to a validly enacted

state law if that law is rationally related to a legitimate state interest.

Bowers held, first, that criminal prohibitions of homosexual sodomy are not subject to heightened scrutiny because they do not implicate a "fundamental right" under the Due Process Clause. Noting that "[p]roscriptions against that conduct have ancient roots," that "[s]odomy was a criminal offense at common law and was forbidden by the laws of the original 13 States when they ratified the Bill of Rights," *ibid.*, and that many States had retained their bans on sodomy, *Bowers* concluded that a right to engage in homosexual sodomy was not " 'deeply rooted in this Nation's history and tradition.' "

The Court today does not overrule this holding. Not once does it describe homosexual sodomy as a "fundamental right" or a "fundamental liberty interest," nor does it subject the Texas statute to strict scrutiny. Instead, having failed to establish that the right to homosexual sodomy is " 'deeply rooted in this Nation's history and tradition,' " the Court concludes that the application of Texas's statute to petitioners' conduct fails the rational-basis test, and overrules *Bowers*' holding to the contrary. . . .

The Texas statute undeniably seeks to further the belief of its citizens that certain forms of sexual behavior are "immoral and unacceptable,"—the same interest furthered by criminal laws against fornication, bigamy, adultery, adult incest, bestiality, and obscenity. *Bowers* held that this *was* a legitimate state interest. The Court today reaches the opposite conclusion. The Texas statute, it says, "furthers *no legitimate state interest* which can justify its intrusion into the personal and private life of the individual." The Court embraces instead Justice STEVENS' declaration in his *Bowers* dissent, that "the fact that the governing majority in a State has traditionally viewed a particular practice as immoral is not a sufficient reason for upholding a law prohibiting the practice." This effectively decrees the end of all morals legislation. If, as the Court asserts, the promotion of majoritarian sexual morality is not even a *legitimate* state interest, none of the above-mentioned laws can survive rational-basis review.

In *PHE, Inc. v. State*, 877 So.2d 1244 (Miss. 2004), the Mississippi Supreme Court upheld a law prohibiting "knowingly selling, advertising, publishing or exhibiting any three-dimensional device designed or marketed as useful primarily for the stimulation of human genitalia" ("sexual devices") is illegal. The court stated:

"The positive law of this state affords each person a substantial zone of freedom which, at his election, he may keep private. This zone surrounds person and place and without his consent may not be invaded by other persons . . . or by the state." *Pro-Choice Miss. v. Fordice*, 716 So.2d 645, 654 (Miss.1998). . . . The right to privacy includes the right to "autonomous bodily integrity." *Pro-Choice*, 716

So.2d at 653. "[A] right to privacy exists for citizens and that right entitles citizens 'to be left alone.' " *Miller v. State,* 636 So.2d 391, 394 (Miss.1994) (quoting Warren and Brandeis, *The Right to Privacy,* 4 Harv. L.Rev. 193, 193, 195 (1890)). "It requires little awareness of personal prejudice and human nature to know that, generally speaking, no aspects of life [are] more personal and private than those having to do with one's sexual organs and reproductive system." *Young,* 572 So.2d at 382. "The right to privacy is so personal that its protection does not require the giving of a reason for its exercise. That one is a person, unique and individual, is enough." *In re Brown,* 478 So.2d at 1040.

We find that there is no "independent fundamental right of access to purchase [sexual devices]," just as the United States Supreme Court found that there was no independent fundamental right of access to purchase contraceptives. *Carey v. Population Servs. Int'l,* 431 U.S. 678 (1977). However, the plaintiffs argue that "such access is essential to the exercise of the constitutionally protected right [of privacy to engage in adult consensual sexual activities]."

People who are sexually dysfunctional (presumably those people who cannot achieve sexual enjoyment and fulfillment without a sexual device) should be treated by a physician or a psychologist. Sexual dysfunction may be caused by medicinal side effects, diabetes, hormonal problems, endocrine problems, cardiovascular illness, neurological impairments, psychological problems or hypertension. Miss.Code Ann. § 97–29–107(1)(b) (Rev.2000) expressly provides that physicians and psychologists may prescribe sexual devices for their patients, and the patients may purchase the sexual devices from the physicians and psychologists. The novelty and gag gifts which the vendor plaintiffs sell have no medical purpose.

The only conclusion we can reach is that the sale of or access to sexual devices sold by novelty stores is not protected under the right to privacy guaranteed under the Mississippi Constitution.

Chapter 12

EXCUSES

B. INSANITY

1. M'NAGHTEN AND THE IRRESISTIBLE IMPULSE TEST

On p. 492, before the problems, add the following new note:

8. In *Sell v. United States*, 539 U.S. 166 (2003), the Court held that the Constitution allows the government to administer antipsychotic drugs involuntarily to a mentally ill criminal defendant—in order to render that defendant competent to stand trial for serious, but nonviolent, crimes—in limited circumstances. Relying on its prior decisions in *Washington v. Harper*, 494 U.S. 210 (1990) and *Riggins v. Nevada,* 504 U.S. 127 (1992), the Court stated that:

> In *Harper,* this Court recognized that an individual has a "significant" constitutionally protected "liberty interest" in "avoiding the unwanted administration of antipsychotic drugs." [In] *Riggins,* the Court [suggested] that, in principle, forced medication in order to render a defendant competent to stand trial for murder was constitutionally permissible.... These two cases, *Harper* and *Riggins,* indicate that the Constitution permits the Government involuntarily to administer antipsychotic drugs to a mentally ill defendant facing serious criminal charges in order to render that defendant competent to stand trial, but only if the treatment is medically appropriate, is substantially unlikely to have side effects that may undermine the fairness of the trial, and, taking account of less intrusive alternatives, is necessary significantly to further important governmental trial-related interests.

> This standard will permit involuntary administration of drugs solely for trial competence purposes in certain instances. But those instances may be rare. That is because the standard says or fairly implies the following: First, a court must find that *important* governmental interests are at stake. The Government's interest in bringing to trial an individual accused of a serious crime is important.... Second, the court must conclude that involuntary medication will *significantly further* those concomitant state interests. It must find that administration of the drugs is substantially likely to render the defendant competent to stand trial.... Third, the court must conclude that involuntary medi-

8

cation is *necessary* to further those interests.... Fourth, [the] court must conclude that administration of the drugs is *medically appropriate, i.e.*, in the patient's best medical interest in light of his medical condition . . . . .

[In order to make this evaluation, the court should] focus upon such questions as: Why is it medically appropriate forcibly to administer antipsychotic drugs to an individual who (1) is *not* dangerous *and* (2) *is* competent to make up his own mind about treatment? Can bringing such an individual to trial *alone* justify in whole (or at least in significant part) administration of a drug that may have adverse side effects, including side effects that may to some extent impair a defense at trial? [Courts must also consider w]hether a particular drug will tend to sedate a defendant, interfere with communication with counsel, prevent rapid reaction to trial developments, or diminish the ability to express emotions are matters important in determining the permissibility of medication to restore competence, but not necessarily relevant when dangerousness is primarily at issue. We cannot tell whether the side effects of antipsychotic medication were likely to undermine the fairness of a trial in Sell's case.

2. *OTHER TESTS*

On p. 511, at the end of the problems, add the following new problem:

12. A stay-at-home mother called 911 just after midnight and stated that "I've just killed my boys." She also stated that God ordered her to do it. When they arrived at the scene, police found a 6 year-old and 8 year-old boy in the front yard with their skulls smashed. They also found an alive 14 month old baby in his crib with a fractured skull. The evidence revealed that the mother had suffered from delusional psychotic disorder and had been through three major psychotic episodes over the prior three years. Does the fact that the mother had the awareness to contact police after the killings suggest that she was not insane?

Chapter 14

SENTENCING

Ordinarily it is a relatively simple matter to ascertain a client's potential "exposure" to a given criminal provision. All crimes contain an express or implied penalty. In the vast majority of cases, the actual punishment is contained in the definition of the offense by reference to statutes defining ranges of imprisonment terms and fines. In some instances, a punishment for a violation of one statute is found by reference to the "class" of the crime.

The possible punishment for each particular offense can be ascertained with relative ease. Where certain enhanced punishments are being sought by the government, pretrial notice will afford knowledge of this possibility. Nevertheless, simply because a punishment is set forth in the statute does not mean that a defendant will always be subject to these penalties. There are certain statutory and constitutional limitations on sentencing which may tend to lessen a particular penalty. In general, these include limitations on resentencing, alterations in the punishment, and certain notice rules. While it is seldom successful, counsel may attack a sentence which constitutes cruel and unusual punishment, violates double jeopardy prohibitions, or violates concepts of equal protection. See. e.g., *Hodgson v. Vermont*, 168 U.S. 262 (1897).

A. NONCAPITAL SENTENCING ALTERNATIVES

Fines and Costs. The punishment for a violation of the law may include a fine in addition to or, in some cases, instead of imprisonment. Due to certain constitutional limitations, a person may not usually be confined for failure to pay the fine or costs.

The general authority for the imposition of fines for violations of the criminal statutes is found in the statutes themselves. The procedure for the collection of fines is governed largely by statute. The controlling question is whether the defendant may be incarcerated for failure to pay the fine. Fines cannot be imposed upon any person determined by the court to be statutorily indigent. While incarceration is still a possibility for an intentional refusal to pay, the court must explore alternative means of satisfaction of the fine. *Bearden v. Georgia*, 461 U.S. 660

(1983). In instances where the defendant desires to appeal a fine, the trial judge may grant a stay of the payment and require bail.

In some jurisdictions, the sentencing court may issue a criminal garnishment order for all fines, court costs, restitution, and reimbursement charges, combining them in a single order of garnishment. Any convicted person owing fines, court costs, restitution, or reimbursement before or after his or her release from incarceration is subject to a lien upon his or her interest, present or future, in any real property.

The costs associated with litigation are also governed by statute. It appears that the defendant is responsible for the payment of costs only upon conviction. However, the defendant cannot be incarcerated for failure to pay costs. *Bearden v. Georgia*, 461 U.S. 660 (1983). Moreover, court costs cannot be imposed upon an indigent defendant.

Recently, states have begun to provide that the sentencing court may order a person incarcerated to reimburse the state or local government for the costs of incarceration. The sentencing court determines the amount to be paid based on the actual per diem, per person, cost of incarceration, the cost of medical services provided to a prisoner less any copayment paid by the prisoner, and the prisoner's ability to pay all or part of the incarceration costs.

Restitution. By statute, a person convicted of certain types of crimes such as a crime involving the taking of, injury to, or destruction of property can be ordered to restore the property or its value to the victim. An order of restitution may defer payment until the person is released from custody. However, the decision by a trial judge not to use this remedy does not deprive the victim of a civil action for the injury sustained.

Forfeiture or Confiscation of Property. A person convicted of certain types of crimes such as controlled substances, intoxicating liquors, eavesdropping devices, deadly weapons, gambling devices, and obscene matter can be ordered to forfeit property used in connection with commission of the offense. Forfeitures, as payments in kind, are "fines" if they constitute punishment for an offense. *Austin v. United States*, 509 U.S. 602 (1993). Thus, forfeiture of vehicles and realty used to facilitate commission of drug trafficking is allowed, because it serves as a punishment under the Eighth Amendment's Excessive Fines Clause.

In *Alexander v. United States*, 509 U.S. 544 (1993), as part of his punishment for violating federal obscenity laws and RICO, the trial court ordered the defendant to forfeit his businesses and almost $9 million acquired through racketeering activity. The Court found that the forfeiture was a permissible criminal punishment, not a prior restraint on speech, because it merely prevented him from financing his activities with assets derived from his prior racketeering offenses. RICO is oblivious to the expressive or nonexpressive nature of the assets forfeited. Petitioner's assets were forfeited because they were directly related to past racketeering violations.

Generally, under the Due Process Clause, the Government must provide notice and a meaningful opportunity to be heard before seizing real property subject to civil forfeiture. *United States v. James Daniel Good Real Property*, 510 U.S. 43 (1993). However, due process does not preclude forfeiture of property used for unlawful purposes by a defendant but which belongs to another person. *Bennis v. Michigan*, 516 U.S. 442 (1996).

Probation and Conditional Discharge. Probation is granted when the sentencing court suspends the execution of a sentence of imprisonment conditionally and releases the defendant under the supervision of a probation officer. Some jurisdictions grant "conditional discharge" when a defendant is released without supervision. These forms of release are regarded as "legislative clemencies," not constitutional rights, granted as a matter of grace.

Eligibility for probation or conditional discharge usually prohibit their use after convictions for such offenses as a capital offense, recidivist status, serious felonies involving the use of a firearm or while the defendant was already on probation of conditional discharge from another felony conviction, or a sex-related offense against a minor. Otherwise, many states require that a defendant be considered for probation or conditional discharge unless the court finds imprisonment to be necessary to protect the public.

Conditions of release are usually stated in writing and furnished to the defendant. All defendant are required to refrain from committing another offense, as well as other conditions such as restitution which the court deems to be reasonably necessary to enable the defendant to lead a law-abiding life. In addition to reasonable conditions, a court may require a defendant to submit to a period of imprisonment in the local jail at times to be determined by the court. This is known as a "split sentence." The court may initiate proceedings to determine whether to revoke the release because of a violation of its conditions.

Home Incarceration. Many states now permit defendants convicted of minor offenses to serve all or part of a definite term of imprisonment under conditions of home incarceration. Some provisions prohibit home incarceration for minor offenders with outstanding charges or a recent violent crime conviction. The sentencing judge may have discretion to order home incarceration as another type of "split sentence" for the defendant to serve part of the sentence at home and part of it in the local jail. As with probation and conditional discharge, a defendant under home incarceration signs an agreement listing all of the conditions for confinement.

Continuous Confinement for a Definite Term or Indeterminate Term. An indeterminate sentence is set within statutory limits, with the parole board having responsibility for deciding precisely when the defendant is eligible for early release. About two-thirds of the states use indeterminate sentences. A determinate sentence (also known as "flat time,"is for a fixed period without the possibility of early release, but supervision often accompanies that release.

B. DEATH AS A PUNISHMENT

1. *THE PROBLEM OF FAIRNESS*

The death penalty is currently in effect in about three fourths of the states and the federal system. Methods of execution include electrocution, firing squad, gas chamber, hanging, and lethal injection. In *Furman v. Georgia*, 408 U.S. 238 (1972), the Court found that Georgia had not applied the death penalty fairly. Statistics on executions showed that black males who committed murder were executed far more frequently than white males, even though black males were not committing most of the crimes. The Court stated that capital punishment cannot be used unless the states can prove that it is being applied fairly.

Since *Furman*, even those supportive of the death penalty as an appropriate punishment have become concerned about the manner in which it is used. Responding to growing criticism about the administration of the death penalty, a dozen states have commissioned studies of their penalty system to examine racial and geographic disparities within states, as well as serious problems with court-appointed lawyers and the appeals process. For example, Illinois Governor George H. Ryan appointed the Illinois Commission on Capital Punishment in March, 2000 after declaring a moratorium on the execution of death row inmates two months earlier. The Commission's report issued two years later recommended 85 reforms to the capital punishment system in Illinois. The report has fueled a nationwide debate on the death penalty. Before leaving office in January, 2003, Governor Ryan commuted the death sentences of 167 of the state's death row inmates, and pardon four inmates completely. The commission recommendations included:

- Creating a statewide review panel to conduct a pre-trial review of prosecutorial decisions to seek capital punishment. The panel would be comprised of four prosecutors and a retired judge.
- Significantly reducing the current list of death eligibility factors from twenty to five including: murder of a peace officer or firefighter; murder in a correctional facility; the murder of two or more persons; the intentional murder of a person involving torture; and any murder committed by a suspected felon in order to obstruct the justice system.
- No person may be sentenced to death based solely on uncorroborated single eyewitness or accomplice testimony or the uncorroborated testimony of jail house informants.
- Recommending other reforms concerning the use of jail house informants who purport to have information about the case or statements allegedly made by the defendant, including requiring a preliminary hearing to be conducted by the court as to the reliability of such witnesses and their proposed testimony, full-disclosure of benefits conferred for such testimony, early disclo-

sure to the defense about the background of such witnesses and special cautionary instructions to the jury.

- Videotaping the entire interrogation of homicide suspects at a police station, and not merely the confession.

- Allowing trial judges to concur or reverse a jury's death sentence verdict. This will allow the trial judge to take into account potential improper influences such as passion and prejudice that may have influenced a jury's verdict, consider potential residual doubt about the defendant's absolute guilt, consider trial strategies of counsel, credibility of witnesses and the actual presentation of evidence, which may differ from what was anticipated in making pre-trial rulings in either admitting or excluding evidence.

- The Illinois Supreme Court should review all death sentences to determine if the sentence is excessive or disproportionate to the penalty imposed in similar cases, if death was the appropriate sentence given aggravating and mitigating factors and whether the sentence was imposed due to some arbitrary factor.

- Support the Supreme Court's recommendation for a capital case trial bar and requiring judges to be pre-certified before presiding over capital cases. As part of regular training for judges and counsel, as suggested by the Supreme Court and the Commission, improvements must be made in disseminating information and creating manuals and check lists to be used by counsel and the courts. There must also be better reporting of information concerning capital cases so that the fairness and accuracy of the capital punishment system can be adequately assessed.

- To eliminate confusion and improper speculation, juries should be instructed as to all the possible sentencing alternatives before they consider the appropriateness of imposing a death sentence.

- Like defendants in any other criminal case, capital defendants should be afforded the opportunity to make a statement to those who will be deciding whether to impose the ultimate punishment allowed by the state, a sentence of death.

2. *THE TYPICAL CAPITAL CASE*

The procedure for the trial of capital cases has been fashioned in response to federal precedent on the issue. The government must establish at least one aggravating circumstance beyond a reasonable doubt in order to impose the death penalty. Current capital punishment provisions are the product of a lengthy series of statutes and court opinions. See, e.g., *Gregg v. Georgia*, 428 U.S. 153 (1976).

In *California v. Brown*, 479 U.S. 538 (1987), the Court stated that there are two prerequisites to a valid death sentence. First, "death penalty statutes [must] be structured so as to prevent the penalty from being administered in an arbitrary and unpredictable fashion. ... Second, ... the capital defendant generally must be allowed to introduce any relevant mitigating evidence." Later cases have defined the potential for imposition of the death penalty. For example, in *Tison v. Arizona*, 481 U.S. 137 (1987), the Court stated that the death penalty is not disproportionate for a murder committed with wanton indifference. *Atkins v. Virginia*, 536 U.S. 304 (2002) held that the Eighth Amendment prohibits capital punishment upon a prisoner who is insane or mentally retarded. And in *Roper v. Simmons*, 125 S.Ct. 1183 (2005), the Court held that the Eighth Amendment forbids imposition of the death penalty on persons who were under the age of 18 at the time they committed their crimes.

The prosecution must give defense counsel adequate notice that it will seek the death penalty. The defendant's guilt is initially determined at a "guilt" phase, and if the defendant is found guilty, a second hearing (the "penalty" phase) is conducted to determine the punishment. If the guilt phase of the proceeding is tried without a jury, the judge alone presides over the penalty phase. Likewise, if a jury has found guilt, the penalty phase is conducted as soon as possible before the same jury. When a defendant pleads guilty to a capital offense, the defendant may demand that a jury be impanelled to determine punishment.

At a pretrial conference, the defendant may allege that a sentence of death is being sought on the basis of race. The defendant must state with particularity how the evidence supports a claim that racial considerations played a significant part in the decision to seek a death sentence in his or her case. Relevant evidence may include statistical evidence or other evidence that death sentences were sought significantly more frequently either upon persons of one race than upon persons of another race, or as punishment for capital offenses against persons of one race than as punishment for capital offenses against persons of another race. The defendant has the burden of proving by clear and convincing evidence that race was the basis of the decision to seek the death penalty. The prosecution may offer evidence in rebuttal of the claims or evidence of the defendant. If the court finds that race was the basis of the decision to seek the death sentence, the court orders that a death sentence cannot be sought in that case.

In *Zant v. Stephens*, 462 U.S. 862 (1983), the Court held that all evidence may be introduced in a capital sentencing hearing even beyond factors in aggravation and mitigation as long as it is relevant, reliable and not prejudicial. Evidence is relevant to punishment if it is relevant to a statutory aggravating circumstance or to a statutory mitigating circumstance later raised by the defendant. See *Bell v. Ohio*, 438 U.S. 637 (1978).

Each jurisdiction defines the aggravating circumstances which must be proved before the death penalty can be imposed. A common aggravating circumstance is that the defendant has been previously convicted of a capital offense. *Romano v. Oklahoma*, 512 U.S. 1 (1994). A prior conviction cannot be used as an aggravating circumstance, however, if an appeal of the conviction is pending.

A second typical aggravating circumstance is that the defendant committed murder or kidnaping while engaged in the commission of a serious form of a felony such as arson, robbery, burglary, rape, or sodomy. See *Schiro v. Farley*, 510 U.S. 222 (1994). The focus of this aggravating circumstance is the commission of one of the listed offenses, regardless of whether the defendant actually could be convicted of the offense. For example, suppose the defendant argued that first degree burglary could not be an aggravating circumstance because the defendant was a 16 year old child and statutorily could not be tried as an adult for that crime. The fact that the person charged is under a legal disability by reason of age which prevents his being convicted of an offense in no way suggests that the offense has not been committed, or that if the child did in fact commit the offense, it cannot be proved as an aggravating circumstance in conviction of another offense for which he can be tried, convicted and punished as an adult.

A third aggravating circumstance is that by committing murder or kidnaping, the defendant knowingly created a great risk of death to two or more persons in a public place by means of a destructive device or weapon normally hazardous to more than one person. This aggravator is not improper merely because it duplicates one of the elements of the homicide. See *Lowenfield v. Phelps*, 484 U.S. 231 (1988). Presumably, this circumstance applies only in multiple murders or threats to several persons at or shortly prior to or shortly after an act of murder or kidnapping.

Another aggravating circumstance may deals with defendants who either pay for or receive remuneration for a murder. This circumstance appears to apply to the purchaser as well as the perpetrator. Moreover, it applies to persons who commit murder and expect to profit from the victim's death. While many statutes contain no minimum level of profit, the proof may permit the jury to infer that it would be substantial thereby adding to the motive for the crime.

A fifth type of aggravating circumstance may apply to the murder of a prison employee by a defendant who was a prisoner at the time of the homicide. The murder must have occurred while the prison employee was engaged in the performance of duties. A sixth aggravating circumstance deals with the intentional murders of more than one person.

Recently added aggravating circumstances by some states include the intentional killing of a state or local public official or police officer, sheriff or deputy sheriff while the official was engaged in the lawful performance of duties, and a defendant who murdered the victim, either when an emergency protective order or a domestic violence order was in effect, or when any other order designed to protect the victim from the defendant (such as an order issued as a condition of a bond, conditional release, probation, parole, or pretrial diversion) was in effect.

Although there is no burden to do so, as a practical matter the defense may introduce proof of any mitigating circumstances for consideration by the jury. *California v. Brown*, 479 U.S. 538 (1987). The purpose of the mitigating factors appears to be avoidance of the death penalty. The listed circumstances relate generally to matters which were insufficiently persuasive for the factfinder on the issue of guilt. Typical statutory mitigating circumstances include: a lack of a significant history of prior criminal activity, the defendant was under extreme mental or emotional disturbance, the victim participated in the act, the defendant believed he had a moral justification for the conduct, the defendant was only an accomplice, the defendant acted under duress, the defendant suffered from some diminished capacity, or the youth of the defendant. Evidence of statutory mitigating circumstances should be admitted, regardless of its cumulative effect and how long the witness has known the defendant. However, exclusion of mitigating testimony may be harmless.

At the conclusion of all the proof the parties have the right of closing argument with the defense usually having the right of the final argument. Other than the order of argument, in general the rules regarding final jury argument are similar to those in the regular trial. Because of the nature of the hearing there are additional areas of defense objection not usually available in a regular trial. Of particular note is the prohibition of minimizing the jury's responsibility in assessing the death penalty. See *Romano v. Oklahoma*, 512 U.S. 1 (1994). For example, a prosecutor cannot argue to the jury that responsibility for determining the appropriateness of a death sentence rests not with the jury but with an appellate court. *Caldwell v. Mississippi*, 472 U.S. 320 (1985).

At the conclusion of the arguments the judge must instruct the jury in a manner similar to instructions in the guilt phase. Most states use the following format for instructions during the penalty phase. First, with regard to the statutory aggravating and mitigating circumstances, the judge must charge only those factors raised by the proof. *Delo v. Lashley*, 507 U.S. 272 (1993). Second, the judge must instruct the jury as to the authorized sentences. Third, the judge must instruct the jury that imposition of the death penalty is permitted only if it finds the existence of at least one aggravating circumstance beyond a reasonable doubt. Fourth, the judge should instruct the jury on the necessity of unanimity and the presumption of innocence. Finally, the court defines the meaning of "mitigating circumstances." See Penry v. Lynaugh, 492 U.S. 302 (1989).

If the jury finds at least one aggravating circumstance beyond a reasonable doubt, its recommendation as to punishment of death must include a written designation of the aggravating circumstance. If the jury does not find at least one aggravating circumstance, the judge cannot impose a sentence of death. In this situation, the judge can impose a sentence of life. When a sentence of death is not imposed, any error committed during the proceeding is subject to a harmless error analysis. An appeal usually is automatic in cases in which the death penalty is imposed. If a death sentence is set aside because of an error in the penalty phase only, a new trial shall apply to the issue of punishment only.

Exercise

Check the statutes in your state to learn whether the death penalty is available as a punishment for homicide. If the death penalty is not used, locate a state in which it is permitted and find the following:

1. What is the notice provision for informing the defendant that the prosecution will seek the death penalty? How far in advance of trial must the notice occur? Is there a provision for notifying the defendant that the prosecution has decided not to seek the death penalty?

2. How many aggravating factors can be the basis for seeking the death penalty? How often has the list changed? Have any factors been removed by the legislature or ruled too vague by the courts? Do recent additions reflect increased concerns about the safety or importance of certain occupations, e.g., prison guards?

3. Are specific mitigating factors listed in the statute? How often has the list changed? Have any factors been removed by the legislature? Do recent additions reflect increased concerns about a defendant's background that a jury should be know?

4. If the jury finds the presence of an aggravating factor, is the death penalty the only possible punishment, or can other penalties still be considered? Even if the jury finds the presence of an aggravating factor, can the mitigating evidence offset the aggravating factor so that the death penalty is not imposed?

5. Can you think of additional aggravating or mitigating factors that the legislature should recognize?

C. PROPORTIONALITY OF PUNISHMENT

EWING v. CALIFORNIA

538 U.S. 11 (2003).

Justice O'Connor announced the judgment of the Court and delivered an opinion in which The Chief Justice and Justice Kennedy join.

In this case, we decide whether the Eighth Amendment prohibits the State of California from sentencing a repeat felon to a prison term of 25 years to life under the State's "Three Strikes and You're Out" law.

I

A

California's three strikes law reflects a shift in the State's sentencing policies toward incapacitating and deterring repeat offenders who threaten the public safety. The law was designed "to ensure longer prison sentences and greater punishment for those who commit a felony and have been previously convicted of serious and/or violent felony offenses." On March 3, 1993, California Assemblymen Bill Jones and Jim Costa introduced Assembly Bill 971, the legislative version of what would later become the three strikes law. The Assembly Committee on Public Safety defeated the bill only weeks later. Public outrage over the defeat sparked a voter initiative to add Proposition 184, based loosely on the bill, to the ballot in the November 1994 general election.

On October 1, 1993, while Proposition 184 was circulating, 12–year-old Polly Klaas was kidnaped from her home in Petaluma, California. Her admitted killer, Richard Allen Davis, had a long criminal history that included two prior kidnaping convictions. Davis had served only half of his most recent sentence (16 years for kidnaping, assault, and burglary). Had Davis served his entire sentence, he would still have been in prison on the day that Polly Klaas was kidnaped. * * *

California thus became the second State to enact a three strikes law. * * * Between 1993 and 1995, 24 States and the Federal Government enacted three strikes laws. Though the three strikes laws vary from State to State, they share a common goal of protecting the public safety by providing lengthy prison terms for habitual felons.

B

California's current three strikes law consists of two virtually identical statutory schemes "designed to increase the prison terms of repeat felons." When a defendant is convicted of a felony, and he has previously been convicted of one or more prior felonies defined as "serious" or "violent" in Cal.Penal Code Ann. §§ 667.5 and 1192.7, sentencing is conducted pursuant to the three strikes law. * * *

If the defendant has one prior "serious" or "violent" felony conviction, he must be sentenced to "twice the term otherwise provided as punishment for the current felony conviction." If the defendant has two or more prior "serious" or "violent" felony convictions, he must receive "an indeterminate term of life imprisonment." Defendants sentenced to life under the three strikes law become eligible for parole on a date calculated by reference to a "minimum term," which is the greater of (a) three times the term otherwise provided for the current conviction, (b) 25 years, or (c) the term determined by the court pursuant to § 1170 for the underlying conviction, including any enhancements.

Under California law, certain offenses may be classified as either felonies or misdemeanors. These crimes are known as "wobblers." Some crimes that would otherwise be misdemeanors become "wobblers" because of the defendant's prior record. For example, petty theft, a misdemeanor, becomes a "wobbler" when the defendant has previously served a prison term for committing specified theft-related crimes. Other crimes, such as grand theft, are "wobblers" regardless of the defendant's prior record. Both types of "wobblers" are triggering offenses under the three strikes law only when they are treated as felonies. Under California law, a "wobbler" is presumptively a felony and "remains a felony except when the discretion is actually exercised" to make the crime a misdemeanor.

In California, prosecutors may exercise their discretion to charge a "wobbler" as either a felony or a misdemeanor. Likewise, California trial courts have discretion to reduce a "wobbler" charged as a felony to a misdemeanor either before preliminary examination or at sentencing to avoid imposing a three strikes sentence. In exercising this discretion, the court may consider "those factors that direct similar sentencing decisions," such as "the nature and circumstances of the offense, the defendant's appreciation of and attitude toward the offense, . . . [and] the general objectives of sentencing."

California trial courts can also vacate allegations of prior "serious" or "violent" felony convictions, either on motion by the prosecution or sua sponte. In ruling whether to vacate allegations of prior felony convictions, courts consider whether, "in light of the nature and circumstances of [the defendant's] present felonies and prior serious and/or violent felony convictions, and the particulars of his background, character, and prospects, the defendant may be deemed outside the [three strikes'] scheme's spirit, in whole or in part." Thus, trial courts may avoid imposing a three strikes sentence in two ways: first, by reducing "wobblers" to misdemeanors (which do not qualify as triggering offenses), and second, by vacating allegations of prior "serious" or "violent" felony convictions.

C

On parole from a 9–year prison term, petitioner Gary Ewing walked into the pro shop of the El Segundo Golf Course in Los Angeles County on March 12, 2000. He walked out with three golf clubs, priced at $399 apiece, concealed in his pants leg. A shop employee, whose suspicions were aroused when he observed Ewing limp out of the pro shop, telephoned the police. The police apprehended Ewing in the parking lot.

Ewing is no stranger to the criminal justice system. In 1984, at the age of 22, he pleaded guilty to theft. * * * Only 10 months later, Ewing stole the golf clubs at issue in this case. He was charged with, and ultimately convicted of, one count of felony grand theft of personal property in excess of $400. As required by the three strikes law, the prosecutor formally alleged, and the trial court later found, that Ewing had been convicted previously of four serious or violent felonies for the three burglaries and the robbery in the Long Beach apartment complex.

At the sentencing hearing, Ewing asked the court to reduce the conviction for grand theft, a "wobbler" under California law, to a misdemeanor so as to avoid a three strikes sentence. Ewing also asked the trial court to exercise its discretion to dismiss the allegations of some or all of his prior serious or violent felony convictions, again for purposes of avoiding a three strikes sentence. Before sentencing Ewing, the trial court took note of his entire criminal history, including the fact that he was on parole when he committed his latest offense. The court also heard arguments from defense counsel and a plea from Ewing himself.

In the end, the trial judge determined that the grand theft should remain a felony. The court also ruled that the four prior strikes for the three burglaries and the robbery in Long Beach should stand. As a newly convicted felon with two or more "serious" or "violent" felony convictions in his past, Ewing was sentenced under the three strikes law to 25 years to life.

The California Court of Appeal affirmed in an unpublished opinion. Relying on our decision in *Rummel v. Estelle*, 445 U.S. 263, 100 S.Ct. 1133, 63 L.Ed.2d 382 (1980), the court rejected Ewing's claim that his sentence was grossly disproportionate under the Eighth Amendment. Enhanced sentences under recidivist statutes like the three strikes law, the court reasoned, serve the "legitimate goal" of deterring and incapacitating repeat offenders. The Supreme Court of California denied Ewing's petition for review, and we granted certiorari. We now affirm.

II

A

The Eighth Amendment, which forbids cruel and unusual punishments, contains a "narrow proportionality principle" that "applies to noncapital sentences." We have most recently addressed the proportionality principle as applied to terms of years in a series of cases beginning with *Rummel v. Estelle, supra.*

In *Rummel*, we held that it did not violate the Eighth Amendment for a State to sentence a three-time offender to life in prison with the possibility of parole. Like Ewing, Rummel was sentenced to a lengthy prison term under a recidivism statute. Rummel's two prior offenses were a 1964 felony for "fraudulent use of a credit card to obtain $80 worth of goods or services," and a 1969 felony conviction for "passing a forged check in the amount of $28.36." His triggering offense was a conviction for felony theft—"obtaining $120.75 by false pretenses."

This Court ruled that "[h]aving twice imprisoned him for felonies, Texas was entitled to place upon Rummel the onus of one who is simply unable to bring his conduct within the social norms prescribed by the criminal law of the State." The recidivism statute "is nothing more than a societal decision that when such a person commits yet another felony, he should be subjected to the admittedly serious penalty of incarceration for life, subject only to the State's judgment as to whether to grant him parole." We noted that this Court "has on occasion stated that the Eighth Amendment prohibits imposition of a sentence that is grossly disproportionate to the severity of the crime." But "[o]utside the context of capital punishment, successful challenges to the proportionality of particular sentences have been exceedingly rare." Although we stated that the proportionality principle "would ... come into play in the extreme example ... if a legislature made overtime parking a felony punishable by life imprisonment," we held that "the mandatory life sentence imposed upon this petitioner does not constitute cruel and unusual punishment under the Eighth and Fourteenth Amendments"

In *Hutto v. Davis*, 454 U.S. 370, 102 S.Ct. 703, 70 L.Ed.2d 556 (1982) (per curiam), the defendant was sentenced to two consecutive terms of 20 years in prison for possession with intent to distribute nine ounces of marijuana and distribution of marijuana. We held that such a sentence was constitutional: "In short, *Rummel* stands for the proposition that federal courts should be reluctant to review legislatively mandated terms of imprisonment, and that successful challenges to the proportionality of particular sentences should be exceedingly rare."

Three years after *Rummel*, in *Solem v. Helm*, 463 U.S. 277, 279, 103 S.Ct. 3001, 77 L.Ed.2d 637 (1983), we held that the Eighth Amendment prohibited "a life sentence without possibility of parole for a seventh nonviolent felony." The triggering offense in Solem was "uttering a 'no account' check for $100." We specifically stated that the Eighth Amendment's ban on cruel and unusual punishments "prohibits ... sentences that are disproportionate to the crime committed," and that the "constitutional principle of proportionality has been recognized explicitly in this Court for almost a century." The *Solem* Court then explained that three factors may be relevant to a determination of whether a sentence is so disproportionate that it violates the Eighth Amendment: "(i) the gravity of the offense and the harshness of the penalty; (ii) the sentences imposed on other criminals in the same jurisdiction; and (iii) the sentences imposed for commission of the same crime in other jurisdictions."

Applying these factors in *Solem*, we struck down the defendant's sentence of life without parole. We specifically noted the contrast between that sentence and the sentence in *Rummel*, pursuant to which the defendant was eligible for parole. Indeed, we explicitly declined to overrule *Rummel*: "[O]ur conclusion today is not inconsistent with *Rummel v. Estelle*."

Eight years after *Solem*, we grappled with the proportionality issue again in *Harmelin* [*v. Michigan*, 501 U.S. 957 (1991)]. *Harmelin* was not a recidivism case, but rather involved a first-time offender convicted of possessing 672 grams of cocaine. He was sentenced to life in prison without possibility of parole. A majority of the Court rejected Harmelin's claim that his sentence was so grossly disproportionate that it violated the Eighth Amendment. The Court, however, could not agree on why his proportionality argument failed. Justice Scalia, joined by The Chief Justice, wrote that the proportionality principle was "an aspect of our death penalty jurisprudence, rather than a generalizable aspect of Eighth Amendment law." He would thus have declined to apply gross disproportionality principles except in reviewing capital sentences.

Justice Kennedy, joined by two other Members of the Court, concurred in part and concurred in the judgment. Justice Kennedy specifically recognized that "[t]he Eighth Amendment proportionality principle also applies to noncapital sentences." He then identified four principles of proportionality review—"the primacy of the legislature, the variety of legitimate penological schemes, the nature of our federal system, and the requirement that proportionality review be guided by objective factors"—that "inform the final one: The Eighth Amendment does not require strict proportionality between crime and sentence. Rather, it forbids only extreme sentences that are 'grossly disproportionate' to the crime." Justice Kennedy's concurrence also stated that *Solem* "did not mandate" comparative analysis "within and between jurisdictions."

The proportionality principles in our cases distilled in Justice Kennedy's concurrence guide our application of the Eighth Amendment in the new context that we are called upon to consider.

B

* * * Throughout the States, legislatures enacting three strikes laws made a deliberate policy choice that individuals who have repeatedly engaged in serious or violent criminal behavior, and whose conduct has not been deterred by more conventional approaches to punishment, must be isolated from society in order to protect the public safety. Though three strikes laws may be relatively new, our tradition of deferring to state legislatures in making and implementing such important policy decisions is longstanding.

Our traditional deference to legislative policy choices finds a corollary in the principle that the Constitution "does not mandate adoption of any one penological theory." A sentence can have a variety of justifications, such as incapacitation, deterrence, retribution, or rehabilitation. Some or all of these justifications may play a role in a State's sentencing scheme. Selecting the sentencing rationales is generally a policy choice to be made by state legislatures, not federal courts.

When the California Legislature enacted the three strikes law, it made a judgment that protecting the public safety requires incapacitating criminals who have already been convicted of at least one serious or violent crime. * * *

California's justification is no pretext. Recidivism is a serious public safety concern in California and throughout the Nation. According to a recent report, approximately 67 percent of former inmates released from state prisons were charged with at least one "serious" new crime within three years of their release. * * *

The State's interest in deterring crime also lends some support to the three strikes law. We have long viewed both incapacitation and deterrence as rationales for recidivism statutes: "[A] recidivist statute['s] ... primary goals are to deter repeat offenders and, at some point in the life of one who repeatedly commits criminal offenses serious enough to be punished as felonies, to segregate that person from the rest of society for an extended period of time." Rummel, supra. Four years after the passage of California's three strikes law, the recidivism rate of parolees returned to prison for the commission of a new crime dropped by nearly 25 percent. * * *

III

Against this backdrop, we consider Ewing's claim that his three strikes sentence of 25 years to life is unconstitutionally disproportionate to his offense of "shoplifting three golf clubs." We first address the gravity of the offense compared to the harshness of the penalty. At the threshold, we note that Ewing incorrectly frames the issue. The gravity of his offense was not merely "shoplifting three golf clubs." Rather, Ewing was convicted of felony grand theft for stealing nearly $1,200 worth of merchandise after previously having been convicted of at least two "violent" or "serious" felonies. Even standing alone, Ewing's theft should not be taken lightly. His crime was certainly not "one of the most passive felonies a person could commit." To the contrary, the Supreme Court of California has noted the "seriousness" of grand theft in the context of proportionality review.

That grand theft is a "wobbler" under California law is of no moment. Though California courts have discretion to reduce a felony grand theft charge to a misdemeanor, it remains a felony for all purposes "unless and until the trial court imposes a misdemeanor sentence." * * *

In weighing the gravity of Ewing's offense, we must place on the scales not only his current felony, but also his long history of felony recidivism. Any other approach would fail to accord proper deference to the policy judgments that find expression in the legislature's choice of sanctions. In imposing a three strikes sentence, the State's interest is not merely punishing the offense of conviction, or the "triggering" offense: "[I]t is in addition the interest ... in dealing in a harsher manner with those who by repeated criminal acts have shown that they are simply incapable of conforming to the norms of society as established by its criminal law." To give full effect to the State's choice of this legitimate penological goal, our proportionality review of Ewing's sentence must take that goal into account.

Ewing's sentence is justified by the State's public-safety interest in incapacitating and deterring recidivist felons, and amply supported by his own long, serious criminal record. Ewing has been convicted of numerous misdemeanor and felony offenses, served nine separate terms of incarceration, and committed most of his crimes while on probation or parole. His prior "strikes" were serious felonies including robbery and three residential burglaries. To be sure, Ewing's sentence is a long one. But it reflects a rational legislative judgment, entitled to deference, that offenders who have committed serious or violent felonies and who continue to commit felonies must be incapacitated. The State of California "was entitled to place upon [Ewing] the onus of one who is simply unable to bring his conduct within the social norms prescribed by the criminal law of the State." Ewing's is not "the rare case in which a threshold comparison of the crime committed and the sentence imposed leads to an inference of gross disproportionality."

We hold that Ewing's sentence of 25 years to life in prison, imposed for the offense of felony grand theft under the three strikes law, is not grossly disproportionate and therefore does not violate the Eighth Amendment's prohibition on cruel and unusual punishments. The judgment of the California Court of Appeal is affirmed.

Justice BREYER, with whom Justice Stevens, Justice Souter, and Justice Ginsburg join, dissenting.

The constitutional question is whether the "three strikes" sentence imposed by California upon repeat-offender Gary Ewing is "grossly disproportionate" to his crime. The sentence amounts to a real prison term of at least 25 years. The sentence-triggering criminal conduct consists of the theft of three golf clubs priced at a total of $1,197. The offender has a criminal history that includes four felony convictions arising out of three separate burglaries (one armed). In *Solem v. Helm*, the Court found grossly disproportionate a somewhat longer sentence imposed on a recidivist offender for triggering criminal conduct that was somewhat less severe. In my view, the differences are not determinative, and the Court should reach the same ultimate conclusion here.

I

This Court's precedent sets forth a framework for analyzing Ewing's Eighth Amendment claim. The Eighth Amendment forbids, as "cruel and unusual punishments," prison terms (including terms of years) that are "grossly disproportionate." In applying the "gross disproportionality" principle, courts must keep in mind that "legislative policy" will primarily determine the appropriateness of a punishment's "severity," and hence defer to such legislative policy judgments. * * *

If courts properly respect those judgments, they will find that the sentence fails the test only in rare instances. * * * And they will only " 'rarely' " find it necessary to " 'engage in extended analysis' " before rejecting a claim that a sentence is "grossly disproportionate."

The plurality applies Justice Kennedy's analytical framework in *Harmelin*. And, for present purposes, I will consider Ewing's Eighth Amendment claim on those terms. To implement this approach, courts faced with a "gross disproportionality" claim must first make "a threshold comparison of the crime committed and the sentence imposed." If a claim crosses that threshold—itself a rare occurrence—then the court should compare the sentence at issue to other sentences "imposed on other criminals" in the same, or in other, jurisdictions. The comparative analysis will "validate" or invalidate "an initial judgment that a sentence is grossly disproportionate to a crime."

I recognize the warnings implicit in the Court's frequent repetition of words such as "rare." Nonetheless I believe that the case before us is a "rare" case—one in which a court can say with reasonable confidence that the punishment is "grossly disproportionate" to the crime.

II

Ewing's claim crosses the gross disproportionality "threshold." First, precedent makes clear that Ewing's sentence raises a serious disproportionality question. Ewing is a recidivist. Hence the two cases most directly in point are those in which the Court considered the constitutionality of recidivist sentencing: *Rummel* and *Solem*. Ewing's claim falls between these two cases. It is stronger than the claim presented in *Rummel*, where the Court upheld a recidivist's sentence as constitutional. It is weaker than the claim presented in *Solem*, where the Court struck down a recidivist sentence as unconstitutional.

Three kinds of sentence-related characteristics define the relevant comparative spectrum: (a) the length of the prison term in real time, i.e., the time that the offender is likely actually to spend in prison; (b) the sentence-triggering criminal conduct, i.e., the offender's actual behavior or other offense-related circumstances; and (c) the offender's criminal history.

In *Rummel*, the Court held constitutional (a) a sentence of life imprisonment with parole available within 10 to 12 years, (b) for the offense of obtaining $120 by false pretenses, (c) committed by an offender with two prior felony convictions (involving small amounts of money). In *Solem*, the Court held unconstitutional (a) a sentence of life imprisonment without parole, (b) for the crime of writing a $100 check on a nonexistent bank account, (c) committed by an offender with six prior felony convictions (including three for burglary). Which of the three pertinent comparative factors made the constitutional difference?

The third factor, prior record, cannot explain the difference. The offender's prior record was worse in *Solem*, where the Court found the sentence too long, than in *Rummel*, where the Court upheld the sentence. The second factor, offense conduct, cannot explain the difference. The nature of the triggering offense—viewed in terms of the actual monetary loss—in the two cases was about the same. The one critical factor that explains the difference in the outcome is the length of the likely prison term measured in real time. In *Rummel*, where the Court upheld the sentence, the state sentencing statute authorized parole for the offender, *Rummel*, after 10 or 12 years. In *Solem*, where the Court struck down the sentence, the sentence required the offender, Helm, to spend the rest of his life in prison.

Now consider the present case. The third factor, offender characteristics—i.e., prior record—does not differ significantly here from that in *Solem*. * * *

The difference in length of the real prison term—the first, and critical, factor in *Solem* and *Rummel*—is considerably more important. Ewing's sentence here amounts, in real terms, to at least 25 years without parole or good-time credits. That sentence is considerably shorter than Helm's sentence in *Solem*, which amounted, in real terms, to life in prison. Nonetheless Ewing's real prison term is more than twice as long as the term at issue in *Rummel*, which amounted, in real terms, to at least 10 or 12 years. And, Ewing's sentence, unlike *Rummel*'s (but like Helm's sentence in *Solem*), is long enough to consume the productive remainder of almost any offender's life. (It means that Ewing himself, seriously ill when sentenced at age 38, will likely die in prison.)

The upshot is that the length of the real prison term—the factor that explains the *Solem /Rummel* difference in outcome—places Ewing closer to *Solem* than to *Rummel*, though the greater value of the golf clubs that Ewing stole moves Ewing's case back slightly in *Rummel*'s direction. Overall, the comparison places Ewing's sentence well within the twilight zone between *Solem* and *Rummel*—a zone where the argument for unconstitutionality is substantial, where the cases themselves cannot determine the constitutional outcome.

Second, Ewing's sentence on its face imposes one of the most severe punishments available upon a recidivist who subsequently engaged in one of the less serious forms of criminal conduct. I do not deny the seriousness of shoplifting, which an amicus curiae tells us costs retailers in the range of $30 billion annually. * * *

To the contrary, well-publicized instances of shoplifting suggest that the offense is often punished without any prison sentence at all. On the other hand, shoplifting is a frequently committed crime; but "frequency," standing alone, cannot make a critical difference. Otherwise traffic offenses would warrant even more serious punishment.

This case, of course, involves shoplifting engaged in by a recidivist. One might argue that any crime committed by a recidivist is a serious crime potentially warranting a 25–year sentence. But this Court rejected that view in *Solem*, and in *Harmelin*, with the recognition that "no penalty is per se constitutional."

Third, some objective evidence suggests that many experienced judges would consider Ewing's sentence disproportionately harsh. The United States Sentencing Commission (having based the federal Sentencing Guidelines primarily upon its review of how judges had actually sentenced offenders) does not include shoplifting (or similar theft-related offenses) among the crimes that might trigger especially long sentences for recidivists

III

Believing Ewing's argument a strong one, sufficient to pass the threshold, I turn to the comparative analysis. A comparison of Ewing's sentence with other sentences requires answers to two questions. First, how would other jurisdictions (or California at other times, i.e., without the three strikes penalty) punish the same offense conduct? Second, upon what other conduct would other jurisdictions (or California) impose the same prison term? Moreover, since hypothetical punishment is beside the point, the relevant prison time, for comparative purposes, is real prison time, i.e., the time that an offender must actually serve.

Sentencing statutes often shed little light upon real prison time. That is because sentencing laws normally set maximum sentences, giving the sentencing judge discretion to choose an actual sentence within a broad range, and because many States provide good-time credits and parole, often permitting release after, say, one-third of the sentence has been served. Thus, the statutory maximum is rarely the sentence imposed, and the sentence imposed is rarely the sentence that is served. For the most part, the parties' briefs discuss sentencing statutes. Nonetheless, that discussion, along with other readily available information, validates my initial belief that Ewing's sentence, comparatively speaking, is extreme.

As to California itself, we know the following: First, between the end of World War II and 1994 (when California enacted the three strikes law), no one like Ewing could have served more than 10 years in prison. We know that for certain because the maximum sentence for Ewing's crime of conviction, grand theft, was for most of that period 10 years. We also know that the time that any offender actually served was likely far less than 10 years. This is because statistical data shows that the median time actually served for grand theft (other than auto theft) was about two years, and 90 percent of all those convicted of that crime served less than three or four years.

Second, statistics suggest that recidivists of all sorts convicted during that same time period in California served a small fraction of Ewing's real-time sentence. On average, recidivists served three to four additional (recidivist-related) years in prison, with 90 percent serving less than an additional real seven to eight years.

Third, we know that California has reserved, and still reserves, Ewing-type prison time, i.e., at least 25 real years in prison, for criminals convicted of crimes far worse than was Ewing's. Statistics for the years 1945 to 1981, for example, indicate that typical (nonrecidivist) male first-degree murderers served between 10 and 15 real years in prison, with 90 percent of all such murderers serving less than 20 real years. Moreover, California, which has moved toward a real-time sentencing system (where the statutory punishment approximates the time served), still punishes far less harshly those who have engaged in far more serious conduct. * * *

As to other jurisdictions, we know the following: The United States, bound by the federal Sentencing Guidelines, would impose upon a recidivist, such as Ewing, a sentence that, in any ordinary case, would not exceed 18 months in prison. * * *

With three exceptions, we do not have before us information about actual time served by Ewing-type offenders in other States. We do know, however, that the law would make it legally impossible for a Ewing-type offender to serve more than 10 years in prison in 33 jurisdictions, as well as the federal courts, more than 15 years in 4 other States, and more than 20 years in 4 additional States. In nine other States, the law might make it legally possible to impose a sentence of 25 years or more—

though that fact by itself, of course, does not mean that judges have actually done so. * * *

Notes

1. Proportionality limitations may apply to forfeitures as well. In *United States v. Bajakajian*, 524 U.S. 321 (1998), the defendant was arrested while trying to take $357,144 on a flight to Cyprus, because he had failed to report that he possessed or had control of more than $10,000. After a bench trial on a criminal forfeiture charge, the trial court found the entire amount subject to forfeiture under a criminal forfeiture statute. The court, however, ordered only $15,000 forfeited, reasoning that forfeiture of more than that amount would be "grossly disproportional" to Bajakajian's culpability and thus unconstitutional under the Excessive Fines Clause. The court expressly found that all of the money came from a lawful source and was to be used for a lawful purpose. The Supreme Court agreed that the forfeiture of currency permissible under the statute constituted punishment, because the forfeiture only became possible upon conviction of willfully violating the reporting statute. After concluding that the forfeiture qualified as a "fine," the Court turned to the question of excessiveness. Bajakajian's crime was "solely a reporting offense," and the harm Bajakajian's caused was "minimal" in the sense that the government would be deprived only of information that the $357,144 left the country. Thus, the gravity of the crime compared to the amount in forfeiture sought would be "grossly disproportional."

2. *Enhanced Sentences for Recidivists.* Recidivist offender statutes like the one applied in *Ewing* are used by about half the states. A defendant may be sentenced to a maximum of life imprisonment upon proof of a requisite number of prior convictions where the defendant is convicted of certain classifications of felonies. A person cannot be convicted as a recidivist unless a term of imprisonment is imposed as punishment for the underlying charge. Recidivist provisions do not create an independent offense but merely serves to enhance the punishment for a crime committed by a person who qualifies as a recidivist. A conviction for a capital offense such as murder is not subject to enhancement.

A defendant is entitled to notice of being charged as a recidivist before the trial of the underlying substantive offense. A separate indictment meets this requirement just as does a separate count in the indictment charging the substantive offense to which it refers. It is common practice for the indictment to specify the nature, time and place of the prior conviction.

Assuming the defendant is properly charged as a recidivist, trial initially takes place on the underlying felony. During this initial trial, no mention is made of the prior convictions, except for impeachment. The determination of whether the defendant is a recidivist must occur in a separate proceeding from the trial on the underlying felony. This penalty phase usually is conducted with the same jury. The defendant is not entitled to separate juries for the guilt and penalty phases. The evidence at the hearing is very narrow. The only function of the jury is to hear proof of prior convictions and to determine if a defendant's record of recidivism warrants punishment. Accordingly, the courts have denied the defendant an opportunity to introduce evidence of mitigation. During the hearing, the prosecution must prove every element of the recidivist charge beyond a reasonable doubt. A defendant charged with being a recidivist may plead guilty to the charge

In many jurisdictions, there are two degrees of recidivist status, the elements of which are indistinguishable except for the number of previous felony convictions required. For example, a recidivist in the second degree must have been convicted of one previous felony before committing the current felony. A recidivist in the first degree must have been convicted of two or more previous felonies prior to committing the current felony. Naturally the penalties for a recidivist in the first degree are more severe. Except for prior convictions, any fact increasing sentence beyond the statutory maximum for the crime of conviction must be proved beyond a reasonable doubt. *Apprendi v. New Jersey, infra.*

For both degrees, the defendant's prior conviction must have occurred prior to the date of the commission of the current felony. Likewise, for first degree status, the second felony must have been committed after the conviction of the first felony. For example, if a defendant is convicted and paroled, then commits another felony and is again incarcerated and released, upon committing a third felony, he has two prior felony convictions and is a first-degree offender. However, if the defendant's second conviction did not occur until after commission of the third felony, he has one prior felony conviction for offender status. The prior conviction must be for a felony in the sentencing jurisdiction or conviction of a crime in any other jurisdiction. If the defendant has been convicted of a crime in another state which is a felony in the sentencing jurisdiction, the conviction counts as a prior felony conviction for purposes of the recidivist statute. The prior conviction must have included imposition of a sentence of one year or more or of death.

A defendant who is indicted as a recidivist may challenge the validity of any prior conviction. The defendant must file a motion to suppress any evidence of prior convictions before trial, alleging that a prior conviction was obtained by constitutionally impermissible means. At a hearing on the motion to suppress, the burden is on the prosecution to prove the judgments of conviction for each of the prior offenses. This burden is sustained by a duly authenticated record of a judgment and conviction. When a defendant is found to be a recidivist, the sentence for the principal crime is replaced and enhanced by an indeterminate sentence.

Typically, if a defendant is found to be a recidivist in the second degree, the sentence imposed is "for the next highest degree than the offense for which [he was] convicted." For example, if the principal conviction is for a Class B felony, the enhanced sentence may be for a Class A felony. The sentence ranges for a first degree recidivist may range from twenty to fifty years or life imprisonment for the principal conviction of a Class A or Class B felony, and ten to twenty years for a Class C or Class D felony.

3. *Limitations on Sentencing* Suppose the defendant is convicted of a felony and is sentenced to twenty years, but the defendant is successful in obtaining a new trial. Could the judge or jury then sentence the defendant to thirty years? The answer, in non-capital cases, depends on who is imposing the sentence. In *North Carolina v. Pearce*, 395 U.S. 711 (1969), the Court held that, absent other factors, a defendant could not be given a higher

sentence on a retrial following reversal of a conviction. In the context of jury sentencing where a different jury imposes a higher sentence on retrial than the jury in the initial trial, the correlating control and the threat are both absent. The foregoing principle is not applicable to capital cases. When a defendant is sentenced to life and succeeds in obtaining a new trial, he or she is no longer subject to the death penalty on any retrial. *Bullington v. Missouri*, 451 U.S. 430 (1981). This proposition, grounded on double jeopardy, applies even if a jury is waived. However, if an appellate court corrects a mistaken legal interpretation of an aggravating factor which does not alter the validity of the punishment, a retrial after a reversal for the trial error can result again in a death sentence. *Poland v. Arizona*, 476 U.S. 147 (1986).

Pearce does not totally prohibit a greater sentence in another situation. Where the same judge imposes the sentence, a higher sentence may be fixed if the judge finds a "change of circumstances." In *Wasman v. United States*, 468 U.S. 559 (1984), the Court clarified the perception that an increased sentence could only be based on circumstances occurring after the original sentence. The defendant had been charged with another criminal offense at the time of the original sentence but had been convicted of this offense by the time of the higher sentence. The Court found that a conviction which took place after the original sentence could be considered even though the conduct took place prior to the initial sentence. The Court concluded that a judge may justify an increased sentence by affirmatively identifying relevant conduct or events that occurred subsequent to the original sentencing proceeding.

When the legislature increases the punishment the defendant gains the benefit of the prior lesser punishment. This result is mandated by the proposition that such an increase is a prohibited *ex post facto* law. *Lindsey v. Washington*, 301 U.S. 397 (1937).

4. *Death Penalty for Juveniles.* In *Roper v. Simmons*, 125 S.Ct. 1183 (2005), the Court in a 5–4 decision held that the Eighth Amendment forbids imposition of the death penalty on persons who were under the age of 18 at the time they committed their crimes. As in *Atkins v. Virginia*, 536 U.S. 304 (2002) regarding the death penalty for the insane or mentally retarded, the majority found a national consensus against the death penalty. A majority of states had legislatively rejected it and the infrequency of its use even where it was authorized provided sufficient evidence that society regards juveniles as "categorically less culpable than the average criminal." In addition, although international opinion against the death penalty was not controlling, the Court noted that it confirmed the majority's view that the death penalty is a disproportionate penalty for criminals under the age of 18.

Exercise

Check the statutes in your state to learn whether an enhanced sentence is available for recidivists. If the enhanced sentences are is not used, locate a state in which it is permitted and find the following:

1. What is the notice provision for informing the defendant that the prosecution will seek an enhanced sentence? How far in advance of trial must the notice occur? Is there a provision for notifying the defendant that the prosecution has decided not to seek an enhanced sentence?

2. Can a prior felony conviction be used both to create an offense or enhance a punishment of the second crime and again to enhance the punishment as a recidivist? For example, possession of a handgun by a convicted felon requires proof of a prior felony. Can that same prior felony also be used to enhance the penalty for the current possessory offense?

3. Is there a minimum age for the defendant in order to receive an enhanced recidivist sentence? Is there a minimum age for the defendant when he committed the prior crimes for which enhanced sentencing is now sought?

4. Is the prior felony conviction limited to a felony in your state, or can a felony conviction anywhere be considered? Does it matter whether the felony in another jurisdiction is not considered a felony in your state?

5. Is there a limit on the age of the prior felony conviction, e.g., within five years prior to the date of the commission of the current felony?

6. How does the prosecution prove the prior felony conviction?

7. Is there more than one degree or type of enhanced recidivist sentencing?

D. SENTENCING PROCEDURES

If the defendant has been convicted, the case should proceed to sentencing without unreasonable delay. However, it is customary to postpone sentencing for a short period of time to enable the court to obtain a presentence report. Normally, the judge who presided at the trial conducts the sentencing. Following a felony or misdemeanor conviction, the judge must consider the defendant for probation or conditional discharge as an alternative to imprisonment. If the record does not clearly reflect a consideration of sentencing alternatives, the case must be remanded for proper sentencing.

Regardless of whether the defendant is eligible for alternative sentencing, the court cannot impose a sentence for a felony other than a capital offense without the consideration of a presentence report. The report must be prepared and reviewed by the court before sentencing. The report must be prepared by a probation officer, must include an analysis of the defendant's background and may include a victim impact statement under appropriate circumstances. *Payne v. Tennessee*, 501 U.S. 808 (1991). Before imposing sentence, the trial court must advise the defendant or counsel of the contents of any presentence report. If the defendant wishes to controvert the contents of any report, the court must afford a fair opportunity and a reasonable period of time to challenge them. However, the court need not disclose the sources of confidential information contained in the report.

WILLIAMS v. NEW YORK
337 U.S. 241 (1949).

Mr. Justice BLACK delivered the opinion of the Court.

A jury in a New York state court found appellant guilty of murder in the first degree. The jury recommended life imprisonment, but the trial judge imposed sentence of death. In giving his reasons for imposing the death sentence the judge discussed in open court the evidence upon which the jury had convicted stating that this evidence had been considered in the light of additional information obtained through the court's "Probation Department, and through other sources." [A state statute required that the court "shall cause the defendant's previous criminal record to be submitted to it, * * * and may seek any information that will aid the court in determining the proper treatment of such defendant." Williams argued that his sentence violated due process, because it was provided by witnesses he had not confronted or cross-examined.]

The narrow contention here makes it unnecessary to set out the facts at length. The record shows a carefully conducted trial lasting more than two weeks in which appellant was represented by three appointed lawyers who conducted his defense with fidelity and zeal. The evidence proved a wholly indefensible murder committed by a person engaged in a burglary. * * *

About five weeks after the verdict of guilty with recommendation of life imprisonment, and after a statutory pre-sentence investigation report to the judge, the defendant was brought to court to be sentenced. Asked what he had to say, appellant protested his innocence. After each of his three lawyers had appealed to the court to accept the jury's recommendation of a life sentence, the judge gave reasons why he felt that the death sentence should be imposed. He narrated the shocking details of the crime as shown by the trial evidence, expressing his own complete belief in appellant's guilt. He stated that the pre-sentence investigation revealed many material facts concerning appellant's background which though relevant to the question of punishment could not properly have been brought to the attention of the jury in its consideration of the question of guilt. He referred to the experience appellant 'had had on thirty other burglaries in and about the same vicinity' where the murder had been committed. The appellant had not been convicted of these burglaries although the judge had information that he had confessed to some and had been identified as the perpetrator of some of the others. The judge also referred to certain activities of appellant as shown by the probation report that indicated appellant possessed "a morbid sexuality" and classified him as a "menace to society." The accuracy of the statements made by the judge as to appellant's background and past practices were not challenged by appellant or his counsel, nor was the judge asked to disregard any of them or to afford appellant a chance to refute or discredit any of them by cross-examination or otherwise.

The case presents a serious and difficult question. The question relates to the rules of evidence applicable to the manner in which a judge may obtain information to guide him in the imposition of sentence upon an already convicted defendant. Within limits fixed by statutes, New York judges are given a broad discretion to decide the type and extent of punishment for convicted defendants. Here, for example, the judge's discretion was to sentence to life imprisonment or death. To aid a judge in exercising this discretion intelligently the New York procedural policy encourages him to consider information about the convicted person's past life, health, habits, conduct, and mental and moral propensities. The sentencing judge may consider such information even though obtained outside the courtroom from persons whom a defendant has not been permitted to confront or cross-examine. It is the consideration of information obtained by a sentencing judge in this manner that is the basis for appellant's broad constitutional challenge to the New York statutory policy.

Appellant urges that the New York statutory policy is in irreconcilable conflict with the underlying philosophy of a second procedural policy grounded in the due process of law clause of the Fourteenth Amendment. That policy as stated in Re Oliver, 333 U.S. 257, is in part that no person shall be tried and convicted of an offense unless he is given reasonable notice of the charges against him and is afforded an opportunity to examine adverse witnesses. That the due process clause does provide these salutary and time-tested protections where the question for consideration is the guilt of a defendant seems entirely clear from the genesis and historical evolution of the clause.

Tribunals passing on the guilt of a defendant always have been hedged in by strict evidentiary procedural limitations. But both before and since the American colonies became a nation, courts in this country and in England practiced a policy under which a sentencing judge could exercise a wide discretion in the sources and types of evidence used to assist him in determining the kind the extent of punishment to be imposed within limits fixed by law. Out-of-court affidavits have been used frequently, and of course in the smaller communities sentencing judges naturally have in mind their knowledge of the personalities and backgrounds of convicted offenders. A recent manifestation of the historical latitude allowed sentencing judges appears in Rule 32 of the Federal Rules of Criminal Procedure. That rule provides for consideration by federal judges of reports made by probation officers containing information about a convicted defendant, including such information "as may be helpful in imposing sentence or in granting probation or in the correctional treatment of the defendant. . . . "

In addition to the historical basis for different evidentiary rules governing trial and sentencing procedures there are sound practical reasons for the distinction. In a trial before verdict the issue is whether a defendant is guilty of having engaged in certain criminal conduct of which he has been specifically accused. Rules of evidence have been fashioned for criminal trials which narrowly confine the trial contest to evidence that is strictly relevant to the particular offense charged. These rules rest in part on a necessity to prevent a time consuming and confusing trial of collateral issues. They were also designed to prevent tribunals concerned solely with the issue of guilt of a particular offense from being influenced to convict for that offense by evidence that the defendant had habitually engaged in other misconduct. A sentencing judge, however, is not confined to the narrow issue of guilt. His task within fixed statutory or constitutional limits is to determine the type and extent of punishment after the issue of guilt has been determined. Highly relevant—if not essential—to his selection of an appropriate sentence is the possession of the fullest information possible concerning the defendant's life and characteristics. And modern concepts individualizing punishment have made it all the more necessary that a sentencing judge not be denied an opportunity to obtain pertinent information by a requirement of rigid adherence to restrictive rules of evidence properly applicable to the trial.

Undoubtedly the New York statutes emphasize a prevalent modern philosophy of penology that the punishment should fit the offender and not merely the crime. The belief no longer prevails that every offense in a like legal category calls for an identical punishment without regard to the past life and habits of a particular offender. This whole country has traveled far from the period in which the death sentence was an automatic and commonplace result of convictions—even for offenses today deemed trivial. Today's philosophy of individualizing sentences makes sharp distinctions for example between first and repeated offenders. Indeterminate sentences, the ultimate termination of which are sometimes decided by nonjudicial agencies have to a large extent taken the place of the old rigidly fixed punishments. The practice of probation which relies heavily on non-judicial implementation has been accepted as a wise policy. Execution of the United States parole system rests on the discretion of an administrative parole board. Retribution is no longer the dominant objective of the criminal law. Reformation and rehabilitation of offenders have become important goals of criminal jurisprudence.

Modern changes in the treatment of offenders make it more necessary now than a century ago for observance of the distinctions in the evidential procedure in the trial and sentencing processes. For indeterminate sentences and probation have resulted in an increase in the discretionary powers exercised in fixing punishments. In general, these modern changes have not resulted in making the lot of offenders harder. On the contrary a strong motivating force for the changes has been the belief that by careful study of the lives and personalities of convicted offenders many could be less severely punished and restored sooner to complete freedom and useful citizenship. This belief to a large a large extent has been justified.

Under the practice of individualizing punishments, investigation techniques have been given an important role. Probation workers making reports of their investigations have not been trained to prosecute but to aid offenders. Their reports have been given a high value by conscientious judges who want to sentence persons on the best available information rather than on guesswork and inadequate information. To deprive sentencing judges of this kind of information would undermine modern penological procedural policies that have been cautiously adopted throughout the nation after careful consideration and experimentation. We must recognize that most of the information now relied upon by judges to guide them in the intelligent imposition of sentences would be unavailable if information were restricted to that given in open court by witnesses subject to cross-examination. And the modern probation report draws on information concerning every aspect of a defendant's life. The type and extent of this information make totally impractical if not impossible open court testimony with cross-examination. Such a procedure could endlessly delay criminal administration in a retrial of collateral issues.

The considerations we have set out admonish us against treating the due-process clause as a uniform command that courts throughout the Nation abandon their age-old practice of seeking information from out-of-court sources to guide their judgment toward a more enlightened and just sentence. New York criminal statutes set wide limits for maximum and minimum sentences. Under New York statutes a state judge cannot escape his grave responsibility of fixing sentence. In determining whether a defendant shall receive a one-year minimum or a twenty-year maximum sentence, we do not think the Federal Constitution restricts the view of the sentencing judge to the information received in open court. The due-process clause should not be treated as a device for freezing the evidential procedure of sentencing in the mold of trial procedure. So to treat the due-process clause would hinder if not preclude all courts—state and federal—from making progressive efforts to improve the administration of criminal justice. * * * *

Affirmed.

Mr. Justice MURPHY, dissenting. * * * The record before us indicates that the judge exercised his discretion to deprive a man of his life, in reliance on material made available to him in a probation report, consisting almost entirely of evidence that would have been inadmissible at the trial. Some, such as allegations of prior crimes, was irrelevant. Much was incompetent as hearsay. All was damaging, and none was subject to scrutiny by the defendant.

Due process of law includes at least the idea that a person accused of crime shall be accorded a fair hearing through all the stages of the proceedings against him. I agree with the Court as to the value and humaneness of liberal use of probation reports as developed by modern penologists, but, in a capital case, against the unanimous recommendation of a jury, where the report would concededly not have been admissible at the trial, and was not subject to examination by the defendant, I am forced to conclude that the high commands of due process were not obeyed.

Notes

1. Formal sentencing consists of pronouncing sentence in accordance with the previous plea or adjudication of guilt. Any pending motions which may affect the need for sentencing should be decided before sentencing is pronounced. The defendant should be given the common law right of allocution, to identify any reason why the sentence should not be pro-

nounced or why a particular sentence is appropriate. It thus affords regularity to the proceedings and reduces the likelihood of a subsequent attack on the judgment. If the sentence is predicated upon a contested adjudication, the defendant must be advised of rights regarding appeal.

2. In making a sentence determination, the judge should consider the presentence report, sentencing alternatives if any, evidence concerning the nature and characteristics of the criminal conduct, and whether to run any multiple sentences concurrently or consecutively. In addition, the judge may consider the defendant's untruthfulness or refusal to cooperate with law enforcement authorities. The judge "must be permitted to consider any and all information that reasonably might bear on the proper sentence for the particular defendant, given the crime committed." *Wasman v. United States*, 468 U.S. 559 (1984).

APPRENDI v. NEW JERSEY

530 U.S. 466 (2000).

Justice STEVENS delivered the opinion of the Court. [A New Jersey hate crime statute provided for an "extended term" of imprisonment if the trial judge found, by a preponderance of the evidence, that "[t]he defendant in committing the crime acted with a purpose to intimidate an individual or group of individuals because of race, color, gender, handicap, religion, sexual orientation or ethnicity." The extended term authorized by the hate crime law is imprisonment for "between 10 and 20 years." After his indictment, Apprendi agreed to plead guilty to possession of a firearm for an unlawful purpose, punishable by five to ten years. The plea agreement allowed the prosecution to request that the sentence be enhanced due to a biased purpose. After an adversarial hearing, the trial court concluded that the crime was motivated by racial bias.]

* * * The question presented is whether the Due Process Clause of the Fourteenth Amendment requires that a factual determination authorizing an increase in the maximum prison sentence for an offense from 10 to 20 years be made by a jury on the basis of proof beyond a reasonable doubt. * * *

* * * Our answer to that question was foreshadowed by our opinion in Jones v. United States, 526 U.S. 227 (1999), construing a federal statute. We there noted that "under the Due Process Clause of the Fifth Amendment and the notice and jury trial guarantees of the Sixth Amendment, any fact (other than prior conviction) that increases the maximum penalty for a crime must be charged in an indictment, submitted to a jury, and proven beyond a reasonable doubt." The Fourteenth Amendment commands the same answer in this case involving a state statute.

* * * At stake in this case are constitutional protections of surpassing importance: the proscription of any deprivation of liberty without "due process of law," Amdt. 14, and the guarantee that "[i]n all criminal

prosecutions, the accused shall enjoy the right to a speedy and public trial, by an impartial jury," Amdt. 6. * * *

Any possible distinction between an "element" of a felony offense and a "sentencing factor" was unknown to the practice of criminal indictment, trial by jury, and judgment by court as it existed during the years surrounding our Nation's founding. As a general rule, criminal proceedings were submitted to a jury after being initiated by an indictment containing "all the facts and circumstances which constitute the offence, . . . stated with such certainty and precision, that the defendant . . . may be enabled to determine the species of offence they constitute, in order that he may prepare his defence accordingly . . . and that there may be no doubt as to the judgment which should be given, if the defendant be convicted." J. Archbold, Pleading and Evidence in Criminal Cases 44 (15th ed. 1862) The defendant's ability to predict with certainty the judgment from the face of the felony indictment flowed from the invariable linkage of punishment with crime. * * *

* * * Just as the circumstances of the crime and the intent of the defendant at the time of commission were often essential elements to be alleged in the indictment, so too were the circumstances mandating a particular punishment. "Where a statute annexes a higher degree of punishment to a common-law felony, if committed under particular circumstances, an indictment for the offence, in order to bring the defendant within that higher degree of punishment, must expressly charge it to have been committed under those circumstances, and must state the circumstances with certainty and precision. [2 M. Hale, Pleas of the Crown *170]." Archbold, Pleading and Evidence in Criminal Cases, at 51. If, then, "upon an indictment under the statute, the prosecutor prove the felony to have been committed, but fail in proving it to have been committed under the circumstances specified in the statute, the defendant shall be convicted of the common-law felony only." Id., at 188. * * *

We should be clear that nothing in this history suggests that it is impermissible for judges to exercise discretion—taking into consideration various factors relating both to offense and offender—in imposing a judgment within the range prescribed by statute. We have often noted that judges in this country have long exercised discretion of this nature in imposing sentence within statutory limits in the individual case. * * * As in *Williams* [*v. New York*], our periodic recognition of judges' broad discretion in sentencing—since the 19th-century shift in this country from statutes providing fixed-term sentences to those providing judges discretion within a permissible range, has been regularly accompanied by the qualification that that discretion was bound by the range of sentencing options prescribed by the legislature. * * *

We do not suggest that trial practices cannot change in the course of centuries and still remain true to the principles that emerged from the Framers' fears "that the jury right could be lost not only by gross denial, but by erosion." But practice must at least adhere to the basic principles undergirding the requirements of trying to a jury all facts necessary to constitute a statutory offense, and proving those facts beyond reasonable doubt. As we made clear in *Winship*, the "reasonable doubt" requirement "has [a] vital role in our criminal procedure for cogent reasons." Prosecution subjects the criminal defendant both to "the possibility that he may lose his liberty upon conviction and ... the certainty that he would be stigmatized by the conviction." We thus require this, among other, procedural protections in order to "provid[e] concrete substance for the presumption of innocence," and to reduce the risk of imposing such deprivations erroneously. Ibid. If a defendant faces punishment beyond that provided by statute when an offense is committed under certain circumstances but not others, it is obvious that both the loss of liberty and the stigma attaching to the offense are heightened; it necessarily follows that the defendant should not—at the moment the State is put to proof of those circumstances—be deprived of protections that have, until that point, unquestionably attached.

Since *Winship*, we have made clear beyond peradventure that *Winship*'s due process and associated jury protections extend, to some degree, "to determinations that [go] not to a defendant's guilt or innocence, but simply to the length of his sentence." *Almendarez-Torres*, 523 U.S., at 251, (Scalia, J., dissenting). This was a primary lesson of *Mullaney v. Wilbur*, 421 U.S. 684 (1975), in which we invalidated a Maine statute that presumed that a defendant who acted with an intent to kill possessed the "malice aforethought" necessary to constitute the State's murder offense (and therefore, was subject to that crime's associated punishment of life imprisonment). The statute placed the burden on the defendant of proving, in rebutting the statutory presumption, that he acted with a lesser degree of culpability, such as in the heat of passion, to win a reduction in the offense from murder to manslaughter (and thus a reduction of the maximum punishment of 20 years).

The State had posited in *Mullaney* that requiring a defendant to prove heat-of-passion intent to overcome a presumption of murderous intent did not implicate *Winship* protections because, upon conviction of either offense, the defendant would lose his liberty and face societal stigma just the same. Rejecting this argument, we acknowledged that criminal law "is concerned not only with guilt or innocence in the abstract, but also with the degree of criminal culpability" assessed. Because the "consequences "of a guilty verdict for murder and for manslaughter differed substantially, we dismissed the possibility that a State could circumvent the protections of *Winship* merely by "redefin[ing] the elements that constitute different crimes, characterizing them as factors that bear solely on the extent of punishment."

It was in *McMillan v. Pennsylvania*, 477 U.S. 79 (1986), that this Court, for the first time, coined the term "sentencing factor" to refer to a fact that was not found by a jury but that could affect the sentence imposed by the judge. * * * Articulating for the first time, and then applying, a multifactor set of criteria for determining whether the *Winship* protections applied to bar such a system, we concluded that the

Pennsylvania statute did not run afoul of our previous admonitions against relieving the State of its burden of proving guilt, or tailoring the mere form of a criminal statute solely to avoid *Winship*'s strictures.

We did not, however, there budge from the position that (1) constitutional limits exist to States' authority to define away facts necessary to constitute a criminal offense, id., at 85–88, 106 S.Ct. 2411, and (2) that a state scheme that keeps from the jury facts that "expos[e] [defendants] to greater or additional punishment," may raise serious constitutional concern. * * *

Finally, * * * *Almendarez-Torres v. United States*, 523 U.S. 224 (1998), represents at best an exceptional departure from the historic practice that we have described. * * * Because Almendarez–Torres had admitted the three earlier convictions for aggravated felonies—all of which had been entered pursuant to proceedings with substantial procedural safeguards of their own—no question concerning the right to a jury trial or the standard of proof that would apply to a contested issue of fact was before the Court. Although our conclusion in that case was based in part on our application of the criteria we had invoked in *McMillan*, the specific question decided concerned the sufficiency of the indictment. More important, * * * our conclusion in *Almendarez-Torres* turned heavily upon the fact that the additional sentence to which the defendant was subject was "the prior commission of a serious crime." * * * Both the certainty that procedural safeguards attached to any "fact" of prior conviction, and the reality that Almendarez–Torres did not challenge the accuracy of that "fact" in his case, mitigated the due process and Sixth Amendment concerns otherwise implicated in allowing a judge to determine a "fact" increasing punishment beyond the maximum of the statutory range.

Even though it is arguable that *Almendarez-Torres* was incorrectly decided, and that a logical application of our reasoning today should apply if the recidivist issue were contested, Apprendi does not contest the decision's validity and we need not revisit it for purposes of our decision today to treat the case as a narrow exception to the general rule we recalled at the outset. Given its unique facts, it surely does not warrant rejection of the otherwise uniform course of decision during the entire history of our jurisprudence.

In sum, our reexamination of our cases in this area, and of the history upon which they rely, confirms the opinion that we expressed in *Jones*. Other than the fact of a prior conviction, any fact that increases the penalty for a crime beyond the prescribed statutory maximum must be submitted to a jury, and proved beyond a reasonable doubt. With that exception, we endorse the statement of the rule set forth in the concurring opinions in that case: "[I]t is unconstitutional for a legislature to remove from the jury the assessment of facts that increase the prescribed range of penalties to which a criminal defendant is exposed. It is equally clear that such facts must be established by proof beyond a reasonable doubt."

The New Jersey statutory scheme that Apprendi asks us to invalidate allows a jury to convict a defendant of a second-degree offense based on its finding beyond a reasonable doubt that he unlawfully possessed a prohibited weapon; after a subsequent and separate proceeding, it then allows a judge to impose punishment identical to that New Jersey provides for crimes of the first degree, based upon the judge's finding, by a preponderance of the evidence, that the defendant's "purpose" for unlawfully possessing the weapon was "to intimidate" his victim on the basis of a particular characteristic the victim possessed. In light of the constitutional rule explained above, and all of the cases supporting it, this practice cannot stand.

* * * [T]his Court has previously considered and rejected the argument that the principles guiding our decision today render invalid state capital sentencing schemes requiring judges, after a jury verdict holding a defendant guilty of a capital crime, to find specific aggravating factors before imposing a sentence of death. *Walton v. Arizona*, 497 U.S. 639, 647–649 (1990); *id.*, at 709–714 (Stevens, J., dissenting). For reasons we have explained, the capital cases are not controlling:

> "Neither the cases cited, nor any other case, permits a judge to determine the existence of a factor which makes a crime a capital offense. What the cited cases hold is that, once a jury has found the defendant guilty of all the elements of an offense which carries as its maximum penalty the sentence of death, it may be left to the judge to decide whether that maximum penalty, rather than a lesser one, ought to be imposed.... The person who is charged with actions that expose him to the death penalty has an absolute entitlement to jury trial on all the elements of the charge." *Almendarez-Torres*, 523 U.S., at 257, n. 2, (Scalia, J., dissenting) (emphasis deleted).

* * * Accordingly, the judgment of the Supreme Court of New Jersey is reversed, and the case is remanded for further proceedings not inconsistent with this opinion.

Justice O'CONNOR, with whom The Chief Justice, Justice Kennedy, and Justice Breyer join, dissenting.

* * * Today, in what will surely be remembered as a watershed change in constitutional law, the Court imposes as a constitutional rule the principle it first identified in *Jones.*

Our Court has long recognized that not every fact that bears on a defendant's punishment need be charged in an indictment, submitted to a jury, and proved by the government beyond a reasonable doubt. Rather, we have held that the "legislature's definition of the elements of the offense is usually dispositive." *McMillan* Although we have recognized that "there are obviously constitutional limits beyond which the States may not go in this regard," and that "in certain limited circumstances *Winship*'s reasonable-doubt requirement applies to facts not formally identified as elements of the offense charged," we have proceeded with caution before deciding that a certain fact must be treated as an offense element despite the legislature's choice not to characterize it as such. We have therefore declined to establish any bright-line rule for making such judgments and have instead approached each case individually, sifting through the considerations most relevant to determining whether the legislature has acted properly within its broad power to define crimes and their punishments or instead has sought to evade the constitutional requirements associated with the characterization of a fact as an offense element.

In one bold stroke the Court today casts aside our traditional cautious approach and instead embraces a universal and seemingly bright-line rule limiting the power of Congress and state legislatures to define criminal offenses and the sentences that follow from convictions thereunder. * * * [T]the Court marshals virtually no authority to support its extraordinary rule. Indeed, it is remarkable that the Court cannot identify a single instance, in the over 200 years since the ratification of the Bill of Rights, that our Court has applied, as a constitutional requirement, the rule it announces today.

* * * None of the history contained in the Court's opinion requires the rule it ultimately adopts. The history cited by the Court can be divided into two categories: first, evidence that judges at common law had virtually no discretion in sentencing, and, second, statements from a 19th-century criminal procedure treatise that the government must charge in an indictment and prove at trial the elements of a statutory offense for the defendant to be sentenced to the punishment attached to that statutory offense. The relevance of the first category of evidence can be easily dismissed. Indeed, the Court does not even claim that the historical evidence of nondiscretionary sentencing at common law supports its "increase in the maximum penalty" rule. Rather, almost as quickly as it recites that historical practice, the Court rejects its relevance to the constitutional question presented here due to the conflicting American practice of judges exercising sentencing discretion and our decisions recognizing the legitimacy of that American practice.

* * * Apparently, then, the historical practice on which the Court places so much reliance consists of only two quotations taken from an 1862 criminal procedure treatise. A closer examination of the two statements reveals that neither supports the Court's "increase in the maximum penalty" rule. Both of the excerpts pertain to circumstances in which a common-law felony had also been made a separate statutory offense carrying a greater penalty. Taken together, the statements from the Archbold treatise demonstrate nothing more than the unremarkable proposition that a defendant could receive the greater statutory punishment only if the indictment expressly charged and the prosecutor proved the facts that made up the statutory offense, as opposed to simply those facts that made up the common-law offense. In other words, for the defendant to receive the statutory punishment, the prosecutor had to charge in the indictment and prove at trial the elements of the statutory offense. * * * No Member of this Court questions the proposition that a State must charge in the indictment and prove at trial beyond a reasonable doubt the actual elements of the offense. This case, however,

concerns the distinct question of when a fact that bears on a defendant's punishment, but which the legislature has not classified as an element of the charged offense, must nevertheless be treated as an offense element. The excerpts drawn from the Archbold treatise do not speak to this question at all. The history on which the Court's opinion relies provides no support for its "increase in the maximum penalty" rule. * * *

* * * [T]he Court appears to hold that the Constitution requires that a fact be submitted to a jury and proved beyond a reasonable doubt only if that fact, as a formal matter, extends the range of punishment beyond the prescribed statutory maximum. A State could, however, remove from the jury (and subject to a standard of proof below "beyond a reasonable doubt") the assessment of those facts that define narrower ranges of punishment, within the overall statutory range, to which the defendant may be sentenced. Thus, apparently New Jersey could cure its sentencing scheme, and achieve virtually the same results, by drafting its weapons possession statute in the following manner: First, New Jersey could prescribe, in the weapons possession statute itself, a range of 5 to 20 years' imprisonment for one who commits that criminal offense. Second, New Jersey could provide that only those defendants convicted under the statute who are found by a judge, by a preponderance of the evidence, to have acted with a purpose to intimidate an individual on the basis of race may receive a sentence greater than 10 years' imprisonment.

The Court's proffered distinction of *Walton v. Arizona*, [497 U.S. 639 (1990)] suggests that it means to announce a rule of only this limited effect. The Court claims the Arizona capital sentencing scheme is consistent with the constitutional principle underlying today's decision because Arizona's first-degree murder statute itself authorizes both life imprisonment and the death penalty. " '[O]nce a jury has found the defendant guilty of all the elements of an offense which carries as its maximum penalty the sentence of death, it may be left to the judge to decide whether that maximum penalty, rather than a lesser one, ought to be imposed.' " Of course, an Arizona sentencing judge can impose the maximum penalty of death only if the judge first makes a statutorily required finding that at least one aggravating factor exists in the defendant's case. Thus, the Arizona first-degree murder statute authorizes a maximum penalty of death only in a formal sense. In real terms, however, the Arizona sentencing scheme removes from the jury the assessment of a fact that determines whether the defendant can receive that maximum punishment. The only difference, then, between the Arizona scheme and the New Jersey scheme we consider here—apart from the magnitude of punishment at stake—is that New Jersey has not prescribed the 20–year maximum penalty in the same statute that it defines the crime to be punished. It is difficult to understand, and the Court does not explain, why the Constitution would require a state legislature to follow such a meaningless and formalistic difference in drafting its criminal statutes.

Under another reading of the Court's decision, it may mean only that the Constitution requires that a fact be submitted to a jury and proved beyond a reasonable doubt if it, as a formal matter, *increases* the range of punishment *beyond that which could legally be imposed absent that fact.* A State could, however, remove from the jury (and subject to a standard of proof below "beyond a reasonable doubt") the assessment of those facts that, as a formal matter, decrease the range of punishment *below that which could legally be imposed absent that fact.* Thus, consistent with our decision in Patterson, New Jersey could cure its sentencing scheme, and achieve virtually the same results, by drafting its weapons possession statute in the following manner: First, New Jersey could prescribe, in the weapons possession statute itself, a range of 5 to 20 years' imprisonment for one who commits that criminal offense. Second, New Jersey could provide that a defendant convicted under the statute whom a judge finds, by a preponderance of the evidence, not to have acted with a purpose to intimidate an individual on the basis of race may receive a sentence no greater than 10 years' imprisonment.

* * * If either of the above readings is all that the Court's decision means, "the Court's principle amounts to nothing more than chastising [the New Jersey Legislature] for failing to use the approved phrasing in expressing its intent as to how [unlawful weapons possession] should be punished." *Jones,* 526 U.S., at 267 (Kennedy, J., dissenting). If New Jersey can, consistent with the Constitution, make precisely the same differences in punishment turn on precisely the same facts, and can remove the assessment of those facts from the jury and subject them to a standard of proof below "beyond a reasonable doubt," it is impossible to say that the Fifth, Sixth, and Fourteenth Amendments require the Court's rule. For the same reason, the "structural democratic constraints" that might discourage a legislature from enacting either of the above hypothetical statutes would be no more significant than those that would discourage the enactment of New Jersey's present sentence-enhancement statute. In all three cases, the legislature is able to calibrate punishment perfectly, and subject to a maximum penalty only those defendants whose cases satisfy the sentence-enhancement criterion. * * *

Given the pure formalism of the above readings of the Court's opinion, one suspects that the constitutional principle underlying its decision is more far reaching. The actual principle underlying the Court's decision may be that any fact (other than prior conviction) that has the effect, *in real terms,* of increasing the maximum punishment beyond an otherwise applicable range must be submitted to a jury and proved beyond a reasonable doubt. The principle thus would apply not only to schemes like New Jersey's, under which a factual determination exposes the defendant to a sentence beyond the prescribed statutory maximum, but also to all determinate-sentencing schemes in which the length of a defendant's sentence within the statutory range turns on specific factual determinations (e.g., the federal Sentencing Guidelines).

* * * I would reject any such principle. As explained above, it is inconsistent with our precedent and would require the Court to overrule, at a minimum, decisions like *Patterson* and *Walton.*

One important purpose of the Sixth Amendment's jury trial guarantee is to protect the criminal defendant against potentially arbitrary judges. It effectuates this promise by preserving, as a constitutional matter, certain fundamental decisions for a jury of one's peers, as opposed to a judge. * * * Clearly, the concerns animating the Sixth Amendment's jury trial guarantee, if they were to extend to the sentencing context at all, would apply with greater strength to a discretionary-sentencing scheme than to determinate sentencing. In the former scheme, the potential for mischief by an arbitrary judge is much greater, given that the judge's decision of where to set the defendant's sentence within the prescribed statutory range is left almost entirely to discretion. In contrast, under a determinate-sentencing system, the discretion the judge wields within the statutory range is tightly constrained. Accordingly, our approval of discretionary-sentencing schemes, in which a defendant is not entitled to have a jury make factual findings relevant to sentencing despite the effect those findings have on the severity of the defendant's sentence, demonstrates that the defendant should have no right to demand that a jury make the equivalent factual determinations under a determinate-sentencing scheme.

The Court appears to hold today, however, that a defendant is entitled to have a jury decide, by proof beyond a reasonable doubt, every fact relevant to the determination of sentence under a determinate-sentencing scheme. If this is an accurate description of the constitutional principle underlying the Court's opinion, its decision will have the effect of invalidating significant sentencing reform accomplished at the federal and state levels over the past three decades.

* * * [I]t is ironic that the Court, in the name of constitutional rights meant to protect criminal defendants from the potentially arbitrary exercise of power by prosecutors and judges, appears to rest its decision on a principle that would render unconstitutional efforts by Congress and the state legislatures to place constraints on that very power in the sentencing context.

Finally, perhaps the most significant impact of the Court's decision will be a practical one—its unsettling effect on sentencing conducted under current federal and state determinate-sentencing schemes. As I have explained, the Court does not say whether these schemes are constitutional, but its reasoning strongly suggests that they are not. Thus, with respect to past sentences handed down by judges under determinate-sentencing schemes, the Court's decision threatens to unleash a flood of petitions by convicted defendants seeking to invalidate their sentences in whole or in part on the authority of the Court's decision today. Statistics compiled by the United States Sentencing Commission reveal that almost a half-million cases have been sentenced under the Sentencing Guidelines since 1989 * * * [and] federal criminal prosecutions represented only about 0.4% of the total number of criminal prosecutions in federal and state courts. * * * Because many States, like New Jersey, have determinate-sentencing schemes, the number of individual sentences drawn into question by the Court's decision could be colossal.

* * * I would evaluate New Jersey's sentence-enhancement statute by analyzing the factors we have examined in past cases. First, the New Jersey statute does not shift the burden of proof on an essential ingredient of the offense by presuming that ingredient upon proof of other elements of the offense. Second, the magnitude of the New Jersey sentence enhancement, as applied in petitioner's case, is constitutionally permissible. * * * The 10–year increase in the maximum penalty to which petitioner was exposed falls well within the range we have found permissible. See *Almendarez-Torres* (approving 18–year enhancement). Third, the New Jersey statute gives no impression of having been enacted to evade the constitutional requirements that attach when a State makes a fact an element of the charged offense. For example, New Jersey did not take what had previously been an element of the weapons possession offense and transform it into a sentencing factor.

In sum, New Jersey "simply took one factor that has always been considered by sentencing courts to bear on punishment"—a defendant's motive for committing the criminal offense—"and dictated the precise weight to be given that factor" when the motive is to intimidate a person because of race. * * *

Justice BREYER, with whom The Chief Justice joins, dissenting. The majority * * * rule would seem to promote a procedural ideal—that of juries, not judges, determining the existence of those facts upon which increased punishment turns. But the real world of criminal justice cannot hope to meet any such ideal. It can function only with the help of procedural compromises, particularly in respect to sentencing. And those compromises, which are themselves necessary for the fair functioning of the criminal justice system, preclude implementation of the procedural model that today's decision reflects. At the very least, the impractical nature of the requirement that the majority now recognizes supports the proposition that the Constitution was not intended to embody it.

* * * [I]t is important for present purposes to understand why judges, rather than juries, traditionally have determined the presence or absence of such sentence-affecting facts in any given case. And it is important to realize that the reason is not a theoretical one, but a practical one. It * * * reflect[s] an * * * administrative need for procedural compromise. There are, to put it simply, far too many potentially relevant sentencing factors to permit submission of all (or even many) of them to a jury. As the Sentencing Guidelines state the matter,

> "[a] bank robber with (or without) a gun, which the robber kept hidden (or brandished), might have frightened (or merely warned), injured seriously (or less seriously), tied up (or simply pushed) a guard, a teller or a customer, at night (or at noon), for a bad (or arguably less bad) motive, in an effort to obtain money for other crimes (or for other purposes), in the company of a few (or many) other robbers, for the first (or fourth) time that day, while sober (or

under the influence of drugs or alcohol), and so forth." Sentencing Guidelines, Part A, at 1.2.

The Guidelines note that "a sentencing system tailored to fit every conceivable wrinkle of each case can become unworkable and seriously compromise the certainty of punishment and its deterrent effect." Ibid. To ask a jury to consider all, or many, such matters would do the same.

At the same time, to require jury consideration of all such factors— say, during trial where the issue is guilt or innocence—could easily place the defendant in the awkward (and conceivably unfair) position of having to deny he committed the crime yet offer proof about how he committed it, e.g., "I did not sell drugs, but I sold no more than 500 grams." And while special postverdict sentencing juries could cure this problem, they have seemed (but for capital cases) not worth their administrative costs.

* * * [T]he majority also makes no constitutional objection to a legislative delegation to a commission of the authority to create guidelines that determine how a judge is to exercise sentencing discretion. But if the Constitution permits Guidelines, why does it not permit Congress similarly to guide the exercise of a judge's sentencing discretion? That is, if the Constitution permits a delegatee (the commission) to exercise sentencing-related rulemaking power, how can it deny the delegator (the legislature) what is, in effect, the same rulemaking power?

The majority appears to offer two responses. First, it argues for a limiting principle that would prevent a legislature with broad authority from transforming (jury-determined) facts that constitute elements of a crime into (judge-determined) sentencing factors, thereby removing procedural protections that the Constitution would otherwise require. ("[C]onstitutional limits" prevent States from "defin[ing] away facts necessary to constitute a criminal offense"). The majority's cure, however, is not aimed at the disease.

* * * [T]he solution to the problem lies, not in prohibiting legislatures from enacting sentencing factors, but in sentencing rules that determine punishments on the basis of properly defined relevant conduct, with sensitivity to the need for procedural protections where sentencing factors are determined by a judge (for example, use of a "reasonable doubt" standard), and invocation of the Due Process Clause where the history of the crime at issue, together with the nature of the facts to be proved, reveals unusual and serious procedural unfairness. Cf. *McMillan*, 477 U.S. at 88 (upholding statute in part because it "gives no impression of having been tailored to permit the [sentencing factor] to be a tail which wags the dog of the substantive offense").

Second, the majority, in support of its constitutional rule, emphasizes the concept of a statutory "maximum." * * * From a defendant's perspective, the legislature's decision to cap the possible range of punishment at a statutorily prescribed "maximum" would affect the actual sentence imposed no differently than a sentencing commission's (or a sentencing judge's) similar determination. Indeed, as a practical matter, a legislated mandatory "minimum" is far more important to an actual defendant. A judge and a commission, after all, are legally free to select any sentence below a statute's maximum, but they are not free to subvert a statutory minimum.

* * * I am willing, consequently, to assume that the majority's rule would provide a degree of increased procedural protection in respect to those particular sentencing factors currently embodied in statutes. I nonetheless believe that any such increased protection provides little practical help and comes at too high a price. For one thing, by leaving mandatory minimum sentences untouched, the majority's rule simply encourages any legislature interested in asserting control over the sentencing process to do so by creating those minimums. That result would mean significantly less procedural fairness, not more. For another thing, this Court's case law, prior to *Jones* led legislatures to believe that they were permitted to increase a statutory maximum sentence on the basis of a sentencing factor. * * * [T]he rationale that underlies the Court's rule suggests a principle—jury determination of all sentencing-related facts—that, unless restricted, threatens the workability of every criminal justice system (if applied to judges) or threatens efforts to make those systems more uniform, hence more fair (if applied to commissions). * * *

Notes

1. Soon after *Apprendi* was decided, scores of challengers attempted to take advantage of what Justice O'Connor had termed a "watershed change in constitutional law." *Harris v. United States*, 536 U.S. 545 (2002) held that *Apprendi* is inapplicable to mandatory minimum sentences. Under federal law, carrying a firearm in relation to a drug trafficking offense requires a mandatory minimum sentence of five years. The judge, rather than jury, in Harris's case found that he had flourished a gun and sentenced him to seven years. Justice Kennedy's opinion first decided that the mandatory minimum provision was a sentence enhancement provision rather than a separate offense. This view affirmed *McMillan v. Pennsylvania*, 477 U.S. 79 (1986), which permitted a legislature to specify a condition for a mandatory minimum without making the condition an element of the crime. *Apprendi* did not apply to the mandatory minimum concept at issue, because that decision required a jury determination beyond a reasonable doubt for any fact that increased the penalty for a crime above the prescribed statutory *maximum* sentence. A "judge may impose the minimum, the maximum, or any other sentence within the range without seeking further authorization from" a jury.

2. By contrast, the Court in *Ring v. Arizona*, 536 U.S. 584 (2002) concluded that it violated *Apprendi* for a sentencing judge sitting without a jury to find an aggravating circumstance necessary for imposition of the death penalty. When the judge made that finding, the defendant was exposed to a penalty greater than that authorized by the jury's verdict alone, in violation of *Apprendi*.

The Court stated in *Schriro v. Summerlin*, 542 U.S. 348 (2004), that *Ring* did not apply retroactively to cases like Summerlin's which was already final on direct review when *Ring* was decided. New substantive rules generally apply retroactively; new procedural rules like *Ring* apply retroactively only if they implicate the fundamental fairness and accuracy of the proceeding. *Ring* altered only the method of deciding whether the defendant was subject to the death penalty and therefore was not a "watershed rule of criminal procedure."

3. However, the failure of a federal indictment to allege a drug quantity that was necessary for and could result in an enhanced statutory maximum sentence violates *Apprendi*. In *United States v. Cotton*, 535 U.S. 625 (2002), the defendants never objected to the error at trial, thereby requiring a plain error analysis. The parties on appeal agreed that the omission of the drug quantity was an error that affected the defendant's substantial rights. However, the Court found that the error did not seriously affect the fairness, integrity, or public reputation of judicial proceedings and therefore did not constitute plain error requiring a reversal of the conviction.

UNITED STATES v. BOOKER

125 S.Ct. 738 (2005).

Justice STEVENS delivered the opinion of the Court in part [in which Justice SCALIA, Justice SOUTER, Justice THOMAS, and Justice GINSBURG join].

The question presented ... is whether an application of the Federal Sentencing Guidelines violated the Sixth Amendment. In each case, the courts below held that binding rules set forth in the Guidelines limited the severity of the sentence that the judge could lawfully impose on the defendant based on the facts found by the jury at his trial. In both cases the courts rejected, on the basis of our decision in *Blakely v. Washington*, 542 U.S. 296, 124 S.Ct. 2531 (2004), the Government's recommended application of the Sentencing Guidelines because the proposed sentences were based on additional facts that the sentencing judge found by a preponderance of the evidence. We hold that both courts correctly concluded that the Sixth Amendment as construed in *Blakely* does apply to the Sentencing Guidelines. In a separate opinion authored by Justice Breyer, the Court concludes that in light of this holding, two provisions of the Sentencing Reform Act of 1984(SRA) that have the effect of making the Guidelines mandatory must be invalidated in order to allow the statute to operate in a manner consistent with congressional intent.

I

Respondent Booker was charged with possession with intent to distribute at least 50 grams of cocaine base (crack). Having heard evidence that he had 92.5 grams in his duffel bag, the jury found him guilty of violating 21 U.S.C. § 841(a)(1). That statute prescribes a minimum sentence of 10 years in prison and a maximum sentence of life for that offense. § 841(b)(1)(A)(iii).

Based upon Booker's criminal history and the quantity of drugs found by the jury, the Sentencing Guidelines required the District Court

Judge to select a "base" sentence of not less than 210 nor more than 262 months in prison. See United States Sentencing Commission, Guidelines Manual §§ 2D1.1(c)(4), 4A1.1 (Nov.2003) (hereinafter USSG). The judge, however, held a post-trial sentencing proceeding and concluded by a preponderance of the evidence that Booker had possessed an additional 566 grams of crack and that he was guilty of obstructing justice. Those findings mandated that the judge select a sentence between 360 months and life imprisonment; the judge imposed a sentence at the low end of the range. Thus, instead of the sentence of 21 years and 10 months that the judge could have imposed on the basis of the facts proved to the jury beyond a reasonable doubt, Booker received a 30–year sentence.

Over the dissent of Judge Easterbrook, the Court of Appeals for the Seventh Circuit held that this application of the Sentencing Guidelines conflicted with our holding in *Apprendi v. New Jersey*, 530 U.S. 466, 490 (2000), that "[o]ther than the fact of a prior conviction, any fact that increases the penalty for a crime beyond the prescribed statutory maximum must be submitted to a jury, and proved beyond a reasonable doubt." 375 F.3d 508, 510 (2004). The majority relied on our holding in *Blakely v. Washington*, 542 U.S. 296, 124 S.Ct. 2531 (2004), that "the 'statutory maximum' for *Apprendi* purposes is the maximum sentence a judge may impose solely on the basis of the facts reflected in the jury verdict or admitted by the defendant." *Id.*, at ___, 124 S.Ct., at 2537. The court held that the sentence violated the Sixth Amendment, and remanded with instructions to the District Court either to sentence respondent within the sentencing range supported by the jury's findings or to hold a separate sentencing hearing before a jury. * * *

II

It has been settled throughout our history that the Constitution protects every criminal defendant "against conviction except upon proof beyond a reasonable doubt of every fact necessary to constitute the crime with which he is charged." *In re Winship*, 397 U.S. 358, 364, (1970). It is equally clear that the "Constitution gives a criminal defendant the right to demand that a jury find him guilty of all the elements of the crime with which he is charged." *United States v. Gaudin*, 515 U.S. 506, 511, (1995). These basic precepts, firmly rooted in the common law, have provided the basis for recent decisions interpreting modern criminal statutes and sentencing procedures. * * *

In *Blakely v. Washington*, 542 U.S. 296, 124 S.Ct. 2531 (2004), we dealt with a determinate sentencing scheme similar to the Federal Sentencing Guidelines. There the defendant pleaded guilty to kidnaping, a class B felony punishable by a term of not more than 10 years. Other provisions of Washington law, comparable to the Federal Sentencing Guidelines, mandated a "standard" sentence of 49–to–53 months, unless the judge found aggravating facts justifying an exceptional sentence. Although the prosecutor recommended a sentence in the standard range, the judge found that the defendant had acted with " 'deliberate cruelty' " and sentenced him to 90 months. *Id.*, at ___, 124 S.Ct., at 2534.

* * * The application of Washington's sentencing scheme violated the defendant's right to have the jury find the existence of " 'any particular fact' " that the law makes essential to his punishment. 542 U.S., at ___, 124 S.Ct., at 2536. That right is implicated whenever a judge seeks to impose a sentence that is not solely based on "facts reflected in the jury verdict or admitted by the defendant." *Id.*, at ___, 124 S.Ct., at 2537 (emphasis deleted). We rejected the State's argument that the jury verdict was sufficient to authorize a sentence within the general 10–year sentence for Class B felonies, noting that under Washington law, the judge was required to find additional facts in order to impose the greater 90–month sentence. Our precedents, we explained, make clear "that the 'statutory maximum' for Apprendi purposes is the maximum sentence a judge may impose solely on the basis of the facts reflected in the jury verdict or admitted by the defendant." *Ibid.* at ___, 124 S.Ct., at 2537 (emphasis in original). The determination that the defendant acted with deliberate cruelty, like the determination in Apprendi that the defendant acted with racial malice, increased the sentence that the defendant could have otherwise received. Since this fact was found by a judge using a preponderance of the evidence standard, the sentence violated Blakely's Sixth Amendment rights.

As the dissenting opinions in *Blakely* recognized, there is no distinction of constitutional significance between the Federal Sentencing Guidelines and the Washington procedures at issue in that case. See, e.g., 542 U.S., at ___, 124 S.Ct., at 2540 (opinion of O'CONNOR, J.) ("The structure of the Federal Guidelines likewise does not, as the Government half-heartedly suggests, provide any grounds for distinction. . . . If anything, the structural differences that do exist make the Federal Guidelines more vulnerable to attack"). This conclusion rests on the premise, common to both systems, that the relevant sentencing rules are mandatory and impose binding requirements on all sentencing judges.

If the Guidelines as currently written could be read as merely advisory provisions that recommended, rather than required, the selection of particular sentences in response to differing sets of facts, their use would not implicate the Sixth Amendment. We have never doubted the authority of a judge to exercise broad discretion in imposing a sentence within a statutory range. See *Apprendi*, 530 U.S., at 481, 120 S.Ct. 2348; *Williams v. New York*, 337 U.S. 241, 246, 69 S.Ct. 1079, 93 L.Ed. 1337 (1949). Indeed, everyone agrees that the constitutional issues presented by these cases would have been avoided entirely if Congress had omitted from the SRA the provisions that make the Guidelines binding on district judges; it is that circumstance that makes the Court's answer to the second question presented possible. For when a trial judge exercises his discretion to select a specific sentence within a defined range, the defendant has no right to a jury determination of the facts that the judge deems relevant.

The Guidelines as written, however, are not advisory; they are mandatory and binding on all judges. While subsection (a) of § 3553 of the sentencing statute lists the Sentencing Guidelines as one factor to be considered in imposing a sentence, subsection (b) directs that the court "shall impose a sentence of the kind, and within the range" established by the Guidelines, subject to departures in specific, limited cases. Because they are binding on judges, we have consistently held that the Guidelines have the force and effect of laws. See, e.g., Mistretta v. United States, 488 U.S. 361, 391, 109 S.Ct. 647, 102 L.Ed.2d 714 (1989); Stinson v. United States, 508 U.S. 36, 42, 113 S.Ct. 1913, 123 L.Ed.2d 598 (1993).

The availability of a departure in specified circumstances does not avoid the constitutional issue, just as it did not in *Blakely* itself. The Guidelines permit departures from the prescribed sentencing range in cases in which the judge "finds that there exists an aggravating or mitigating circumstance of a kind, or to a degree, not adequately taken into consideration by the Sentencing Commission in formulating the guidelines that should result in a sentence different from that described." 18 U.S.C.A. § 3553(b)(1) (Supp.2004). At first glance, one might believe that the ability of a district judge to depart from the Guidelines means that she is bound only by the statutory maximum. Were this the case, there would be no *Apprendi* problem. Importantly, however, departures are not available in every case, and in fact are unavailable in most. In most cases, as a matter of law, the Commission will have adequately taken all relevant factors into account, and no departure will be legally permissible. In those instances, the judge is bound to impose a sentence within the Guidelines range. It was for this reason that we rejected a similar argument in *Blakely*, holding that although the Washington statute allowed the judge to impose a sentence outside the sentencing range for " 'substantial and compelling reasons,' " that exception was not available for *Blakely* himself. 542 U.S., at ___, 124 S.Ct., at 2535. The sentencing judge would have been reversed had he invoked the departure section to justify the sentence.

Booker's case illustrates the mandatory nature of the Guidelines. The jury convicted him of possessing at least 50 grams of crack in violation of 21 U.S.C. § 841(b)(1)(A)(iii) based on evidence that he had 92.5 grams of crack in his duffel bag. Under these facts, the Guidelines specified an offense level of 32, which, given the defendant's criminal history category, authorized a sentence of 210–to–262 months. See USSG § 2D1.1(c)(4). Booker's is a run-of-the-mill drug case, and does not present any factors that were inadequately considered by the Commission. The sentencing judge would therefore have been reversed had he not imposed a sentence within the level 32 Guidelines range. Booker's actual sentence, however, was 360 months, almost 10 years longer than the Guidelines range supported by the jury verdict alone. To reach this sentence, the judge found facts beyond those found by the jury: namely, that Booker possessed 566 grams of crack in addition to the 92.5 grams in his duffel bag. The jury never heard any evidence of the additional drug quantity, and the judge found it true by a preponderance of the evidence. Thus, just as in *Blakely*, "the jury's verdict alone does not authorize the sentence. The judge acquires that authority only upon finding some additional fact." 542 U.S., at ___, 124 S.Ct., at 2538. There is no relevant distinction between the sentence imposed pursuant to the Washington statutes in *Blakely* and the sentences imposed pursuant to the Federal Sentencing Guidelines in these cases.

In his dissent, Justice Breyer argues on historical grounds that the Guidelines scheme is constitutional across the board. He points to traditional judicial authority to increase sentences to take account of any unusual blameworthiness in the manner employed in committing a crime, an authority that the Guidelines require to be exercised consistently throughout the system. This tradition, however, does not provide a sound guide to enforcement of the Sixth Amendment's guarantee of a jury trial in today's world.

It is quite true that once determinate sentencing had fallen from favor, American judges commonly determined facts justifying a choice of a heavier sentence on account of the manner in which particular defendants acted. *Apprendi*, 530 U.S., at 481, 120 S.Ct. 2348. In 1986, however, our own cases first recognized a new trend in the legislative regulation of sentencing when we considered the significance of facts selected by legislatures that not only authorized, or even mandated, heavier sentences than would otherwise have been imposed, but increased the range of sentences possible for the underlying crime. Provisions for such enhancements of the permissible sentencing range reflected growing and wholly justified legislative concern about the proliferation and variety of drug crimes and their frequent identification with firearms offences.

The effect of the increasing emphasis on facts that enhanced sentencing ranges, however, was to increase the judge's power and diminish that of the jury. It became the judge, not the jury, that determined the upper limits of sentencing, and the facts determined were not required to be raised before trial or proved by more than a preponderance. * * *

III

The Government advances three arguments in support of its submission that we should not apply our reasoning in *Blakely* to the Federal Sentencing Guidelines. It contends that *Blakely* is distinguishable because the Guidelines were promulgated by a commission rather than the Legislature; that principles of *stare decisis* require us to follow four earlier decisions that are arguably inconsistent with *Blakely*; and that the application of *Blakely* to the Guidelines would conflict with separation of powers principles reflected in *Mistretta v. United States*, 488 U.S. 361 (1989). These arguments are unpersuasive. * * *

IV

All of the foregoing support our conclusion that our holding in *Blakely* applies to the Sentencing Guidelines. We recognize ... that in some cases jury factfinding may impair the most expedient and efficient sentencing of defendants. But the interest in fairness and reliability protected by the right to a jury trial—a common-law right that defendants enjoyed for centuries and that is now enshrined in the Sixth Amendment—has always outweighed the interest in concluding trials swiftly. *Blakely*, 542 U.S., at ___, 124 S.Ct., at 2542–43. As Blackstone put it:

> [H]owever convenient these [new methods of trial] may appear at first (as doubtless all arbitrary powers, well executed, are the most convenient) yet let it be again remembered, that delays, and little inconveniences in the forms of justice, are the price that all free nations must pay for their liberty in more substantial matters; that these inroads upon this sacred bulwark of the nation are fundamentally opposite to the spirit of our constitution; and that, though begun in trifles, the precedent may gradually increase and spread, to the utter disuse of juries in questions of the most momentous concerns. 4 Commentaries on the Laws of England 343–344 (1769).

Accordingly, we reaffirm our holding in *Apprendi*: Any fact (other than a prior conviction) which is necessary to support a sentence exceeding the maximum authorized by the facts established by a plea of guilty or a jury verdict must be admitted by the defendant or proved to a jury beyond a reasonable doubt.

Justice BREYER delivered the opinion of the Court in part. [in which THE CHIEF JUSTICE, Justice O'CONNOR, Justice KENNEDY, and Justice GINSBURG join].

* * * We answer the question of remedy by finding the provision of the federal sentencing statute that makes the Guidelines mandatory incompatible with today's constitutional holding. We conclude that this provision must be severed and excised, as must one other statutory section which depends upon the Guidelines' mandatory nature. So modified, the Federal Sentencing Act, see Sentencing Reform Act of 1984 makes the Guidelines effectively advisory. It requires a sentencing court to consider Guidelines ranges, but it permits the court to tailor the sentence in light of other statutory concerns as well.

I

We answer the remedial question by looking to legislative intent. We seek to determine what "Congress would have intended" in light of the Court's constitutional holding. In this instance, we must determine which of the two following remedial approaches is the more compatible with the legislature's intent as embodied in the 1984 Sentencing Act.

One approach, that of Justice Stevens' dissent, would retain the Sentencing Act (and the Guidelines) as written, but would engraft onto the existing system today's Sixth Amendment "jury trial" requirement. The addition would change the Guidelines by preventing the sentencing court from increasing a sentence on the basis of a fact that the jury did not find (or that the offender did not admit).

The other approach, which we now adopt, would (through severance and excision of two provisions) make the Guidelines system advisory while maintaining a strong connection between the sentence imposed and the offender's real conduct—a connection important to the increased uniformity of sentencing that Congress intended its Guidelines system to achieve. Both approaches would significantly alter the system that Congress designed. But today's constitutional holding means that it is no longer possible to maintain the judicial factfinding that Congress thought would underpin the mandatory Guidelines system that it sought to create and that Congress wrote into the Act in 18 U.S.C.A. §§ 3553(a) and 3661 (main ed. and Supp.2004). Hence we must decide whether we would deviate less radically from Congress' intended system (1) by superimposing the constitutional requirement announced today or (2) through elimination of some provisions of the statute. * * *

In today's context—a highly complex statute, interrelated provisions, and a constitutional requirement that creates fundamental change—we cannot assume that Congress, if faced with the statute's invalidity in key applications, would have preferred to apply the statute in as many other instances as possible. Neither can we determine likely congressional intent mechanically. We cannot simply approach the problem grammatically, say, by looking to see whether the constitutional requirement and the words of the Act are linguistically compatible.

Nor do simple numbers provide an answer. It is, of course, true that the numbers show that the constitutional jury trial requirement would lead to additional decisionmaking by juries in only a minority of cases. Prosecutors and defense attorneys would still resolve the lion's share of criminal matters through plea bargaining, and plea bargaining takes place without a jury. Many of the rest involve only simple issues calling for no upward Guidelines adjustment. And in at least some of the remainder, a judge may find adequate room to adjust a sentence within the single Guidelines range to which the jury verdict points, or within the overlap between that range and the next highest.

But the constitutional jury trial requirement would nonetheless affect every case. It would affect decisions about whether to go to trial. It would affect the content of plea negotiations. It would alter the judge's role in sentencing. Thus we must determine likely intent not by counting proceedings, but by evaluating the consequences of the Court's constitutional requirement in light of the Act's language, its history, and its basic purposes.

While reasonable minds can, and do, differ about the outcome, we conclude that the constitutional jury trial requirement is not compatible with the Act as written and that some severance and excision are necessary. * * * In essence, in what follows, we explain both (1) why Congress would likely have preferred the total invalidation of the Act to an Act with the Court's Sixth Amendment requirement engrafted onto it, and (2) why Congress would likely have preferred the excision of some of the Act, namely the Act's mandatory language, to the invalidation of the entire Act. That is to say, in light of today's holding, we compare maintaining the Act as written with jury factfinding added (the dissenters' proposed remedy) to the total invalidation of the statute, and conclude that Congress would have preferred the latter. We then compare our own remedy to the total invalidation of the statute, and conclude that Congress would have preferred our remedy.

II

Several considerations convince us that, were the Court's constitutional requirement added onto the Sentencing Act as currently written, the requirement would so transform the scheme that Congress created that Congress likely would not have intended the Act as so modified to stand. First, the statute's text states that "[t]he court" when sentencing will consider "the nature and circumstances of the offense and the history and characteristics of the defendant." 18 U.S.C.A. § 3553(a)(1). In context, the words "the court" mean "the judge without the jury," not "the judge working together with the jury." A further statutory provision, by removing typical "jury trial" evidentiary limitations, makes this clear. See § 3661 (ruling out any "limitation . . . on the information concerning the [offender's] background, character, and conduct" that the "court . . . may receive"). The Act's history confirms it. See, e.g., S.Rep. No. 98–225, p. 51 (1983) (the Guidelines system "will guide the judge in making" sentencing decisions) (emphasis added); id., at 52 (before sentencing, "the judge" must consider "the nature and circumstances of the offense"); id., at 53 ("the judge" must conduct "a comprehensive examination of the characteristics of the particular offense and the particular offender").

This provision is tied to the provision of the Act that makes the Guidelines mandatory, see § 3553(b)(1) (Supp.2004). They are part and parcel of a single, unified whole—a whole that Congress intended to apply to all federal sentencing.

This provision makes it difficult to justify Justice Stevens' approach, for that approach requires reading the words "the court" as if they meant "the judge working together with the jury." Unlike Justice Stevens, we do not believe we can interpret the statute's language to save its constitutionality, because we believe that any such reinterpretation, even if limited to instances in which a Sixth Amendment problem arises, would be "plainly contrary to the intent of Congress." *United States v. X–Citement Video, Inc.*, 513 U.S. 64, 78 (1994). * * *

Second, Congress' basic statutory goal—a system that diminishes sentencing disparity—depends for its success upon judicial efforts to determine, and to base punishment upon, the real conduct that underlies the crime of conviction. That determination is particularly important in the federal system where crimes defined as, for example, "obstruct[ing], delay[ing], or affect[ing] commerce or the movement of any article or commodity in commerce, by . . . extortion," 18 U.S.C. § 1951(a), or, say, using the mail "for the purpose of executing" a "scheme or artifice to defraud," § 1341, can encompass a vast range of very different kinds of underlying conduct. But it is also important even in respect to ordinary crimes, such as robbery, where an act that meets the statutory definition can be committed in a host of different ways. Judges have long looked to real conduct when sentencing. Federal judges have long relied upon a presentence report, prepared by a probation officer, for information (often unavailable until after the trial) relevant to the manner in which the convicted offender committed the crime of conviction.

Congress expected this system to continue. That is why it specifically inserted into the Act the provision cited above, which (recodifying prior law) says that

> "[n]o limitation shall be placed on the information concerning the background, character, and conduct of a person convicted of an offense which a court of the United States may receive and consider for the purpose of imposing an appropriate sentence." 18 U.S.C. § 3661.

This Court's earlier opinions assumed that this system would continue. That is why the Court, for example, held in *United States v. Watts*, 519 U.S. 148 (1997), that a sentencing judge could rely for sentencing purposes upon a fact that a jury had found unproved (beyond a reasonable doubt).

The Sentencing Guidelines also assume that Congress intended this system to continue. That is why, among other things, they permit a judge to reject a plea-bargained sentence if he determines, after reviewing the presentence report, that the sentence does not adequately reflect the seriousness of the defendant's actual conduct.

To engraft the Court's constitutional requirement onto the sentencing statutes, however, would destroy the system. It would prevent a judge from relying upon a presentence report for factual information, relevant to sentencing, uncovered after the trial. In doing so, it would, even compared to pre-Guidelines sentencing, weaken the tie between a sentence and an offender's real conduct. It would thereby undermine the sentencing statute's basic aim of ensuring similar sentences for those who have committed similar crimes in similar ways.

Several examples help illustrate the point. Imagine Smith and Jones, each of whom violates the Hobbs Act in very different ways. See 18 U.S.C. § 1951(a) (forbidding "obstruct[ing], delay[ing], or affect[ing] commerce or the movement of any article or commodity in commerce, by . . . extortion"). Smith threatens to injure a co-worker unless the co-worker advances him a few dollars from the interstate company's till; Jones, after similarly threatening the co-worker, causes far more harm by seeking far more money, by making certain that the co-worker's family is aware of the threat, by arranging for deliveries of dead animals to the co-worker's home to show he is serious, and so forth. The offenders' behavior is very different; the known harmful consequences of their actions are different; their punishments both before, and after, the Guidelines would have been different. But, under the dissenters' approach, unless prosecutors decide to charge more than the elements of the crime, the judge would have to impose similar punishments.

Now imagine two former felons, Johnson and Jackson, each of whom engages in identical criminal behavior: threatening a bank teller with a gun, securing $50,000, and injuring an innocent bystander while fleeing the bank. Suppose prosecutors charge Johnson with one crime (say, illegal gun possession, and Jackson with another (say, bank robbery. Before the Guidelines, a single judge faced with such similar real conduct would have been able (within statutory limits) to impose similar sentences upon the two similar offenders despite the different charges brought against them. The Guidelines themselves would ordinarily have required judges to sentence the two offenders similarly. But under the dissenters' system, in these circumstances the offenders likely would receive different punishments. * * *

This point is critically important. Congress' basic goal in passing the Sentencing Act was to move the sentencing system in the direction of increased uniformity. That uniformity does not consist simply of similar sentences for those convicted of violations of the same statute—a uniformity consistent with the dissenters' remedial approach. It consists, more importantly, of similar relationships between sentences and real conduct, relationships that Congress' sentencing statutes helped to advance and that Justice Stevens' approach would undermine. * * *

Third, the sentencing statutes, read to include the Court's Sixth Amendment requirement, would create a system far more complex than Congress could have intended. How would courts and counsel work with an indictment and a jury trial that involved not just whether a defendant robbed a bank but also how? Would the indictment have to allege, in addition to the elements of robbery, whether the defendant possessed a firearm, whether he brandished or discharged it, whether he threatened death, whether he caused bodily injury, whether any such injury was ordinary, serious, permanent or life threatening, whether he abducted or physically restrained anyone, whether any victim was unusually vulnerable, how much money was taken, and whether he was an organizer, leader, manager, or supervisor in a robbery gang? See USSG §§ 2B3.1, 3B1.1. If so, how could a defendant mount a defense against some or all such specific claims should he also try simultaneously to maintain that the Government's evidence failed to place him at the scene of the crime? Would the indictment in a mail fraud case have to allege the number of victims, their vulnerability, and the amount taken from each? How could a judge expect a jury to work with the Guidelines' definitions of, say, "relevant conduct," which includes "all acts and omissions committed, aided, abetted, counseled, commanded, induced, procured, or willfully caused by the defendant; and [in the case of a conspiracy] all reasonably foreseeable acts and omissions of others in furtherance of the jointly undertaken criminal activity"? §§ 1B1.3(a)(1)(A)-(B). How would a jury measure "loss" in a securities fraud case—a matter so complex as to lead the Commission to instruct judges to make "only ... a reasonable estimate"? § 2B1.1, comment., n. 3(C). How would the court take account, for punishment purposes, of a defendant's contemptuous behavior at trial—a matter that the Government could not have charged in the indictment? § 3C1.1.

Fourth, plea bargaining would not significantly diminish the consequences of the Court's constitutional holding for the operation of the Guidelines. Rather, plea bargaining would make matters worse. Congress enacted the sentencing statutes in major part to achieve greater uniformity in sentencing, i.e., to increase the likelihood that offenders who engage in similar real conduct would receive similar sentences. The statutes reasonably assume that their efforts to move the trial-based sentencing process in the direction of greater sentencing uniformity would have a similar positive impact upon plea-bargained sentences, for plea bargaining takes place in the shadow of (i.e., with an eye towards the hypothetical result of) a potential trial.

That, too, is why Congress, understanding the realities of plea bargaining, authorized the Commission to promulgate policy statements that would assist sentencing judges in determining whether to reject a plea agreement after reading about the defendant's real conduct in a presentence report (and giving the offender an opportunity to challenge the report). See 28 U.S.C. § 994(a)(2)(E); USSG § 6B1.2(a). This system has not worked perfectly; judges have often simply accepted an agreed-upon account of the conduct at issue. But compared to pre-existing law, the statutes try to move the system in the right direction, i.e., toward greater sentencing uniformity.

The Court's constitutional jury trial requirement, however, if patched onto the present Sentencing Act, would move the system backwards in respect both to tried and to plea-bargained cases. In respect to tried cases, it would effectively deprive the judge of the ability to use post-verdict-acquired real-conduct information; it would prohibit the judge from basing a sentence upon any conduct other than the conduct the prosecutor chose to charge; and it would put a defendant to a set of difficult strategic choices as to which prosecutorial claims he would contest. The sentence that would emerge in a case tried under such a system would likely reflect real conduct less completely, less accurately, and less often than did a pre-Guidelines, as well as a Guidelines, trial. Because plea bargaining inevitably reflects estimates of what would happen at trial, plea bargaining too under such a system would move in the wrong direction. That is to say, in a sentencing system modified by the Court's constitutional requirement, plea bargaining would likely lead to sentences that gave greater weight, not to real conduct, but rather to the skill of counsel, the policies of the prosecutor, the caseload, and other factors that vary from place to place, defendant to defendant, and crime to crime. Compared to pre-Guidelines plea bargaining, plea bargaining of this kind would necessarily move federal sentencing in the direction of diminished, not increased, uniformity in sentencing. It would tend to defeat, not to further, Congress' basic statutory goal.

Such a system would have particularly troubling consequences with respect to prosecutorial power. Until now, sentencing factors have come before the judge in the presentence report. But in a sentencing system with the Court's constitutional requirement engrafted onto it, any factor that a prosecutor chose not to charge at the plea negotiation would be placed beyond the reach of the judge entirely. Prosecutors would thus exercise a power the Sentencing Act vested in judges: the power to decide, based on relevant information about the offense and the offender, which defendants merit heavier punishment.

In respondent Booker's case, for example, the jury heard evidence that the crime had involved 92.5 grams of crack cocaine, and convicted Booker of possessing more than 50 grams. But the judge, at sentencing, found that the crime had involved an additional 566 grams, for a total of 658.5 grams. A system that would require the jury, not the judge, to make the additional "566 grams" finding is a system in which the prosecutor, not the judge, would control the sentence. That is because it is the prosecutor who would have to decide what drug amount to charge. He could choose to charge 658.5 grams, or 92.5, or less. It is the prosecutor who, through such a charging decision, would control the sentencing range. And it is different prosecutors who, in different cases—say, in two cases involving 566 grams—would potentially insist upon different punishments for similar defendants who engaged in similar criminal conduct involving similar amounts of unlawful drugs— say, by charging one of them with the full 566 grams, and the other with 10. As long as different prosecutors react differently, a system with a patched-on jury factfinding requirement would mean different sentences for otherwise similar conduct, whether in the context of trials or that of plea bargaining. * * *

For all these reasons, Congress, had it been faced with the constitutional jury trial requirement, likely would not have passed the same Sentencing Act. It likely would have found the requirement incompatible with the Act as written. Hence the Act cannot remain valid in its entirety. Severance and excision are necessary.

III

We now turn to the question of which portions of the sentencing statute we must sever and excise as inconsistent with the Court's constitutional requirement. Although, as we have explained, we believe that Congress would have preferred the total invalidation of the statute to the dissenters' remedial approach, we nevertheless do not believe that the entire statute must be invalidated. Most of the statute is perfectly valid.

* * * [W]e must sever and excise two specific statutory provisions: the provision that requires sentencing courts to impose a sentence within the applicable Guidelines range (in the absence of circumstances that justify a departure), see 18 U.S.C. § 3553(b)(1), and the provision that sets forth standards of review on appeal, including de novo review of

departures from the applicable Guidelines range, see § 3742(e). With these two sections excised (and statutory cross-references to the two sections consequently invalidated), the remainder of the Act satisfies the Court's constitutional requirements. As the Court today recognizes in its first opinion in these cases, the existence of § 3553(b)(1) is a necessary condition of the constitutional violation. * * *

Without the "mandatory" provision, the Act nonetheless requires judges to take account of the Guidelines together with other sentencing goals. The Act nonetheless requires judges to consider the Guidelines "sentencing range established for . . . the applicable category of offense committed by the applicable category of defendant," the pertinent Sentencing Commission policy statements, the need to avoid unwarranted sentencing disparities, and the need to provide restitution to victims. And the Act nonetheless requires judges to impose sentences that reflect the seriousness of the offense, promote respect for the law, provide just punishment, afford adequate deterrence, protect the public, and effectively provide the defendant with needed educational or vocational training and medical care.

[D]espite the absence of § 3553(b)(1), the Act continues to provide for appeals from sentencing decisions (irrespective of whether the trial judge sentences within or outside the Guidelines range in the exercise of his discretionary power under § 3553(a)). We concede that the excision of § 3553(b)(1) requires the excision of a different, appeals-related section, namely § 3742(e), which sets forth standards of review on appeal. That section contains critical cross-references to the (now-excised) § 3553(b)(1) and consequently must be severed and excised for similar reasons.

Excision of § 3742(e), however, does not pose a critical problem for the handling of appeals. That is because, as we have previously held, a statute that does not explicitly set forth a standard of review may nonetheless do so implicitly. See *Pierce v. Underwood*, 487 U.S. 552, 558–560 (1988) (adopting a standard of review, where "neither a clear statutory prescription nor a historical tradition" existed, based on the statutory text and structure, and on practical considerations). We infer appropriate review standards from related statutory language, the structure of the statute, and the "sound administration of justice." *Pierce*, supra, at 559–560. And in this instance those factors, in addition to the past two decades of appellate practice in cases involving departures, imply a practical standard of review already familiar to appellate courts: review for "unreasonable [ness]." 18 U.S.C. § 3742(e)(3). * * *

Finally, the Act without its "mandatory" provision and related language remains consistent with Congress' initial and basic sentencing intent. Congress sought to "provide certainty and fairness in meeting the purposes of sentencing, [while] avoiding unwarranted sentencing disparities . . . [and] maintaining sufficient flexibility to permit individualized sentences when warranted." 28 U.S.C. § 991(b)(1)(B); see also USSG § 1A1.1, application note (explaining that Congress sought to achieve "honesty," "uniformity," and "proportionality" in sentencing (emphases deleted)). The system remaining after excision, while lacking the mandatory features that Congress enacted, retains other features that help to further these objectives. * * *

As we have said, the Sentencing Commission remains in place, writing Guidelines, collecting information about actual district court sentencing decisions, undertaking research, and revising the Guidelines accordingly. See 28 U.S.C.A. § 994. The district courts, while not bound to apply the Guidelines, must consult those Guidelines and take them into account when sentencing. See 18 U.S.C.A. §§ 3553(a)(4), (5). * * *

We do not doubt that Congress, when it wrote the Sentencing Act, intended to create a form of mandatory Guidelines system. But, we repeat, given today's constitutional holding, that is not a choice that remains open. Hence we have examined the statute in depth to determine Congress' likely intent in light of today's holding. And we have concluded that today's holding is fundamentally inconsistent with the judge-based sentencing system that Congress enacted into law. In our view, it is more consistent with Congress' likely intent in enacting the Sentencing Reform Act (1) to preserve important elements of that system while severing and excising two provisions (§§ 3553(b)(1) and 3742(e)) than (2) to maintain all provisions of the Act and engraft today's constitutional requirement onto that statutory scheme.

Ours, of course, is not the last word: The ball now lies in Congress' court. The National Legislature is equipped to devise and install, long-term, the sentencing system, compatible with the Constitution, that Congress judges best for the federal system of justice. * * *

V

In respondent Booker's case, the District Court applied the Guidelines as written and imposed a sentence higher than the maximum authorized solely by the jury's verdict. The Court of Appeals held *Blakely* applicable to the Guidelines, concluded that Booker's sentence violated the Sixth Amendment, vacated the judgment of the District Court, and remanded for resentencing. We affirm the judgment of the Court of Appeals and remand the case. On remand, the District Court should impose a sentence in accordance with today's opinions, and, if the sentence comes before the Court of Appeals for review, the Court of Appeals should apply the review standards set forth in this opinion. * * *

As these dispositions indicate, we must apply today's holdings—both the Sixth Amendment holding and our remedial interpretation of the Sentencing Act—to all cases on direct review. See *Griffith v. Kentucky*, 479 U.S. 314, 328 (1987) ("[A] new rule for the conduct of criminal prosecutions is to be applied retroactively to all cases ... pending on direct review or not yet final, with no exception for cases in which the new rule constitutes a 'clear break' with the past"). That fact does not mean that we believe that every sentence gives rise to a Sixth Amendment violation. Nor do we believe that every appeal will lead to a new sentencing hearing. That is because we expect reviewing courts to apply ordinary prudential doctrines, determining, for example, whether the issue was raised below and whether it fails the "plain-error" test. It is also because, in cases not involving a Sixth Amendment violation, whether resentencing is warranted or whether it will instead be sufficient to review a sentence for reasonableness may depend upon application of the harmless-error doctrine.

It is so ordered.

[Justice Breyer's dissent repeated the argument from his *Apprendi* dissent that the jury trial right permits judges to find "sentencing facts." Justice Stevens also dissented, arguing that the prosecution should be permitted to empanel juries to find "sentencing facts" that would increase a sentence above the maximum term of a presumptive range. Justice Scalia's dissenting opinion criticized the severance remedy, preferring a reasonableness standard.]

Notes and Questions

1. *How does* Booker *affect a generation of defendants were sentenced under the Sentencing Guidelines?* Immediately after *Booker*, officials from the United States Sentencing Commission, the Department of Justice, and the Congress were cautious about whether further legislative action was necessary.

The instant impact of *Booker* was to throw into disarray the appeals of hundreds of federal criminal cases. As often happens with systemic change, most of the cases were pragmatic in trying to assess the backlog of cases ripe for resentencing. Defendants sentenced *before Booker* comprised the largest group potentially seeking a new sentencing hearing.

Several circuits quickly decided that *Booker* is not retroactive. See, e.g., *McReynolds v. United States*, 397 F.3d 479 (7th Cir. 2005); *Humphress v. United States*, 398 F.3d 855 (6th Cir.2005); *United States v. Price*, 400 F.3d 844 (10th Cir.2005); *Varela v. United States*, 400 F.3d 864 (11th Cir.2005); *Guzman v. United States*, 404 F.3d 139 (2d Cir. 2005); *Lloyd v. United States*, 407 F.3d 608 (3d Cir. 2005).

A second, smaller group of federal defendants were sentenced after *Blakely v. Washington* indicated a potential *Apprendi* problem with the Federal Guidelines. Some post-*Blakely* courts continued to apply (erroneously, as it turned out) the Guidelines as mandatory; some used them as advisory without considering the statutory factors like age, poor upbringing, education, mental health, drug addiction and other factors previously thought to be inapplicable under the Guidelines.

2. *Appellate Review of Sentences After Booker.* What about cases that were on appeal at the time *Booker* was decided? *United States v. Crosby*, 397 F.3d 103 (2d Cir. 2005) set out a procedure for a limited remand on sentences invalid under *Booker*. As long as the trial court retains jurisdiction of the case, the trial judge may make a finding of whether she would have imposed a materially different sentence and, if she would have, she keeps the

case and resentences. If the case is already on appeal, the circuit would review for "plain error" by the sentencing court when the defendant did not raise an objection. If a defendant raised an objection and the Guidelines calculation was correct, but erroneous because the Guidelines' use was compulsory, the Second Circuit would remand to the trial court for resentencing in conformity with *Booker*. In a deeply divided *en banc* opinion, the Ninth Circuit chose to follow the *Crosby* approach. *United States v. Ameline*, 409 F.3d 1073 (9th Cir. 2005).

Not every circuit has agreed with the *Crosby* approach. For example, in *United States v. Rodriguez*, 398 F.3d 1291 (11th Cir. 2005), the court required that when the defendant did not raise the Booker issue, he must establish a "reasonable probability" that the trial judge would have imposed a different sentence had the Guidelines not been mandatory. That decision brought a swift rebuke from the Seventh Circuit in *United States v. Paladino*, 401 F.3d 471 (7th Cir. 2005).

3. *Appellate Advice for Prospective Trial Court Sentencing.* For future cases, the circuits have attempted to prescribe a sentencing method, now that the mandatory nature of the Guidelines is unconstitutional.

> [A]t this point, we can identify several essential aspects of *Booker* that concern the selection of sentences. First, the Guidelines are no longer mandatory. Second, the sentencing judge must consider the Guidelines and all of the other factors listed in section 3553(a). Third, consideration of the Guidelines will normally require determination of the applicable Guidelines range, or at least identification of the arguably applicable ranges, and consideration of applicable policy statements. Fourth, the sentencing judge should decide, after considering the Guidelines and all the other factors set forth in section 3553(a), whether (i) to impose the sentence that would have been imposed under the Guidelines, i.e., a sentence within the applicable Guidelines range or within permissible departure authority, or (ii) to impose a non-Guidelines sentence. Fifth, the sentencing judge is entitled to find all the facts appropriate for determining either a Guidelines sentence or a non-Guidelines sentence.

United States v. Crosby, 397 F.3d 103 (2d Cir. 2005).

4. *What is a "reasonable" sentence?* Justice Breyer's opinion held that the remedy for the constitutional violation was to make the Guidelines advisory and to replace *de novo* appellate review of sentences with a reasonableness standard of review. Few appellate courts have seized the opportunity to define "reasonableness." One exception is *United States v. Fleming*, 397 F.3d 95 (2d Cir. 2005), in which the court described how an appellate court would assess the reasonableness of a federal sentence.

> The appellate function in this context should exhibit restraint, not micromanagement. In addition to their familiarity with the record, including the presentence report, district judges have discussed sentencing with a probation officer and gained an impression of a defendant from the entirety of the proceedings, including the defendant's opportunity for sentencing allocution. The appellate court proceeds only with the record. Although the brevity or length of a sentence can exceed the bounds of "reasonableness," we anticipate encountering such circumstances infrequently.

In the pending case, the District Court sentenced a defendant who had served three sentences of imprisonment and was appearing for his third violation of a term of supervised release. Judge Gershon considered the current violations "massive." She noted that the Defendant had been given the benefit of a substantial departure for his cooperation in connection with his sentence on the prisoner assault charge. See U.S.S.G. § 7B1.4, comment. (n.4) ("Where the original sentence was the result of a downward departure (e.g., as a reward for substantial assistance), . . . an upward departure may be warranted."). She identified as the "primary purpose" of her sentence "the necessity for both punishment for [Fleming's] behavior and deterrence." The District Court's explanation was sufficient to facilitate appellate review. Under all the circumstances, we cannot say that the two-year sentence was unreasonable.

We observed today in *Crosby* that in many cases it will not be possible to tell whether the district judge would have given a nontrivially different sentence if fully informed of the currently applicable requirements of the [Federal Sentencing Guidelines], the Supreme Court's decision in *Booker*, and our preliminary guidance in *Crosby*. However, the pending appeal is readily distinguishable from a case like Crosby, where we remanded to afford the District Court an opportunity to consider whether to resentence. Here the sentencing judge, functioning under a sentencing regime that, even before *Booker*, was advisory with respect to revocation of supervised release, knew that she was not bound by the policy statements and chose to exercise her discretion. In any case, the two-year sentence was well considered and would obviously be retained if an opportunity for reconsideration were afforded. Nothing additional has been suggested that now needs to be brought to the District Court's attention under prevailing law.

AMERICAN LAW INSTITUTE
MODEL PENAL CODE

(Official Draft, 1962)

PART I. GENERAL PROVISIONS

Article 1. Preliminary

SECTION 1.01. [*Omitted*]

SECTION 1.02. PURPOSES; PRINCIPLES OF CONSTRUCTION

(1) The general purposes of the provisions governing the definition of offenses are:

(a) to forbid and prevent conduct that unjustifiably and inexcusably inflicts or threatens substantial harm to individual or public interests;

(b) to subject to public control persons whose conduct indicates that they are disposed to commit crimes;

(c) to safeguard conduct that is without fault from condemnation as criminal;

(d) to give fair warning of the nature of the conduct declared to constitute an offense;

(e) to differentiate on reasonable grounds between serious and minor offenses.

(2) The general purposes of the provisions governing the sentencing and treatment of offenders are:

(a) to prevent the commission of offenses;

(b) to promote the correction and rehabilitation of offenders;

(c) to safeguard offenders against excessive, disproportionate or arbitrary punishment;

(d) to give fair warning of the nature of the sentences that may be imposed on conviction of an offense;

(e) to differentiate among offenders with a view to a just individualization in their treatment;

(f) to define, coordinate and harmonize the powers, duties and functions of the courts and of administrative officers and agencies responsible for dealing with offenders;

(g) to advance the use of generally accepted scientific methods and knowledge in the sentencing and treatment of offenders;

(h) to integrate responsibility for the administration of the correctional system in a State Department of Correction [or other single department or agency].

(3) The provisions of the Code shall be construed according to the fair import of their terms but when the language is susceptible of differing constructions it shall be interpreted to further the general purposes stated in this Section and the special purposes of the particular provision involved. The discretionary powers conferred by the Code shall be exercised in accordance with the criteria stated in the Code and, insofar as such criteria are not decisive, to further the general purposes stated in this Section.

SECTION 1.03. [*Omitted*]

SECTION 1.04. CLASSES OF CRIMES; VIOLATIONS

(1) An offense defined by this Code or by any other statute of this State, for which a sentence of [death or of] imprisonment is authorized, constitutes a crime. Crimes are classified as felonies, misdemeanors or petty misdemeanors.

(2) A crime is a felony if it is so designated in this Code or if persons convicted thereof may be sentenced [to death or] to imprisonment for a term that, apart from an extended term, is in excess of one year.

(3) A crime is a misdemeanor if it is so designated in the Code or in a statute other than this Code enacted subsequent thereto.

(4) A crime is a petty misdemeanor if it is so designated in this Code or in a statute other than this Code enacted subsequent thereto or if it is defined by a statute other than this Code that now provides that persons convicted thereof may be sentenced to imprisonment for a term of which the maximum is less than one year.

(5) An offense defined by this Code or by any other statute of this State constitutes a violation if it is so designated in this Code or in the law defining the offense or if no other sentence than a fine, or fine and forfeiture or other civil penalty is authorized upon conviction or if it is defined by a statute other than this Code that now provides that the offense shall not constitute a crime. A violation does not constitute a crime and conviction of a violation shall not give rise to any disability or legal disadvantage based on conviction of a criminal offense.

(6) Any offense declared by law to constitute a crime, without specification of the grade thereof or of the sentence authorized upon conviction, is a misdemeanor.

(7) An offense defined by any statute of this State other than this Code shall be classified as provided in this Section and the sentence that may be imposed upon conviction thereof shall hereafter be governed by the Code.

SECTION 1.05.   ALL OFFENSES DEFINED BY STATUTE; APPLICATION OF GENERAL
PROVISIONS OF THE CODE

(1) No conduct constitutes an offense unless it is a crime or violation under this Code or another statute of the State.

(2) The provisions of Part I of the Code are applicable to offenses defined by other statutes, unless the Code otherwise provides.

(3) This Section does not affect the power of a court to punish for contempt or to employ any sanction authorized by law for the enforcement of an order or a civil judgment or decree.

SECTION 1.06.   [*Omitted*]

SECTION 1.07.   METHOD OF PROSECUTION WHEN CONDUCT CONSTITUTES MORE
THAN ONE OFFENSE

(1) *Prosecution for Multiple Offenses; Limitation on Convictions.* When the same conduct of a defendant may establish the commission of more than one offense, the defendant may be prosecuted for each such offense. He may not, however, be convicted of more than one offense if:

(a) one offense is included in the other, as defined in Subsection (4) of this Section; or

(b) one offense consists only of a conspiracy or other form of preparation to commit the other; or

(c) inconsistent findings of fact are required to establish the commission of the offenses; or

(d) the offenses differ only in that one is defined to prohibit a designated kind of conduct generally and the other to prohibit a specific instance of such conduct; or

(e) the offense is defined as a continuing course of conduct and the defendant's course of conduct was uninterrupted, unless the law provides that specific periods of such conduct constitute separate offenses.

(2) *Limitation on Separate Trials for Multiple Offenses.* Except as provided in Subsection (3) of this Section, a defendant shall not be subject to separate trials for multiple offenses based on the same conduct or arising from the same criminal episode, if such offenses are known to the appropriate prosecuting officer at the time of the commencement of the first trial and are within the jurisdiction of a single court.

(3) *Authority of Court to Order Separate Trials.* When a defendant is charged with two or more offenses based on the same conduct or arising from the same criminal episode, the Court, on application of the prosecuting attorney or of the defendant, may order any such charge to be tried separately, if it is satisfied that justice so requires.

(4) *Conviction of Included Offense Permitted.* A defendant may be convicted of an offense included in an offense charged in the indictment [or the information]. An offense is so included when:

(a) it is established by proof of the same or less than all the facts required to establish the commission of the offense charged; or

(b) it consists of an attempt or solicitation to commit the offense charged or to commit an offense otherwise included therein; or

(c) it differs from the offense charged only in the respect that a less serious injury or risk of injury to the same person, property or public interest or a lesser kind of culpability suffices to establish its commission.

(5) *Submission of Included Offense to Jury.* The Court shall not be obligated to charge the jury with respect to an included offense unless there is a rational basis for a verdict acquitting the defendant of the offense charged and convicting him of the included offense.

SECTIONS 1.08.–1.11. [*Omitted*]

SECTION 1.12. PROOF BEYOND A REASONABLE DOUBT; AFFIRMATIVE DEFENSES; BURDEN OF PROVING FACT WHEN NOT AN ELEMENT OF AN OFFENSE; PRESUMPTIONS

(1) No person may be convicted of an offense unless each element of such offense is proved beyond a reasonable doubt. In the absence of such proof, the innocence of the defendant is assumed.

(2) Subsection (1) of the Section does not:

(a) require the disproof of an affirmative defense unless and until there is evidence supporting such defense; or

(b) apply to any defense which the Code or another statute plainly requires the defendant to prove by a preponderance of evidence.

(3) A ground of defense is affirmative, within the meaning of Subsection (2)(a) of the Section, when:

(a) it arises under a section of the Code that so provides; or

(b) it relates to an offense defined by a statute other than the Code and such statute so provides; or

(c) it involves a matter of excuse or justification peculiarly within the knowledge of the defendant on which he can fairly be required to adduce supporting evidence.

(4) When the application of the Code depends upon the finding of a fact which is not an element of an offense, unless the Code otherwise provides:

(a) the burden of proving the fact is on the prosecution or defendant, depending on whose interest or contention will be furthered if the finding should be made; and

(b) the fact must be proved to the satisfaction of the Court or jury, as the case may be.

(5) When the Code establishes a presumption with respect to any fact that is an element of an offense, it has the following consequences:

(a) when there is evidence of the facts that give rise to the presumption, the issue of the existence of the presumed fact must be submitted to the jury, unless the Court is satisfied that the evidence as a whole clearly negatives the presumed fact; and

(b) when the issue of the existence of the presumed fact is submitted to the jury, the Court shall charge that while the presumed fact must, on all the evidence, be proved beyond a reasonable doubt, the law declares that the jury may regard the facts giving rise to the presumption as sufficient evidence of the presumed fact.

(6) A presumption not established by the Code or inconsistent with it has the consequences otherwise accorded it by law.

SECTION 1.13.   GENERAL DEFINITIONS

In this Code, unless a different meaning plainly is required:

(1) "statute" includes the Constitution and a local law or ordinance of a political subdivision of the State;

(2) "act" or "action" means a bodily movement whether voluntary or involuntary;

(3) "voluntary" has the meaning specified in Section 2.01;

(4) "omission" means a failure to act;

(5) "conduct" means an action or omission and its accompanying state of mind, or, where relevant, a series of acts and omissions;

(6) "actor" includes, where relevant, a person guilty of an omission;

(7) "acted" includes, where relevant, "omitted to act";

(8) "person," "he" and "actor" include any natural person and, where relevant, a corporation or an unincorporated association;

(9) "element of an offense" means (i) such conduct or (ii) such attendant circumstance or (iii) such a result of conduct as

(a) is included in the description of the forbidden conduct in the definition of the offense; or

(b) establishes the required kind of culpability; or

(c) negatives an excuse or justification for such conduct; or

(d) negatives a defense under the statute of limitations; or

(e) establishes jurisdiction or venue;

(10) "material element of an offense" means an element that does not relate exclusively to the statute of limitations, jurisdiction, venue or to any other matter similarly unconnected with (i) the harm or evil, incident to conduct, sought to be prevented by the law defining the offense, or (ii) the existence of a justification or excuse for such conduct;

(11) "purposely" has the meaning specified in Section 2.02 and equivalent terms such as "with purpose," "designed" or "with design" have the same meaning;

(12) "intentionally" or "with intent" means purposely;

(13) "knowingly" has the meaning specified in Section 2.02 and equivalent terms such as "knowing" or "with knowledge" have the same meaning;

(14) "recklessly" has the meaning specified in Section 2.02 and equivalent terms such as "recklessness" or "with recklessness" have the same meaning;

(15) "negligently" has the meaning specified in Section 2.02 and equivalent terms such as "negligence" or "with negligence" have the same meaning;

(16) "reasonably believes" or "reasonable belief" designates a belief which the actor is not reckless or negligent in holding.

Article 2. General Principles of Liability

SECTION 2.01. REQUIREMENT OF VOLUNTARY ACT; OMISSION AS BASIS OF LIABILITY; POSSESSION AS AN ACT

(1) A person is not guilty of an offense unless his liability is based on conduct which includes a voluntary act or the omission to perform an act of which he is physically capable.

(2) The following are not voluntary acts within the meaning of this Section:

(a) a reflex or convulsion;

(b) a bodily movement during unconsciousness or sleep;

(c) conduct during hypnosis or resulting from hypnotic suggestion;

(d) a bodily movement that otherwise is not a product of the effort or determination of the actor, either conscious or habitual.

(3) Liability for the commission of an offense may not be based on an omission unaccompanied by action unless:

(a) the omission is expressly made sufficient by the law defining the offense; or

(b) a duty to perform the omitted act is otherwise imposed by law.

(4) Possession is an act, within the meaning of this Section, if the possessor knowingly procured or received the thing possessed or was aware of his control thereof for a sufficient period to have been able to terminate his possession.

SECTION 2.02. GENERAL REQUIREMENTS OF CULPABILITY

(1) *Minimum Requirements of Culpability.* Except as provided in Section 2.05, a person is not guilty of an offense unless he acted purposely, knowingly, recklessly or negligently, as the law may require, with respect to each material element of the offense.

(2) *Kinds of Culpability Defined.*

(a) *Purposely.* A person acts purposely with respect to a material element of an offense when:

(i) if the element involves the nature of his conduct or a result thereof, it is his conscious object to engage in conduct of that nature or to cause such a result; and

(ii) if the element involves the attendant circumstances, he is aware of the existence of such circumstances or he believes or hopes that they exist.

(b) *Knowingly.* A person acts knowingly with respect to a material element of an offense when:

(i) if the element involves the nature of his conduct or the attendant circumstances, he is aware that his conduct is of that nature or that such circumstances exist; and

(ii) if the element involves a result of his conduct, he is aware that it is practically certain that his conduct will cause such a result.

(c) *Recklessly.* A person acts recklessly with respect to a material element of an offense when he consciously disregards a substantial and unjustifiable risk that the material element exists or will result from his conduct. The risk must be of such a nature and degree that, considering the nature and purpose of the actor's conduct and the circumstances known to him, its disregard involves a gross deviation from the standard of conduct that a law-abiding person would observe in the actor's situation.

(d) *Negligently.* A person acts negligently with respect to a material element of an offense when he should be aware of a substantial and unjustifiable risk that the material element exists or will result from his conduct. The risk must be of such a nature and degree that the actor's failure to perceive it, considering the nature and purpose of his conduct and the circumstances known to him, involves a gross deviation from the standard of care that a reasonable person would observe in the actor's situation.

(3) *Culpability Required Unless Otherwise Provided.* When the culpability sufficient to establish a material element of an offense is not prescribed by law, such element is established if a person acts purposely, knowingly or recklessly with respect thereto.

(4) *Prescribed Culpability Requirement Applies to All Material Elements.* When the law defining an offense prescribes the kind of culpability that is sufficient for the commission of an offense, without distinguishing among the material elements thereof, such provision shall apply to all the material elements of the offense, unless a contrary purpose plainly appears.

(5) *Substitutes for Negligence, Recklessness and Knowledge.* When the law provides that negligence suffices to establish an element of an offense, such element also is established if a person acts purposely, knowingly or recklessly. When recklessness suffices to establish an element, such element also is established if a person acts purposely or knowingly. When acting knowingly suffices to establish an element, such element also is established if a person acts purposely.

(6) *Requirement of Purpose Satisfied if Purpose Is Conditional.* When a particular purpose is an element of an offense, the element is established although such purpose is conditional, unless the condition negatives the harm or evil sought to be prevented by the law defining the offense.

(7) *Requirement of Knowledge Satisfied by Knowledge of High Probability.* When knowledge of the existence of a particular fact is an element of an offense, such knowledge is established if a person is aware of a high probability of its existence, unless he actually believes that it does not exist.

(8) *Requirement of Wilfulness Satisfied by Acting Knowingly.* A requirement that an offense be committed wilfully is satisfied if a person acts knowingly with respect to the material elements of the offense, unless a purpose to impose further requirements appears.

(9) *Culpability as to Illegality of Conduct.* Neither knowledge nor recklessness or negligence as to whether conduct constitutes an offense or as to the existence, meaning or application of the law determining the elements of an offense is an element of such offense, unless the definition of the offense or the Code so provides.

(10) *Culpability as Determinant of Grade of Offense.* When the grade or degree of an offense depends on whether the offense is committed purposely, knowingly, recklessly or negligently, its grade or degree shall be the lowest for which the determinative kind of culpability is established with respect to any material element of the offense.

SECTION 2.03. CAUSAL RELATIONSHIP BETWEEN CONDUCT AND RESULT; DIVERGENCE BETWEEN RESULT DESIGNED OR CONTEMPLATED AND ACTUAL RESULT OR BETWEEN PROBABLE AND ACTUAL RESULT

(1) Conduct is the cause of a result when:

(a) it is an antecedent but for which the result in question would not have occurred; and

(b) the relationship between the conduct and result satisfies any additional causal requirements imposed by the Code or by the law defining the offense.

(2) When purposely or knowingly causing a particular result is an element of an offense, the element is not established if the actual result is not within the purpose or the contemplation of the actor unless:

(a) the actual result differs from that designed or contemplated, as the case may be, only in the respect that a different person or different property is injured or affected or that the injury or harm designed or contemplated would have been more serious or more extensive than that caused; or

(b) the actual result involves the same kind of injury or harm as that designed or contemplated and is not too remote or accidental in its occurrence to have a [just] bearing on the actor's liability or on the gravity of his offense.

(3) When recklessly or negligently causing a particular result is an element of an offense, the element is not established if the actual result is not within the risk of which the actor is aware or, in the case of negligence, of which he should be aware unless:

(a) the actual result differs from the probable result only in the respect that a different person or different property is injured or affected or that the probable injury or harm would have been more serious or more extensive than that caused; or

(b) the actual result involves the same kind of injury or harm as the probable result and is not too remote or accidental in its occurrence to have a [just] bearing on the actor's liability or on the gravity of his offense.

(4) When causing a particular result is a material element of an offense for which absolute liability is imposed by law, the element is not established unless the actual result is a probable consequence of the actor's conduct.

SECTION 2.04. IGNORANCE OR MISTAKE

(1) Ignorance or mistake as to a matter of fact or law is a defense if:

(a) the ignorance or mistake negatives the purpose, knowledge, belief, recklessness or negligence required to establish a material element of the offense; or

(b) the law provides that the state of mind established by such ignorance or mistake constitutes a defense.

(2) Although ignorance or mistake would otherwise afford a defense to the offense charged, the defense is not available if the defendant would be guilty of another offense had the situation been as he supposed. In such case, however, the ignorance or mistake of the defendant shall reduce the grade and degree of the offense of which he may be convicted to those of the offense of which he would be guilty had the situation been as he supposed.

(3) A belief that conduct does not legally constitute an offense is a defense to a prosecution for that offense based upon such conduct when:

(a) the statute or other enactment defining the offense is not known to the actor and has not been published or otherwise reasonably made available prior to the conduct alleged; or

(b) he acts in reasonable reliance upon an official statement of the law, afterward determined to be invalid or erroneous, contained in (i) a statute or other enactment; (ii) a judicial decision, opinion or judgment; (iii) an administrative order or grant of permission; or (iv) an official interpretation of the public officer or body charged by law with responsibility for the interpretation, administration or enforcement of the law defining the offense.

(4) The defendant must prove a defense arising under Subsection (3) of this Section by a preponderance of evidence.

SECTION 2.05. WHEN CULPABILITY REQUIREMENTS ARE INAPPLICABLE TO VIOLA-
TIONS AND TO OFFENSES DEFINED BY OTHER STATUTES;
EFFECT OF ABSOLUTE LIABILITY IN REDUCING GRADE OF
OFFENSE TO VIOLATION

(1) The requirements of culpability prescribed by Sections 2.01 and 2.02 do not apply to:

(a) offenses which constitute violations, unless the requirement involved is included in the definition of the offense or the Court determines that its application is consistent with effective enforcement of the law defining the offense; or

(b) offenses defined by statutes other than the Code, insofar as a legislative purpose to impose absolute liability for such offenses or with respect to any material element thereof plainly appears.

(2) Notwithstanding any other provision of existing law and unless a subsequent statute otherwise provides:

(a) when absolute liability is imposed with respect to any material element of an offense defined by a statute other than the Code and a conviction is based upon such liability, the offense constitutes a violation; and

(b) although absolute liability is imposed by law with respect to one or more of the material elements of an offense defined by a statute other than the Code, the culpable commission of the offense may be charged and proved, in which event negligence with respect to such elements constitutes sufficient culpability and the classification of the offense and the sentence that may be imposed therefor upon conviction are determined by Section 1.04 and Article 6 of the Code.

SECTION 2.06. LIABILITY FOR CONDUCT OF ANOTHER; COMPLICITY

(1) A person is guilty of an offense if it is committed by his own conduct or by the conduct of another person for which he is legally accountable, or both.

(2) A person is legally accountable for the conduct of another person when:

(a) acting with the kind of culpability that is sufficient for the commission of the offense, he causes an innocent or irresponsible person to engage in such conduct; or

(b) he is made accountable for the conduct of such other person by the Code or by the law defining the offense; or

(c) he is an accomplice of such other person in the commission of the offense.

(3) A person is an accomplice of another person in the commission of an offense if:

(a) with the purpose of promoting or facilitating the commission of the offense, he

(i) solicits such other person to commit it; or

(ii) aids or agrees or attempts to aid such other person in planning or committing it; or

(iii) having a legal duty to prevent the commission of the offense, fails to make proper effort so to do; or

(b) his conduct is expressly declared by law to establish his complicity.

(4) When causing a particular result is an element of an offense, an accomplice in the conduct causing such result is an accomplice in the commission of that offense, if he acts with the kind of culpability, if any, with respect to that result that is sufficient for the commission of the offense.

(5) A person who is legally incapable of committing a particular offense himself may be guilty thereof if it is committed by the conduct of another

person for which he is legally accountable, unless such liability is inconsistent with the purpose of the provision establishing his incapacity.

(6) Unless otherwise provided by the Code or by the law defining the offense, a person is not an accomplice in an offense committed by another person if:

(a) he is a victim of that offense; or

(b) the offense is so defined that his conduct is inevitably incident to its commission; or

(c) he terminates his complicity prior to the commission of the offense and

(i) wholly deprives it of effectiveness in the commission of the offense; or

(ii) gives timely warning to the law enforcement authorities or otherwise makes proper effort to prevent the commission of the offense.

(7) An accomplice may be convicted on proof of the commission of the offense and of his complicity therein, though the person claimed to have committed the offense has not been prosecuted or convicted or has been convicted of a different offense or degree of offense or has an immunity to prosecution or conviction or has been acquitted.

SECTION 2.07.   LIABILITY OF CORPORATIONS, UNINCORPORATED ASSOCIATIONS AND PERSONS ACTING, OR UNDER A DUTY TO ACT, IN THEIR BEHALF

(1) A corporation may be convicted of the commission of an offense if:

(a) the offense is a violation or the offense is defined by a statute other than the Code in which a legislative purpose to impose liability on corporations plainly appears and the conduct is performed by an agent of the corporation acting in behalf of the corporation within the scope of his office or employment, except that if the law defining the offense designates the agents for whose conduct the corporation is accountable or the circumstance under which it is accountable, such provisions shall apply; or

(b) the offense consists of an omission to discharge a specific duty of affirmative performance imposed on corporations by law; or

(c) the commission of the offense was authorized, requested, commanded, performed or recklessly tolerated by the board of directors or by a high managerial agent acting in behalf of the corporation within the scope of his office or employment.

(2) When absolute liability is imposed for the commission of an offense, a legislative purpose to impose liability on a corporation shall be assumed, unless the contrary plainly appears.

(3) An unincorporated association may be convicted of the commission of an offense if:

(a) the offense is defined by a statute other than the Code which expressly provides for the liability of such an association and the conduct is performed by an agent of the association acting in behalf of the association within the scope of his office or employment, except that if the law defining the offense designates the agents for whose conduct the association is accountable or the circumstances under which it is accountable, such provisions shall apply; or

(b) the offense consists of an omission to discharge a specific duty of affirmative performance imposed on associations by law.

(4) As used in the Section:

(a) "corporation" does not include an entity organized as or by a governmental agency for the execution of a governmental program;

(b) "agent" means any director, officer, servant, employee or other person authorized to act in behalf of the corporation or association and, in the case of an unincorporated association, a member of such association;

(c) "high managerial agent" means an officer of a corporation or an unincorporated association, or, in the case of a partnership, a partner, or any other agent of a corporation or association having duties of such responsibilities that his conduct may fairly be assumed to represent the policy of the corporation or association.

(5) In any prosecution of a corporation or an unincorporated association for the commission of an offense included within the terms of Subsection (1)(a) or Subsection (3)(a) of this Section, other than an offense for which absolute liability has been imposed, it shall be a defense if the defendant proves by a preponderance of evidence that the high managerial agent having supervisory responsibility over the subject matter of the offense employed due diligence to prevent its commission. This paragraph shall not apply if it is plainly inconsistent with the legislative purpose in defining the particular offense.

(6)(a) A person is legally accountable for any conduct he performs or causes to be performed in the name of the corporation or an unincorporated association or in its behalf to the same extent as if it were performed in his own name or behalf.

(b) Whenever a duty to act is imposed by law upon a corporation or an unincorporated association, any agent of the corporation or association having responsibility for the discharge of the duty is legally accountable for a reckless omission to perform the required act to the same extent as if the duty were imposed by law directly upon himself.

(c) When a person is convicted of an offense by reason of his legal accountability for the conduct of a corporation or an unincorporated association, he is subject to the sentence authorized by law when a natural person is convicted of an offense of the grade and the degree involved.

SECTION 2.08. INTOXICATION

(1) Except as provided in Subsection (4) of this Section, intoxication of the actor is not a defense unless it negatives an element of the offense.

(2) When recklessness establishes an element of the offense, if the actor, due to self-induced intoxication, is unaware of a risk of which he would have been aware had he been sober, such unawareness is immaterial.

(3) Intoxication does not, in itself, constitute mental disease within the meaning of Section 4.01.

(4) Intoxication that (a) is not self-induced or (b) is pathological is an affirmative defense if by reason of such intoxication the actor at the time of his conduct lacks substantial capacity either to appreciate its criminality [wrongfulness] or to conform his conduct to the requirements of law.

(5) *Definitions.* In this Section unless a different meaning plainly is required:

(a) "intoxication" means a disturbance of mental or physical capacities resulting from the introduction of substances into the body;

(b) "self-induced intoxication" means intoxication caused by substances which the actor knowingly introduces into his body, the tendency of which to cause intoxication he knows or ought to know, unless he introduces them pursuant to medical advice or under such circumstances as would afford a defense to a charge of crime;

(c) "pathological intoxication" means intoxication grossly excessive in degree, given the amount of the intoxicant, to which the actor does not know he is susceptible.

SECTION 2.09. DURESS

(1) It is an affirmative defense that the actor engaged in the conduct charged to constitute an offense because he was coerced to do so by the use of, or a threat to use, unlawful force against his person or the person of another, that a person of reasonable firmness in his situation would have been unable to resist.

(2) The defense provided by this Section is unavailable if the actor recklessly placed himself in a situation in which it was probable that he would be subjected to duress. The defense is also unavailable if he was negligent in placing himself in such a situation, whenever negligence suffices to establish culpability for the offense charged.

(3) It is not a defense that a woman acted on the command of her husband, unless she acted under such coercion as would establish a defense under this Section. [The presumption that a woman acting in the presence of her husband is coerced is abolished.]

(4) When the conduct of the actor would otherwise be justifiable under Section 3.02, this Section does not preclude such defense.

SECTION 2.10. MILITARY ORDERS

It is an affirmative defense that the actor, in engaging in the conduct charged to constitute an offense, does no more than execute an order of his superior in the armed services which he does not know to be unlawful.

SECTION 2.11.   CONSENT

(1) *In General.* The consent of the victim to conduct charged to constitute an offense or to the result thereof is a defense if such consent negatives an element of the offense or precludes the infliction of the harm or evil sought to be prevented by the law defining the offense.

(2) *Consent to Bodily Harm.* When conduct is charged to constitute an offense because it causes or threatens bodily harm, consent to such conduct or to the infliction of such harm is a defense if:

(a) the bodily injury consented to or threatened by the conduct consented to is not serious; or

(b) the conduct and the injury are reasonably foreseeable hazards of joint participation in a lawful athletic contest or competitive sport or other concerted activity not forbidden by law; or

(c) the consent establishes a justification for the conduct under Article 3 of the Code.

(3) *Ineffective Consent.* Unless otherwise provided by the Code or by the law defining the offense, assent does not constitute consent if:

(a) it is given by a person who is legally incompetent to authorize the conduct charged to constitute the offense; or

(b) it is given by a person who by reason of youth, mental disease or defect or intoxication is manifestly unable or known by the actor to be unable to make a reasonable judgment as to the nature or harmfulness of the conduct charged to constitute the offense; or

(c) it is given by a person whose improvident consent is sought to be prevented by the law defining the offense; or

(d) it is induced by force, duress or deception of a kind sought to be prevented by the law defining the offense.

SECTION 2.12.   DE MINIMIS INFRACTIONS

The Court shall dismiss a prosecution if, having regard to the nature of the conduct charged to constitute an offense and the nature of the attendant circumstances, it finds that the defendant's conduct:

(1) was within a customary license of tolerance, neither expressly negatived by the person whose interest was infringed nor inconsistent with the purpose of the law defining the offense; or

(2) did not actually cause or threaten the harm or evil sought to be prevented by the law defining the offense or did so only to an extent too trivial to warrant the condemnation of conviction; or

(3) presents such other extenuations that it cannot reasonably be regarded as envisaged by the legislature in forbidding the offense.

The Court shall not dismiss a prosecution under Subsection (3) of this Section without filing a written statement of its reasons.

SECTION 2.13. ENTRAPMENT

(1) A public law enforcement official or a person acting in cooperation with such an official perpetrates an entrapment if for the purpose of obtaining evidence of the commission of an offense, he induces or encourages another person to engage in conduct constituting such offense by either:

(a) making knowingly false representations designed to induce the belief that such conduct is not prohibited; or

(b) employing methods of persuasion or inducement that create a substantial risk that such an offense will be committed by persons other than those who are ready to commit it.

(2) Except as provided in Subsection (3) of this Section, a person prosecuted for an offense shall be acquitted if he proves by a preponderance of evidence that his conduct occurred in response to an entrapment. The issue of entrapment shall be tried by the Court in the absence of the jury.

(3) The defense afforded by this Section is unavailable when causing or threatening bodily injury is an element of the offense charged and the prosecution is based on conduct causing or threatening such injury to a person other than the person perpetrating the entrapment.

Article 3. General Principles of Justification

SECTION 3.01. JUSTIFICATION AN AFFIRMATIVE DEFENSE; CIVIL REMEDIES UNAFFECTED

(1) In any prosecution based on conduct that is justifiable under this Article, justification is an affirmative defense.

(2) The fact that conduct is justifiable under this Article does not abolish or impair any remedy for such conduct that is available in any civil action.

SECTION 3.02. JUSTIFICATION GENERALLY: CHOICE OF EVILS

(1) Conduct that the actor believes to be necessary to avoid a harm or evil to himself or to another is justifiable, provided that:

(a) the harm or evil sought to be avoided by such conduct is greater than that sought to be prevented by the law defining the offense charged; and

(b) neither the Code nor other law defining the offense provides exceptions or defenses dealing with the specific situation involved; and

(c) a legislative purpose to exclude the justification claimed does not otherwise plainly appear.

(2) When the actor was reckless or negligent in bringing about the situation requiring a choice of harms or evils or in appraising the necessity for his conduct, the justification afforded by this Section is unavailable in a prosecution for any offense for which recklessness or negligence, as the case may be, suffices to establish culpability.

SECTION 3.03. EXECUTION OF PUBLIC DUTY

(1) Except as provided in Subsection (2) of this Section, conduct is justifiable when it is required or authorized by:

(a) the law defining the duties or functions of a public officer or the assistance to be rendered to such officer in the performance of his duties; or

(b) the law governing the execution of legal process; or

(c) the judgment or order of a competent court or tribunal; or

(d) the law governing the armed services or the lawful conduct of war; or

(e) any other provision of law imposing a public duty.

(2) The other sections of this Article apply to:

(a) the use of force upon or toward the person of another for any of the purposes dealt with in such sections; and

(b) the use of deadly force for any purpose, unless the use of such force is otherwise expressly authorized by law or occurs in the lawful conduct of war.

(3) The justification afforded by Subsection (1) of this Section applies:

(a) when the actor believes his conduct to be required or authorized by the judgment or direction of a competent court or tribunal or in the lawful execution of legal process, notwithstanding lack of jurisdiction of the court or defect in the legal process; and

(b) when the actor believes his conduct to be required or authorized to assist a public officer in the performance of his duties, notwithstanding that the officer exceeded his legal authority.

SECTION 3.04. USE OF FORCE IN SELF–PROTECTION

(1) *Use of Force Justifiable for Protection of the Person.* Subject to the provisions of this Section and of Section 3.09, the use of force upon or toward another person is justifiable when the actor believes that such force is immediately necessary for the purpose of protecting himself against the use of unlawful force by such other person on the present occasion.

(2) *Limitations on Justifying Necessity for Use of Force.*

(a) The use of force is not justifiable under this Section:

(i) to resist an arrest that the actor knows is being made by a peace officer, although the arrest is unlawful; or

(ii) to resist force used by the occupier or possessor of property or by another person on his behalf, where the actor knows that the person using the force is doing so under a claim of right to protect the property, except that this limitation shall not apply if:

(1) the actor is a public officer acting in the performance of his duties or a person lawfully assisting him therein or a person making or assisting in a lawful arrest; or

(2) the actor has been unlawfully dispossessed of the property and is making a re-entry or recaption justified by Section 3.06; or

(3) the actor believes that such force is necessary to protect himself against death or serious bodily harm.

(b) The use of deadly force is not justifiable under this Section unless the actor believes that such force is necessary to protect himself against death, serious bodily harm, kidnapping or sexual intercourse compelled by force or threat; nor is it justifiable if:

(i) the actor, with the purpose of causing death or serious bodily injury, provoked the use of force against himself in the same encounter; or

(ii) the actor knows that he can avoid the necessity of using such force with complete safety by retreating or by surrendering possession of a thing to a person asserting a claim of right thereto or by complying with a demand that he abstain from any action that he has no duty to take, except that:

(1) the actor is not obliged to retreat from his dwelling or place of work, unless he was the initial aggressor or is assailed in his place of work by another person whose place of work the actor knows it to be; and

(2) a public officer justified in using force in the performance of his duties or a person justified in using force in his assistance or a person justified in using force in making an arrest or preventing an escape is not obliged to desist from efforts to perform such duty, effect such arrest or prevent such escape because of resistance or threatened resistance by or on behalf of the person against whom such action is directed.

(c) Except as required by paragraphs (a) and (b) of this Subsection, a person employing protective force may estimate the necessity thereof under the circumstances as he believes them to be when the force is used, without retreating, surrendering possession, doing any other act which he has no legal duty to do or abstaining from any lawful action.

(3) *Use of Confinement as Protective Force.* The justification afforded by this Section extends to the use of confinement as protective force only if the actor takes all reasonable measures to terminate the confinement as soon as he knows that he safely can, unless the person confined has been arrested on a charge of crime.

SECTION 3.05. USE OF FORCE FOR THE PROTECTION OF OTHER PERSONS

(1) Subject to the provisions of this Section and of Section 3.09, the use of force upon or toward the person of another is justifiable to protect a third person when:

(a) the actor would be justified under Section 3.04 in using such force to protect himself against the injury he believes to be threatened to the person whom he seeks to protect; and

(b) under the circumstances as the actor believes them to be, the person whom he seeks to protect would be justified in using such protective force; and

(c) the actor believes that his intervention is necessary for the protection of such other person.

(2) Notwithstanding Subsection (1) of this Section:

(a) when the actor would be obliged under Section 3.04 to retreat, to surrender the possession of a thing or to comply with a demand before using force in self-protection, he is not obliged to do so before using force for the protection of another person, unless he knows that he can thereby secure the complete safety of such other person; and

(b) when the person whom the actor seeks to protect would be obliged under Section 3.04 to retreat, to surrender the possession of a thing or to comply with a demand if he knew that he could obtain complete safety by so doing, the actor is obliged to try to cause him to do so before using force in his protection if the actor knows that he can obtain complete safety in that way; and

(c) neither the actor nor the person whom he seeks to protect is obliged to retreat when in the other's dwelling or place of work to any greater extent than in his own.

SECTION 3.06. USE OF FORCE FOR THE PROTECTION OF PROPERTY

(1) *Use of Force Justifiable for Protection of Property.* Subject to the provisions of this Section and of Section 3.09, the use of force upon or toward the person of another is justifiable when the actor believes that such force is immediately necessary:

(a) to prevent or terminate an unlawful entry or other trespass upon land or a trespass against or the unlawful carrying away of tangible, movable property, provided that such land or movable property is, or is believed by the actor to be, in his possession or in the possession of another person for whose protection he acts; or

(b) to effect an entry or re-entry upon land or to retake tangible movable property, provided that the actor believes that he or the person by whose authority he acts or a person from whom he or such other person derives title was unlawfully dispossessed of such land or movable property and is entitled to possession, and provided, further, that:

(i) the force is used immediately or on fresh pursuit after such dispossession; or

(ii) the actor believes that the person against whom he uses force has no claim of right to the possession of the property and, in the case of land, the circumstances, as the actor believes them to be, are of such urgency that it would be an exceptional hardship to postpone the entry or re-entry until a court order is obtained.

(2) *Meaning of Possession.* For the purposes of Subsection (1) of this Section:

(a) a person who has parted with the custody of property to another who refuses to restore it to him is no longer in possession, unless the property is movable and was and still is located on land in his possession;

(b) a person who has been dispossessed of land does not regain possession thereof merely by setting foot thereon;

(c) a person who has a license to use or occupy real property is deemed to be in possession thereof except against the licensor acting under claim of right.

(3) *Limitations on Justifiable Use of Force.*

(a) *Request to Desist.* The use of force is justifiable under this Section only if the actor first requests the person against whom such force is used to desist from his interference with the property, unless the actor believes that:

(i) such request would be useless; or

(ii) it would be dangerous to himself or another person to make the request; or

(iii) substantial harm will be done to the physical condition of the property which is sought to be protected before the request can effectively be made.

(b) *Exclusion of Trespasser.* The use of force to prevent or terminate a trespass is not justifiable under this Section if the actor knows that the exclusion of the trespasser will expose him to substantial danger of serious bodily harm.

(c) *Resistance of Lawful Re-entry or Recaption.* The use of force to prevent an entry or re-entry upon land or the recaption of movable property is not justifiable under this Section, although the actor believes that such re-entry or recaption is unlawful, if:

(i) the re-entry or recaption is made by or on behalf of a person who was actually dispossessed of the property; and

(ii) it is otherwise justifiable under paragraph (1)(b) of this Section.

(d) *Use of Deadly Force.* The use of deadly force is not justifiable under this Section unless the actor believes that:

(i) the person against whom the force is used is attempting to dispossess him of his dwelling otherwise than under a claim of right to its possession; or

(ii) the person against whom the force is used is attempting to commit or consummate arson, burglary, robbery or other felonious theft or property destruction and either:

(1) has employed or threatened deadly force against or in the presence of the actor; or

(2) the use of force other than deadly force to prevent the commission or the consummation of the crime would expose the actor or another in his presence to substantial danger of serious bodily harm.

(4) *Use of Confinement as Protective Force.* The justification afforded by this Section extends to the use of confinement as protective force only if the actor takes all reasonable measures to terminate the confinement as soon as he knows that he can do so with safety to the property, unless the person confined has been arrested on a charge of crime.

(5) *Use of Device to Protect Property.* The justification afforded by this section extends to the use of a device for the purpose of protecting property only if:

(a) the device is not designed to cause or known to create a substantial risk of causing death or serious bodily injury; and

(b) the use of the particular device to protect the property from entry or trespass is reasonable under the circumstances, as the actor believes them to be; and

(c) the device is one customarily used for such a purpose or reasonable care is taken to make known to probable intruders the fact that it is used.

(6) *Use of Force to Pass Wrongful Obstructor.* The use of force to pass a person whom the actor believes to be purposely or knowingly and unjustifiably obstructing the actor from going to a place to which he may lawfully go is justifiable, provided that:

(a) the actor believes that the person against whom he uses force has no claim of right to obstruct the actor; and

(b) the actor is not being obstructed from entry or movement on land which he knows to be in the possession or custody of the person obstructing him, or in the possession or custody of another person by whose authority the obstructor acts, unless the circumstances, as the actor believes them to be, are of such urgency that it would not be reasonable to postpone the entry or movement on such land until a court order is obtained; and

(c) the force used is not greater than would be justifiable if the person obstructing the actor were using force against him to prevent his passage.

SECTION 3.07. USE OF FORCE IN LAW ENFORCEMENT

(1) *Use of Force Justifiable to Effect an Arrest.* Subject to the provisions of this Section and of Section 3.09, the use of force upon or toward the person of another is justifiable when the actor is making or assisting in making an arrest and the actor believes that such force is immediately necessary to effect a lawful arrest.

(2) *Limitations on the Use of Force.*

(a) The use of force is not justifiable under this Section unless:

(i) the actor makes known the purpose of the arrest or believes that it is otherwise known by or cannot reasonably be made known to the person to be arrested; and

(ii) when the arrest is made under a warrant, the warrant is valid or believed by the actor to be valid.

(b) The use of deadly force is not justifiable under this Section unless:

(i) the arrest is for a felony; and

(ii) the person effecting the arrest is authorized to act as a peace officer or is assisting a person whom he believes to be authorized to act as a peace officer; and

(iii) the actor believes that the force employed creates no substantial risk of injury to innocent persons; and

(iv) the actor believes that:

(1) the crime for which the arrest is made involved conduct including the use or threatened use of deadly force; or

(2) there is a substantial risk that the person to be arrested will cause death or serious bodily harm if his apprehension is delayed.

(3) *Use of Force to Prevent Escape From Custody.* The use of force to prevent the escape of an arrested person from custody is justifiable when the force could justifiably have been employed to effect the arrest under which the person is in custody, except that a guard or other person authorized to act as a peace officer is justified in using any force, including deadly force, that he believes to be immediately necessary to prevent the escape of a person from a jail, prison, or other institution for the detention of persons charged with or convicted of a crime.

(4) *Use of Force by Private Person Assisting an Unlawful Arrest.*

(a) A private person who is summoned by a peace officer to assist in effecting an unlawful arrest, is justified in using any force that he would be justified in using if the arrest were lawful, provided that he does not believe the arrest is unlawful.

(b) A private person who assists another private person in effecting an unlawful arrest, or who, not being summoned, assists a peace officer in effecting an unlawful arrest, is justified in using any force that he would be justified in using if the arrest were lawful, provided that (i) he believes the arrest is lawful, and (ii) the arrest would be lawful if the facts were as he believes them to be.

(5) *Use of Force to Prevent Suicide or the Commission of a Crime.*

(a) The use of force upon or toward the person of another is justifiable when the actor believes that such force is immediately necessary to prevent such other person from committing suicide, inflicting serious bodily injury upon himself, committing or consummating the commission of a crime involving or threatening bodily injury, damage to or loss of property or a breach of the peace, except that:

(i) any limitations imposed by the other provisions of this Article on the justifiable use of force in self-protection, for the protection of others, the protection of property, the effectuation of an arrest or the prevention of an escape from custody shall apply notwithstanding the criminality of the conduct against which such force is used; and

(ii) the use of deadly force is not in any event justifiable under this Subsection unless:

(1) the actor believes that there is a substantial risk that the person whom he seeks to prevent from committing a crime

will cause death or serious bodily harm to another unless the commission or the consummation of the crime is prevented and that the use of such force presents no substantial risk of injury to innocent persons; or

(2) the actor believes that the use of such force is necessary to suppress a riot or mutiny after the rioters or mutineers have been ordered to disperse and warned, in any particular manner that the law may require, that such force will be used if they do not obey.

(b) The justification afforded by this Subsection extends to the use of confinement as preventive force only if the actor takes all reasonable measures to terminate the confinement as soon as he knows that he safely can, unless the person confined has been arrested on a charge of crime.

SECTION 3.08.   USE OF FORCE BY PERSONS WITH SPECIAL RESPONSIBILITY FOR CARE, DISCIPLINE OR SAFETY OF OTHER

The use of force upon or toward the person of another is justifiable if:

(1) the actor is the parent or guardian or other person similarly responsible for the general care and supervision of a minor or a person acting at the request of such parent, guardian or other responsible person and:

(a) the force is used for the purpose of safeguarding or promoting the welfare of the minor, including the prevention or punishment of his misconduct; and

(b) the force used is not designed to cause or known to create a substantial risk of causing death, serious bodily injury, disfigurement, extreme pain or mental distress or gross degradation; or

(2) the actor is a teacher or a person otherwise entrusted with the care or supervision for a special purpose of a minor and:

(a) the actor believes that the force used is necessary to further such special purpose, including the maintenance of reasonable discipline in a school, class or other group, and that the use of such force is consistent with the welfare of the minor; and

(b) the degree of force, if it had been used by the parent or guardian of the minor, would not be unjustifiable under Subsection (1)(b) of this Section; or

(3) the actor is the guardian or other person similarly responsible for the general care and supervision of an incompetent person and:

(a) the force is used for the purpose of safeguarding or promoting the welfare of the incompetent person, including the prevention of his misconduct, or, when such incompetent person is in a hospital or other institution for his care and custody, for the maintenance of reasonable discipline in such institution; and

(b) the force used is not designed to cause or known to create a substantial risk of causing death, serious bodily harm, disfigurement, extreme or unnecessary pain, mental distress, or humiliation; or

(4) the actor is a doctor or other therapist or a person assisting him at his direction and:

(a) the force is used for the purpose of administering a recognized form of treatment which the actor believes to be adapted to promoting the physical or mental health of the patient; and

(b) the treatment is administered with the consent of the patient or, if the patient is a minor or an incompetent person, with the consent of his parent or guardian or other person legally competent to consent in his behalf, or the treatment is administered in an emergency when the actor believes that no one competent to consent can be consulted and that a reasonable person, wishing to safeguard the welfare of the patient, would consent; or

(5) the actor is a warden or other authorized official of a correctional institution and:

(a) he believes that the force used is necessary for the purpose of enforcing the lawful rules or procedures of the institution, unless his belief in the lawfulness of the rule or procedure sought to be enforced is erroneous and his error is due to ignorance or mistake as to the provisions of the Code, and other provision of the criminal law or the law governing the administration of the institution; and

(b) the nature or degree of force used is not forbidden by Article 303 or 304 of the Code; and

(c) if deadly force is used, its use is otherwise justifiable under this Article; or

(6) the actor is a person responsible for the safety of a vessel or an aircraft or a person acting at his direction and:

(a) he believes that the force used is necessary to prevent interference with a lawful order, unless his belief in the lawfulness of the order is erroneous and his error is due to ignorance or mistake as to the law defining his authority; and

(b) if deadly force is used, its use is otherwise justifiable under this Article; or

(7) the actor is a person who is authorized or required by law to maintain order or decorum in a vehicle, train or other carrier or in a place where others are assembled, and:

(a) he believes that the force used is necessary for such purpose; and

(b) the force is not designed to cause or known to create a substantial risk of causing death, bodily harm, or extreme mental distress.

SECTION 3.09.   MISTAKE OF LAW AS TO UNLAWFULNESS OF FORCE OR LEGALITY OF ARREST; RECKLESS OR NEGLIGENT USE OF OTHERWISE JUSTIFIABLE FORCE; RECKLESS OR NEGLIGENT INJURY OR RISK OF INJURY TO INNOCENT PERSONS

(1) The justification afforded by Sections 3.04 to 3.07, inclusive, is unavailable when:

(a) the actor's belief in the unlawfulness of the force or conduct against which he employs protective force or his belief in the lawfulness of an arrest which he endeavors to effect by force is erroneous; and

(b) his error is due to ignorance or mistake as to the provisions of the Code, any other provision of the criminal law or the law governing the legality of an arrest or search.

(2) When the actor believes that the use of force upon or toward the person of another is necessary for any of the purposes for which such belief would establish a justification under Sections 3.03 to 3.08 but the actor is reckless or negligent in having such belief or in acquiring or failing to acquire any knowledge or belief which is material to the justifiability of his use of force, the justification afforded by those Sections is unavailable in a prosecution for an offense for which recklessness or negligence, as the case may be, suffices to establish culpability.

(3) When the actor is justified under Sections 3.03 to 3.08 in using force upon or toward the person of another but he recklessly or negligently injures or creates a risk of injury to innocent persons, the justification afforded by those Sections is unavailable in a prosecution for such recklessness or negligence towards innocent persons.

Section 3.10. Justification in Property Crimes

Conduct involving the appropriation, seizure or destruction of, damage to, intrusion on or interference with property is justifiable under circumstances that would establish a defense of privilege in a civil action based thereon unless:

(1) the Code or the law defining the offense deals with the specific situation involved; or

(2) a legislative purpose to exclude the justification claimed otherwise plainly appears.

Section 3.11. Definitions

In this Article, unless a different meaning plainly is required:

(1) "unlawful force" means force, including confinement, which is employed without the consent of the person against whom it is directed and the employment of which constitutes an offense or actionable tort or would constitute such offense or tort except for a defense (such as the absence of intent, negligence, or mental capacity; duress; youth; or diplomatic status) not amounting to a privilege to use the force. Assent constitutes consent, within the meaning of this Section, whether or not it otherwise is legally effective, except assent to the infliction of death or serious bodily harm.

(2) "deadly force" means force which the actor uses with the purpose of causing or which he knows to create a substantial risk of causing death or serious bodily injury. Purposely firing a firearm in the direction of another person or at a vehicle in which another person is believed to be constitutes deadly force. A threat to cause death or serious bodily injury, by the production of a weapon or otherwise, so long as the actor's purpose is limited to creating an apprehension that he will use deadly force if necessary, does not constitute deadly force.

(3) "dwelling" means any building or structure, though movable or temporary, or a portion thereof, that is for the time being the actor's home or place of lodging.

Article 4. Responsibility

SECTION 4.01. MENTAL DISEASE OR DEFECT EXCLUDING RESPONSIBILITY

(1) A person is not responsible for criminal conduct if at the time of such conduct as a result of mental disease or defect he lacks substantial capacity either to appreciate the criminality [wrongfulness] of his conduct or to conform his conduct to the requirements of law.

(2) As used in this Article, the terms "mental disease or defect" do not include an abnormality manifested only by repeated criminal or otherwise antisocial conduct.

SECTION 4.02. EVIDENCE OF MENTAL DISEASE OR DEFECT ADMISSIBLE WHEN RELEVANT TO ELEMENT OF THE OFFENSE; [MENTAL DISEASE OR DEFECT IMPAIRING CAPACITY AS GROUND FOR MITIGATION OF PUNISHMENT IN CAPITAL CASES]

(1) Evidence that the defendant suffered from a mental disease or defect is admissible whenever it is relevant to prove that the defendant did or did not have a state of mind which is an element of the offense.

[(2) Whenever the jury or the Court is authorized to determine or to recommend whether or not the defendant shall be sentenced to death or imprisonment upon conviction, evidence that the capacity of the defendant to appreciate the criminality [wrongfulness] of his conduct or to conform his conduct to the requirements of law was impaired as a result of mental disease or defect is admissible in favor of sentence of imprisonment.]

SECTION 4.03. MENTAL DISEASE OR DEFECT EXCLUDING RESPONSIBILITY IS AFFIRMATIVE DEFENSE; REQUIREMENT OF NOTICE; FORM OF VERDICT AND JUDGMENT WHEN FINDING OF IRRESPONSIBILITY IS MADE

(1) Mental disease or defect excluding responsibility is an affirmative defense.

(2) Evidence of mental disease or defect excluding responsibility is not admissible unless the defendant, at the time of entering his plea of not guilty or within ten days thereafter or at such later time as the Court may for good cause permit, files a written notice of his purpose to rely on such defense.

(3) When the defendant is acquitted on the ground of mental disease or defect excluding responsibility, the verdict and the judgment shall so state.

SECTION 4.04. MENTAL DISEASE OR DEFECT EXCLUDING FITNESS TO PROCEED

No person who as a result of mental disease or defect lacks capacity to understand the proceedings against him or to assist in his defense shall be tried, convicted or sentenced for the commission of an offense so long as such incapacity endures.

SECTION 4.05. PSYCHIATRIC EXAMINATION OF DEFENDANT WITH RESPECT TO MENTAL DISEASE OR DEFECT

(1) Whenever the defendant has filed a notice of intention to rely on the defense of mental disease or defect excluding responsibility, or there is

reason to doubt his fitness to proceed, or reason to believe that mental disease or defect of the defendant will otherwise become an issue in the cause, the Court shall appoint at least one qualified psychiatrist or shall request the Superintendent of the _____ Hospital to designate at least one qualified psychiatrist, which designation may be or include himself, to examine and report upon the mental condition of the defendant. The Court may order the defendant to be committed to a hospital or other suitable facility for the purpose of the examination for a period of not exceeding sixty days or such longer period as the Court determines to be necessary for the purpose and may direct that a qualified psychiatrist retained by the defendant be permitted to witness and participate in the examination.

(2) In such examination any method may be employed which is accepted by the medical profession for the examination of those alleged to be suffering from mental disease or defect.

(3) The report of the examination shall include the following: (a) a description of the nature of the examination; (b) a diagnosis of the mental condition of the defendant; (c) if the defendant suffers from a mental disease or defect, an opinion as to his capacity to understand the proceedings against him and to assist in his own defense; (d) when a notice of intention to rely on the defense of irresponsibility has been filed, an opinion as to the extent, if any, to which the capacity of the defendant to appreciate the criminality [wrongfulness] of his conduct or to conform his conduct to the requirements of law was impaired at the time of the criminal conduct charged; and (e) when directed by the Court, an opinion as to the capacity of the defendant to have a particular state of mind which is an element of the offense charged.

If the examination cannot be conducted by reason of the unwillingness of the defendant to participate therein, the report shall so state and shall include, if possible, an opinion as to whether such unwillingness of the defendant was the result of mental disease or defect.

The report of the examination shall be filed [in triplicate] with the clerk of the Court, who shall cause copies to be delivered to the district attorney and to counsel for the defendant.

SECTION 4.06.   DETERMINATION OF FITNESS TO PROCEED; EFFECT OF FINDING OF UNFITNESS; PROCEEDINGS IF FITNESS IS REGAINED [; POST–COMMITMENT HEARING]

(1) When the defendant's fitness to proceed is drawn in question, the issue shall be determined by the Court. If neither the prosecuting attorney nor counsel for the defendant contests the finding of the report filed pursuant to Section 4.05, the Court may make the determination on the basis of such report. If the finding is contested, the Court shall hold a hearing on the issue. If the report is received in evidence upon such hearing, the party who contests the finding thereof shall have the right to summon and to cross-examine the psychiatrists who joined in the report and to offer evidence upon the issue.

(2) If the Court determines that the defendant lacks fitness to proceed, the proceeding against him shall be suspended, except as provided in

Subsection (3) [Subsections (3) and (4)] of this Section, and the Court shall commit him to the custody of the Commissioner of Mental Hygiene [Public Health or Correction] to be placed in an appropriate institution of the Department of Mental Hygiene [Public Health or Correction] for so long as such unfitness shall endure. When the Court, on its own motion or upon the application of the Commissioner of Mental Hygiene [Public Health or Correction] or the prosecuting attorney, determines, after a hearing if a hearing is requested, that the defendant has regained fitness to proceed, the proceeding shall be resumed. If, however, the Court is of the view that so much time has elapsed since the commitment of the defendant that it would be unjust to resume the criminal proceeding, the Court may dismiss the charge and may order the defendant to be discharged or, subject to the law governing the civil commitment of persons suffering from mental disease or defect, order the defendant to be committed to an appropriate institution of the Department of Mental Hygiene [Public Health].

(3) The fact that the defendant is unfit to proceed does not preclude any legal objection to the prosecution that is susceptible of fair determination prior to trial and without the personal participation of the defendant.

[Alternative: (3) At any time within ninety days after commitment as provided in Subsection (2) of this Section, or at any later time with permission of the Court granted for good cause, the defendant or his counsel or the Commissioner of Mental Hygiene [Public Health or Correction] may apply for a special post-commitment hearing. If the application is made by or on behalf of a defendant not represented by counsel, he shall be afforded a reasonable opportunity to obtain counsel, and if he lacks funds to do so, counsel shall be assigned by the Court. The application shall be granted only if counsel for the defendant satisfies the Court by affidavit or otherwise that as an attorney he has reasonable grounds for a good faith belief that his client has, on the facts and the law, a defense to the charge other than mental disease or defect excluding responsibility.

[(4) If the motion for a special post-commitment hearing is granted, the hearing shall be by the Court without a jury. No evidence shall be offered at the hearing by either party on the issue of mental disease or defect as a defense to, or in mitigation of, the crime charged. After hearing, the Court may in an appropriate case quash the indictment or other charge, or find it to be defective or insufficient, or determine that it is not proved beyond a reasonable doubt by the evidence, or otherwise terminate the proceedings on the evidence or the law. In any such case, unless all defects in the proceedings are promptly cured, the Court shall terminate the commitment ordered under Subsection (2) of this Section and order the defendant to be discharged or, subject to the law governing the civil commitment of persons suffering from mental disease or defect, order the defendant to be committed to an appropriate institution of the Department of Mental Hygiene [Public Health].]

SECTION 4.07. DETERMINATION OF IRRESPONSIBILITY ON BASIS OF REPORT; ACCESS TO DEFENDANT BY PSYCHIATRIST OF HIS OWN CHOICE; FORM OF EXPERT TESTIMONY WHEN ISSUE OF RESPONSIBILITY IS TRIED

(1) If the report filed pursuant to Section 4.05 finds that the defendant at the time of the criminal conduct charged suffered from a mental disease

or defect which substantially impaired his capacity to appreciate the criminality [wrongfulness] of the conduct or to conform his conduct to the requirements of law, and the Court, after a hearing if a hearing is requested by the prosecuting attorney or the defendant, is satisfied that such impairment was sufficient to exclude responsibility, the Court on motion of the defendant shall enter judgement of acquittal on the ground of mental disease or defect excluding responsibility.

(2) When, notwithstanding the report filed pursuant to Section 4.05, the defendant wishes to be examined by a qualified psychiatrist or other expert of his own choice, such examiner shall be permitted to have reasonable access to the defendant for the purposes of such examination.

(3) Upon the trial, the psychiatrists who reported pursuant to Section 4.05 may be called as witnesses by the prosecution, the defendant or the Court. If the issue is being tried before a jury, the jury may be informed that the psychiatrists were designated by the Court or by the Superintendent of the _____ Hospital at the request of the Court, as the case may be. If called by the Court, the witness shall be subject to cross-examination by the prosecution and by the defendant. Both the prosecution and the defendant may summon any other qualified psychiatrist or other expert to testify, but no one who has not examined the defendant shall be competent to testify to an expert opinion with respect to the mental condition or responsibility of the defendant, as distinguished from the validity of the procedure followed by, or the general scientific propositions stated by, another witness.

(4) When a psychiatrist or other expert who has examined the defendant testifies concerning his mental condition, he shall be permitted to make a statement as to the nature of his examination, his diagnosis of the mental condition of the defendant at the time of the commission of the offense charged and his opinion as to the extent, if any, to which the capacity of the defendant to appreciate the criminality [wrongfulness] of his conduct or to conform his conduct to the requirements of law or to have a particular state of mind that is an element of the offense charged was impaired as a result of mental disease or defect at that time. He shall be permitted to make any explanation reasonably serving to clarify his diagnosis and opinion and may be cross-examined as to any matter bearing on his competency or credibility or the validity of his diagnosis or opinion.

SECTION 4.08. LEGAL EFFECT OF ACQUITTAL ON THE GROUND OF MENTAL DISEASE OR DEFECT EXCLUDING RESPONSIBILITY; COMMITMENT; RELEASE OR DISCHARGE

(1) When a defendant is acquitted on the ground of mental disease or defect excluding responsibility, the Court shall order him to be committed to the custody of the Commissioner of Mental Hygiene [Public Health] to be placed in an appropriate institution for custody, care and treatment.

(2) If the Commissioner of Mental Hygiene [Public Health] is of the view that a person committed to his custody, pursuant to paragraph (1) of this Section, may be discharged or released on condition without danger to himself or to others, he shall make application for the discharge or release of such person in a report to the Court by which such person was committed and shall transmit a copy of such application and report to the prosecuting

attorney of the county [parish] from which the defendant was committed. The Court shall thereupon appoint at least two qualified psychiatrists to examine such person and to report within sixty days, or such longer period as the Court determines to be necessary for the purpose, their opinion as to his mental condition. To facilitate such examination and the proceedings thereon, the Court may cause such person to be confined in any institution located near the place where the Court sits, which may hereafter be designated by the Commissioner of Mental Hygiene [Public Health] as suitable for the temporary detention of irresponsible persons.

(3) If the Court is satisfied by the report filed pursuant to paragraph (2) of this Section and such testimony of the reporting psychiatrists as the Court deems necessary that the committed person may be discharged or released on condition without danger to himself or others, the Court shall order his discharge or his release on such conditions as the Court determines to be necessary. If the Court is not so satisfied, it shall promptly order a hearing to determine whether such person may safely be discharged or released. Any such hearing shall be deemed a civil proceeding and the burden shall be upon the committed person to prove that he may safely be discharged or released. According to the determination of the Court upon the hearing, the committed person shall thereupon be discharged or released on such conditions as the Court determines to be necessary, or shall be recommitted to the custody of the Commissioner of Mental Hygiene [Public Health], subject to discharge or release only in accordance with the procedure prescribed above for a first hearing.

(4) If, within [five] years after the conditional release of a committed person, the Court shall determine, after hearing evidence, that the conditions of release have not been fulfilled and that for the safety of such person or for the safety of others his conditional release should be revoked, the Court shall forthwith order him to be recommitted to the Commissioner of Mental Hygiene [Public Health], subject to discharge or release only in accordance with the procedure prescribed above for a first hearing.

(5) A committed person may make application for his discharge or release to the Court by which he was committed, and the procedure to be followed upon such application shall be the same as that prescribed above in the case of an application by the Commissioner of Mental Hygiene [Public Health]. However, no such application by a committed person need be considered until he has been confined for a period of not less than [six months] from the date of the order of commitment, and if the determination of the Court be adverse to the application, such person shall not be permitted to file a further application until [one year] has elapsed from the date of any preceding hearing on an application for his release or discharge.

SECTION 4.09. [*Omitted*]

SECTION 4.10. IMMATURITY EXCLUDING CRIMINAL CONVICTION; TRANSFER OF PROCEEDINGS TO JUVENILE COURT

(1) A person shall not be tried for or convicted of an offense if:

(a) at the time of the conduct charged to constitute the offense he was less than sixteen years of age[, in which case the Juvenile Court shall have exclusive jurisdiction*]; or

(b) at the time of the conduct charged to constitute the offense he was sixteen or seventeen years of age, unless:

(i) the Juvenile Court has no jurisdiction over him, or,

(ii) the Juvenile Court has entered an order waiving jurisdiction and consenting to the institution of criminal proceedings against him.

(2) No court shall have jurisdiction to try or convict a person of an offense if criminal proceedings against him are barred by Subsection (1) of this Section. When it appears that a person charged with the commission of an offense may be of such an age that criminal proceedings may be barred under Subsection (1) of this Section, the Court shall hold a hearing thereon, and the burden shall be on the prosecution to establish to the satisfaction of the Court that the criminal proceeding is not barred upon such grounds. If the Court determines that the proceeding is barred, custody of the person charged shall be surrendered to the Juvenile Court, and the case, including all papers and processes relating thereto, shall be transferred.

Article 5. Inchoate Crimes

SECTION 5.01. CRIMINAL ATTEMPT

(1) *Definition of Attempt.* A person is guilty of an attempt to commit a crime if, acting with the kind of culpability otherwise required for commission of the crime, he:

(a) purposely engages in conduct that would constitute the crime if the attendant circumstances were as he believes them to be; or

(b) when causing a particular result is an element of the crime, does or omits to do anything with the purpose of causing or with the belief that it will cause such result without further conduct on his part; or

(c) purposely does or omits to do anything which, under the circumstances as he believes them to be, is an act or omission constituting a substantial step in a course of conduct planned to culminate in his commission of the crime.

(2) *Conduct That May Be Held Substantial Step Under Subsection (1)(c).* Conduct shall not be held to constitute a substantial step under Subsection (1)(c) of this Section unless it is strongly corroborative of the actor's criminal purpose. Without negativing the sufficiency of other conduct, the following, if strongly corroborative of the actor's criminal purpose, shall not be held insufficient as a matter of law:

(a) lying in wait, searching for or following the contemplated victim of the crime;

(b) enticing or seeking to entice the contemplated victim of the crime to go to the place contemplated for its commission;

* The bracketed words are unnecessary if   amended accordingly.
the Juvenile Court Act so provides or is

(c) reconnoitering the place contemplated for the commission of the crime;

(d) unlawful entry of a structure, vehicle or enclosure in which it is contemplated that the crime will be committed;

(e) possession of materials to be employed in the commission of the crime, that are specially designed for such unlawful use or which can serve no lawful purpose of the actor under the circumstances;

(f) possession, collection or fabrication of materials to be employed in the commission of the crime, at or near the place contemplated for its commission, where such possession, collection or fabrication serves no lawful purpose of the actor under the circumstances;

(g) soliciting an innocent agent to engage in conduct constituting an element of the crime.

(3) *Conduct Designed to Aid Another in Commission of a Crime.* A person who engages in conduct designed to aid another to commit a crime that would establish his complicity under Section 2.06 if the crime were committed by such other person, is guilty of an attempt to commit the crime, although the crime is not committed or attempted by such other person.

(4) *Renunciation of Criminal Purpose.* When the actor's conduct would otherwise constitute an attempt under Subsection (1)(b) or (1)(c) of this Section, it is an affirmative defense that he abandoned his effort to commit the crime or otherwise prevented its commission, under circumstances manifesting a complete and voluntary renunciation of his criminal purpose. The establishment of such defense does not, however, affect the liability of an accomplice who did not join in such abandonment or prevention.

Within the meaning of this Article, renunciation of criminal purpose is not voluntary if it is motivated, in whole or in part, by circumstances, not present or apparent at the inception of the actor's course of conduct, that increase the probability of detection or apprehension or which make more difficult the accomplishment of the criminal purpose. Renunciation is not complete if it is motivated by a decision to postpone the criminal conduct until a more advantageous time or to transfer the criminal effort to another but similar objective or victim.

SECTION 5.02.   CRIMINAL SOLICITATION

(1) *Definition of Solicitation.* A person is guilty of solicitation to commit a crime if with the purpose of promoting or facilitating its commission he commands, encourages or requests another person to engage in specific conduct that would constitute such crime or an attempt to commit such crime or which would establish his complicity in its commission or attempted commission.

(2) *Uncommunicated Solicitation.* It is immaterial under Subsection (1) of this Section that the actor fails to communicate with the person he solicits to commit a crime if his conduct was designed to effect such communication.

(3) *Renunciation of Criminal Purpose.* It is an affirmative defense that the actor, after soliciting another person to commit a crime, persuaded him not to do so or otherwise prevented the commission of the crime, under

circumstances manifesting a complete and voluntary renunciation of his criminal purpose.

SECTION 5.03. CRIMINAL CONSPIRACY

(1) *Definition of Conspiracy.* A person is guilty of conspiracy with another person or persons to commit a crime if with the purpose of promoting or facilitating its commission he:

(a) agrees with such other person or persons that they or one or more of them will engage in conduct that constitutes such crime or an attempt or solicitation to commit such crime; or

(b) agrees to aid such other person or persons in the planning or commission of such crime or of an attempt or solicitation to commit such crime.

(2) *Scope of Conspiratorial Relationship.* If a person guilty of conspiracy, as defined by Subsection (1) of this Section, knows that a person with whom he conspires to commit a crime has conspired with another person or persons to commit the same crime, he is guilty of conspiring with such other person or persons, whether or not he knows their identity, to commit such crime.

(3) *Conspiracy With Multiple Criminal Objectives.* If a person conspires to commit a number of crimes, he is guilty of only one conspiracy so long as such multiple crimes are the object of the same agreement or continuous conspiratorial relationship.

(4) *Joinder and Venue in Conspiracy Prosecutions.*

(a) Subject to the provisions of paragraph (b) of this Subsection, two or more persons charged with criminal conspiracy may be prosecuted jointly if:

(i) they are charged with conspiring with one another; or

(ii) the conspiracies alleged, whether they have the same or different parties, are so related that they constitute different aspects of a scheme of organized criminal conduct.

(b) In any joint prosecution under paragraph (a) of this Subsection:

(i) no defendant shall be charged with a conspiracy in any county [parish or district] other than one in which he entered into such conspiracy or in which an overt act pursuant to such conspiracy was done by him or by a person with whom he conspired; and

(ii) neither the liability of any defendant nor the admissibility against him of evidence of acts or declarations of another shall be enlarged by such joinder; and

(iii) the Court shall order a severance or take a special verdict as to any defendant who so requests, if it deems it necessary or appropriate to promote the fair determination of his guilt or innocence, and shall take any other proper measures to protect the fairness of the trial.

(5) *Overt Act.* No person may be convicted of conspiracy to commit a crime other than a felony of the first or second degree, unless an overt act in

pursuance of such conspiracy is alleged and proved to have been done by him or by a person with whom he conspired.

(6) *Renunciation of Criminal Purpose.* It is an affirmative defense that the actor, after conspiring to commit a crime, thwarted the success of the conspiracy, under circumstances manifesting a complete and voluntary renunciation of his criminal purpose.

(7) *Duration of Conspiracy.* For purposes of Section 1.06(4) [relating to periods of limitation for bringing prosecutions—ed.]:

(a) conspiracy is a continuing course of conduct that terminates when the crime or crimes that are its object are committed or the agreement that they be committed is abandoned by the defendant and by those with whom he conspired; and

(b) such abandonment is presumed if neither the defendant nor anyone with whom he conspired does any overt act in pursuance of the conspiracy during the applicable period of limitation; and

(c) if an individual abandons the agreement, the conspiracy is terminated as to him only if and when he advises those with whom he conspired of his abandonment or he informs the law enforcement authorities of the existence of the conspiracy and of his participation therein.

SECTION 5.04.   INCAPACITY, IRRESPONSIBILITY OR IMMUNITY OF PARTY TO SOLICITATION OR CONSPIRACY

(1) Except as provided in Subsection (2) of this Section, it is immaterial to the liability of a person who solicits or conspires with another to commit a crime that:

(a) he or the person whom he solicits or with whom he conspires does not occupy a particular position or have a particular characteristic that is an element of such crime, if he believes that one of them does; or

(b) the person whom he solicits or with whom he conspires is irresponsible or has an immunity to prosecution or conviction for the commission of the crime.

(2) It is defense to a charge of solicitation or conspiracy to commit a crime that if the criminal object were achieved, the actor would not be guilty of a crime under the law defining the offense or as an accomplice under Section 2.06(5) or 2.06(6)(a) or (b).

SECTION 5.05.   GRADING OF CRIMINAL ATTEMPT, SOLICITATION AND CONSPIRACY; MITIGATION IN CASES OF LESSER DANGER; MULTIPLE CONVICTIONS BARRED

(1) *Grading.* Except as otherwise provided in this Section, attempt, solicitation and conspiracy are crimes of the same grade and degree as the most serious offense that is attempted or solicited or is an object of the conspiracy. An attempt, solicitation or conspiracy to commit a [capital crime or a] felony of the first degree is a felony of the second degree.

(2) *Mitigation.* If the particular conduct charged to constitute a criminal attempt, solicitation or conspiracy is so inherently unlikely to result or

culminate in the commission of a crime that neither such conduct nor the actor presents a public danger warranting the grading of such offense under this Section, the Court shall exercise its power under Section 6.12 to enter judgment and impose sentence for a crime of lower grade or degree or, in extreme cases, may dismiss the prosecution.

(3) *Multiple Convictions.* A person may not be convicted of more than one offense defined by this Article for conduct designed to commit or to culminate in the commission of the same crime.

SECTION 5.06.   POSSESSING INSTRUMENTS OF CRIME; WEAPONS

(1) *Criminal Instruments Generally.* A person commits a misdemeanor if he possesses any instrument of crime with purpose to employ it criminally. "Instrument of crime" means:

(a) anything specially made or specially adapted for criminal use; or

(b) anything commonly used for criminal purposes and possessed by the actor under circumstances that do not negative unlawful purpose.

(2) *Presumption of Criminal Purpose From Possession of Weapon.* If a person possesses a firearm or other weapon on or about his person, in a vehicle occupied by him, or otherwise readily available for use, it is presumed that he had the purpose to employ it criminally, unless:

(a) the weapon is possessed in the actor's home or place of business;

(b) the actor is licensed or otherwise authorized by law to possess such weapon; or

(c) the weapon is of a type commonly used in lawful sport.

"Weapon" means anything readily capable of lethal use and possessed under circumstances not manifestly appropriate for lawful uses it may have; the term includes a firearm that is not loaded or lacks a clip or other component to render it immediately operable, and components that can readily be assembled into a weapon.

(3) *Presumptions as to Possession of Criminal Instruments in Automobiles.* If a weapon or other instrument of crime is found in an automobile, it is presumed to be in the possession of the occupant if there is but one. If there is more than one occupant, it shall be presumed to be in the possession of all, except under the following circumstances:

(a) it is found upon the person of one of the occupants;

(b) the automobile is not a stolen one and the weapon or instrument is found out of view in a glove compartment, car trunk, or other enclosed customary depository, in which case it is presumed to be in the possession of the occupant or occupants who own or have authority to operate the automobile;

(c) in the case of a taxicab, a weapon or instrument found in the passenger's portion of the vehicle shall be presumed to be in the possession of all the passengers, if there are any, and, if not, in the possession of the driver.

SECTION 5.07.   [*Omitted*]

Article 6. Authorized Disposition of Offenders

SECTION 6.01. DEGREES OF FELONIES

(1) Felonies defined by this Code are classified, for the purpose of sentence, into three degrees, as follows:

    (a) felonies of the first degree;

    (b) felonies of the second degree;

    (c) felonies of the third degree.

A felony is of the first or second degree when it is so designated by the Code. A crime declared to be a felony, without specification of degree, is of the third degree.

(2) Notwithstanding any other provision of law, a felony defined by any statute of this State other than this Code shall constitute, for the purpose of sentence, a felony of the third degree.

SECTION 6.02. [*Omitted*]

SECTION 6.03. FINES

A person who has been convicted of an offense may be sentenced to pay a fine not exceeding:

(1) $10,000, when the conviction is of a felony of the first or second degree;

(2) $5,000, when the conviction is of a felony of the third degree;

(3) $1,000, when the conviction is of a misdemeanor;

(4) $500, when the conviction is of a petty misdemeanor or a violation;

(5) any higher amount equal to double the pecuniary gain derived from the offense by the offender;

(6) any higher amount specifically authorized by statute.

SECTION 6.04. PENALTIES AGAINST CORPORATIONS AND UNINCORPORATED ASSOCIATIONS; FORFEITURE OF CORPORATE CHARTER OR REVOCATION OF CERTIFICATE AUTHORIZING FOREIGN CORPORATION TO DO BUSINESS IN THE STATE

(1) The Court may suspend the sentence of a corporation or an unincorporated association that has been convicted of an offense or may sentence it to pay a fine authorized by Section 6.03.

(2)(a) The [prosecuting attorney] is authorized to institute civil proceedings in the appropriate court of general jurisdiction to forfeit the charter of a corporation organized under the laws of this State or to revoke the certificate authorizing a foreign corporation to conduct business in this State. The Court may order the charter forfeited or the certificate revoked upon finding (i) that the board of directors or a high managerial agent acting in behalf of the corporation has, in conducting the corporation's affairs, purposely engaged in a persistent course of criminal conduct and (ii) that for the prevention of future criminal conduct of the same character, the public interest requires the charter of the corporation to be forfeited and the corporation to be dissolved or the certificate to be revoked.

(b) When a corporation is convicted of a crime or a high managerial agent of a corporation, as defined in Section 2.07, is convicted of a crime committed in the conduct of the affairs of the corporation, the Court, in sentencing the corporation or the agent, may direct the [prosecuting attorney] to institute proceedings authorized by paragraph (a) of this Subsection.

(c) The proceedings authorized by paragraph (a) of this Subsection shall be conducted in accordance with the procedures authorized by law for the involuntary dissolution of a corporation or the revocation of the certificate authorizing a foreign corporation to conduct business in this State. Such proceedings shall be deemed additional to any other proceedings authorized by law for the purpose of forfeiting the charter of a corporation or revoking the certificate of a foreign corporation.

SECTION 6.05.   [*Omitted*]

SECTION 6.06.   SENTENCE OF IMPRISONMENT FOR FELONY; ORDINARY TERMS

A person who has been convicted of a felony may be sentenced to imprisonment, as follows:

(1) in the case of a felony of the first degree, for a term the minimum of which shall be fixed by the Court at not less than one year nor more than ten years, and the maximum of which shall be life imprisonment;

(2) in the case of a felony of the second degree, for a term the minimum of which shall be fixed by the Court at not less than one year nor more than three years, and the maximum of which shall be ten years;

(3) in the case of a felony of the third degree, for a term the minimum of which shall be fixed by the Court at not less than one year nor more than two years, and the maximum of which shall be five years.

ALTERNATE SECTION 6.06.   SENTENCE OF IMPRISONMENT FOR FELONY; ORDINARY TERMS

A person who has been convicted of a felony may be sentenced to imprisonment, as follows:

(1) in the case of a felony of the first degree, for a term the minimum of which shall be fixed by the Court at not less than one year nor more than ten years, and the maximum at not more than twenty years or at life imprisonment;

(2) in the case of a felony of the second degree, for a term the minimum of which shall be fixed by the Court at not less than one year nor more than three years, and the maximum at not more than ten years;

(3) in the case of a felony of the third degree, for a term the minimum of which shall be fixed by the Court at not less than one year nor more than two years, and the maximum at not more than five years.

No sentence shall be imposed under this Section of which the minimum is longer than one-half the maximum, or, when the maximum is life imprisonment, longer than ten years.

SECTION 6.07. [*Omitted*]

SECTION 6.08. SENTENCE OF IMPRISONMENT FOR MISDEMEANORS AND PETTY MISDEMEANORS; ORDINARY TERMS

A person who has been convicted of a misdemeanor or a petty misdemeanor may be sentenced to imprisonment for a definite term which shall be fixed by the Court and shall not exceed one year in the case of a misdemeanor or thirty days in the case of a petty misdemeanor.

SECTIONS 6.09.–6.11. [*Omitted*]

SECTION 6.12. REDUCTION OF CONVICTION BY COURT TO LESSER DEGREE OF FELONY OR TO MISDEMEANOR

If, when a person has been convicted of a felony, the Court, having regard to the nature and circumstances of the crime and to the history and character of the defendant, is of the view that it would be unduly harsh to sentence the offender in accordance with the Code, the Court may enter judgment of conviction for a lesser degree of felony or for a misdemeanor and impose sentence accordingly.

SECTION 6.13. [*Omitted*]

Article 7. Authority of Court in Sentencing [*Omitted*]

PART II. DEFINITION OF SPECIFIC CRIMES
OFFENSES INVOLVING DANGER TO THE PERSON
Article 210. Criminal Homicide

SECTION 210.0. DEFINITIONS

In Articles 210–213, unless a different meaning plainly is required:

(1) "human being" means a person who has been born and is alive;

(2) "bodily injury" means physical pain, illness or any impairment of physical condition;

(3) "serious bodily injury" means bodily injury which creates a substantial risk of death or which causes serious, permanent disfigurement, or protracted loss or impairment of the function of any bodily member or organ;

(4) "deadly weapon" means any firearm or other weapon, device, instrument, material or substance, whether animate or inanimate, which in the manner it is used or is intended to be used is known to be capable of producing death or serious bodily injury.

SECTION 210.1. CRIMINAL HOMICIDE

(1) A person is guilty of criminal homicide if he purposely, knowingly, recklessly or negligently causes the death of another human being.

(2) Criminal homicide is murder, manslaughter or negligent homicide.

SECTION 210.2. MURDER

(1) Except as provided in Section 210.3(1)(b), criminal homicide constitutes murder when:

(a) it is committed purposely or knowingly; or

(b) it is committed recklessly under circumstances manifesting extreme indifference to the value of human life. Such recklessness and indifference are presumed if the actor is engaged or is an accomplice in the commission of, or an attempt to commit, or flight after committing or attempting to commit robbery, rape or deviate sexual intercourse by force or threat of force, arson, burglary, kidnapping or felonious escape.

(2) Murder is a felony of the first degree [but a person convicted of murder may be sentenced to death, as provided in Section 210.6].

SECTION 210.3. MANSLAUGHTER

(1) Criminal homicide constitutes manslaughter when:

(a) it is committed recklessly; or

(b) a homicide which would otherwise be murder is committed under the influence of extreme mental or emotional disturbance for which there is reasonable explanation or excuse. The reasonableness of such explanation or excuse shall be determined from the viewpoint of a person in the actor's situation under the circumstances as he believes them to be.

(2) Manslaughter is a felony of the second degree.

SECTION 210.4. NEGLIGENT HOMICIDE

(1) Criminal homicide constitutes negligent homicide when it is committed negligently.

(2) Negligent homicide is a felony of the third degree.

SECTION 210.5. CAUSING OR AIDING SUICIDE

(1) *Causing Suicide as Criminal Homicide.* A person may be convicted of criminal homicide for causing another to commit suicide only if he purposely causes such suicide by force, duress or deception.

(2) *Aiding or Soliciting Suicide as an Independent Offense.* A person who purposely aids or solicits another to commit suicide is guilty of a felony of the second degree if his conduct causes such suicide or an attempted suicide, and otherwise of a misdemeanor.

[SECTION 210.6. SENTENCE OF DEATH FOR MURDER; FURTHER PROCEEDINGS TO DETERMINE SENTENCE*]

(1) *Death Sentence Excluded.* When a defendant is found guilty of murder, the Court shall impose sentence for a felony of the first degree if it is satisfied that:

* The Brackets indicate that the Institute took no position on the desirability of the death penalty.

(a) none of the aggravating circumstances enumerated in Subsection (3) of this Section was established by the evidence at the trial or will be established if further proceedings are initiated under Subsection (2) of this Section; or

(b) substantial mitigating circumstances, established by the evidence at the trial, call for leniency; or

(c) the defendant, with the consent of the prosecuting attorney and the approval of the Court, pleaded guilty to murder as a felony of the first degree; or

(d) the defendant was under 18 years of age at the time of the commission of the crime; or

(e) the defendant's physical or mental condition calls for leniency; or

(f) although the evidence suffices to sustain the verdict, it does not foreclose all doubt respecting the defendant's guilt.

(2) *Determination by Court or by Court and Jury.* Unless the Court imposes sentence under Subsection (1) of this Section, it shall conduct a separate proceeding to determine whether the defendant should be sentenced for a felony of the first degree or sentenced to death. The proceeding shall be conducted before the Court alone if the defendant was convicted by a Court sitting without a jury or upon his plea of guilty or if the prosecuting attorney and the defendant waive a jury with respect to sentence. In other cases it shall be conducted before the Court sitting with the jury which determined the defendant's guilt or, if the Court for good cause shown discharges that jury, with a new jury empanelled for the purpose.

In the proceeding, evidence may be presented as to any matter that the Court deems relevant to sentence, including but not limited to the nature and circumstances of the crime, the defendant's character, background, history, mental and physical condition and any of the aggravating or mitigating circumstances enumerated in Subsections (3) and (4) of this Section. Any such evidence, not legally privileged, which the Court deems to have probative force, may be received, regardless of its admissibility under the exclusionary rules of evidence, provided that the defendant's counsel is accorded a fair opportunity to rebut such evidence. The prosecuting attorney and the defendant or his counsel shall be permitted to present argument for or against sentence of death.

The determination whether sentence of death shall be imposed shall be in the discretion of the Court, except that when the proceeding is conducted before the Court sitting with a jury, the Court shall not impose sentence of death unless it submits to the jury the issue whether the defendant should be sentenced to death or to imprisonment and the jury returns a verdict that the sentence should be death. If the jury is unable to reach a unanimous verdict, the Court shall dismiss the jury and impose sentence for a felony of the first degree.

The Court, in exercising its discretion as to sentence, and the jury, in determining upon its verdict, shall take into account the aggravating and mitigating circumstances enumerated in Subsections (3) and (4) and any other facts that it deems relevant, but it shall not impose or recommend sentence of death unless it finds one of the aggravating circumstances enumerated in Subsection (3) and further finds that there are no mitigating circumstances sufficiently substantial to call for leniency. When the issue is submitted to the jury, the Court shall so instruct and also shall inform the jury of the nature of the sentence of imprisonment that may be imposed, including its implication with respect to possible release upon parole, if the jury verdict is against sentence of death.

Alternative formulation of Subsection (2):

(2) *Determination by Court.* Unless the Court imposes sentence under Subsection (1) of this Section, it shall conduct a separate proceeding to determine whether the defendant should be sentenced for a felony of the first degree or sentenced to death. In the proceeding, the Court, in accordance with Section 7.07 [relating to procedures on sentence], shall consider the report of the presentence investigation and, if a psychiatric examination has been ordered, the report of such examination. In addition, evidence may be presented as to any matter that the Court deems relevant to sentence, including but not limited to the nature and circumstances of the crime, the defendant's character, background, history, mental and physical condition and any of the aggravating or mitigating circumstances enumerated in Subsections (3) and (4) of this Section. Any such evidence, not legally privileged, which the Court deems to have probative force, may be received, regardless of its admissibility under the exclusionary rules of evidence, provided that the defendant's counsel is accorded a fair opportunity to rebut such evidence. The prosecuting attorney and the defendant or his counsel shall be permitted to present argument for or against sentence of death.

The determination whether sentence of death shall be imposed shall be in the discretion of the Court. In exercising such discretion, the Court shall take into account the aggravating and mitigating circumstances enumerated in Subsections (3) and (4) and any other facts that it deems relevant but shall not impose sentence of death unless it finds one of the aggravating circumstances enumerated in Subsection (3) and further finds that there are no mitigating circumstances sufficiently substantial to call for leniency.

(3) *Aggravating Circumstances.*

(a) The murder was committed by a convict under sentence of imprisonment.

(b) The defendant was previously convicted of another murder or of a felony involving the use or threat of violence to the person.

(c) At the time the murder was committed the defendant also committed another murder.

(d) The defendant knowingly created a great risk of death to many persons.

(e) The murder was committed while the defendant was engaged or was an accomplice in the commission of, or an attempt to commit, or flight after committing or attempting to commit robbery, rape or deviate sexual intercourse by force or threat of force, arson, burglary or kidnapping.

(f) The murder was committed for the purpose of avoiding or preventing a lawful arrest or effecting an escape from lawful custody.

(g) The murder was committed for pecuniary gain.

(h) The murder was especially heinous, atrocious or cruel, manifesting exceptional depravity.

(4) *Mitigating Circumstances.*

(a) The defendant has no significant history of prior criminal activity.

(b) The murder was committed while the defendant was under the influence of extreme mental or emotional disturbance.

(c) The victim was a participant in the defendant's homicidal conduct or consented to the homicidal act.

(d) The murder was committed under circumstances which the defendant believed to provide a moral justification or extenuation for his conduct.

(e) The defendant was an accomplice in a murder committed by another person and his participation in the homicidal act was relatively minor.

(f) The defendant acted under duress or under the domination of another person.

(g) At the time of the murder, the capacity of the defendant to appreciate the criminality [wrongfulness] of his conduct or to conform his conduct to the requirements of law was impaired as a result of mental disease or defect or intoxication.

(h) The youth of the defendant at the time of the crime.]

Article 211. Assault; Reckless Endangering; Threats

SECTION 211.0. DEFINITIONS

In this Article, the definitions given in Section 210.0 apply unless a different meaning plainly is required.

SECTION 211.1. ASSAULT

(1) *Simple Assault.* A person is guilty of assault if he:

(a) attempts to cause or purposely, knowingly or recklessly causes bodily injury to another; or

(b) negligently causes bodily injury to another with a deadly weapon; or

(c) attempts by physical menace to put another in fear of imminent serious bodily injury.

Simple assault is a misdemeanor unless committed in a fight or scuffle entered into by mutual consent, in which case it is a petty misdemeanor.

(2) *Aggravated Assault.* A person is guilty of aggravated assault if he:

(a) attempts to cause serious bodily injury to another, or causes such injury purposely, knowingly or recklessly under circumstances manifesting extreme indifference to the value of human life; or

(b) attempts to cause or purposely or knowingly causes bodily injury to another with a deadly weapon.

Aggravated assault under paragraph (a) is a felony of the second degree; aggravated assault under paragraph (b) is a felony of the third degree.

SECTION 211.2. RECKLESSLY ENDANGERING ANOTHER PERSON

A person commits a misdemeanor if he recklessly engages in conduct which places or may place another person in danger of death or serious bodily injury. Recklessness and danger shall be presumed where a person knowingly points a firearm at or in the direction of another, whether or not the actor believed the firearm to be loaded.

SECTION 211.3. TERRORISTIC THREATS

A person is guilty of a felony of the third degree if he threatens to commit any crime of violence with purpose to terrorize another or to cause evacuation of a building, place of assembly, or facility of public transportation, or otherwise to cause serious public inconvenience, or in reckless disregard of the risk of causing such terror or inconvenience.

Article 212. Kidnapping and Related Offenses; Coercion

SECTION 212.0. DEFINITIONS

In this Article, the definitions given in section 210.0 apply unless a different meaning plainly is required.

SECTION 212.1. KIDNAPPING

A person is guilty of kidnapping if he unlawfully removes another from his place of residence or business, or a substantial distance from the vicinity where he is found, or if he unlawfully confines another for a substantial period in a place of isolation, with any of the following purposes:

(a) to hold for ransom or reward, or as a shield or hostage; or

(b) to facilitate commission of any felony or flight thereafter; or

(c) to inflict bodily injury on or to terrorize the victim or another; or

(d) to interfere with the performance of any governmental or political function.

Kidnapping is a felony of the first degree unless the actor voluntarily releases the victim alive and in a safe place prior to trial, in which case it is a felony of the second degree. A removal or confinement is unlawful within the meaning of this Section if it is accomplished by force, threat or deception, or, in the case of a person who is under the age of 14 or incompetent, if it is accomplished without the consent of a parent, guardian or other person responsible for general supervision of his welfare.

SECTION 212.2.   FELONIOUS RESTRAINT

A person commits a felony of the third degree if he knowingly:

(a) restrains another unlawfully in circumstances exposing him to risk of serious bodily injury; or

(b) holds another in a condition of involuntary servitude.

SECTION 212.3.   FALSE IMPRISONMENT

A person commits a misdemeanor if he knowingly restrains another unlawfully so as to interfere substantially with his liberty.

SECTION 212.4.   INTERFERENCE WITH CUSTODY

(1) *Custody of Children.* A person commits an offense if he knowingly or recklessly takes or entices any child under the age of 18 from the custody of its parent, guardian or other lawful custodian, when he has no privilege to do so. It is an affirmative defense that:

(a) the actor believed that his action was necessary to preserve the child from danger to its welfare; or

(b) the child, being at the time not less than 14 years old, was taken away at its own instigation without enticement and without purpose to commit a criminal offense with or against the child.

Proof that the child was below the critical age gives rise to a presumption that the actor knew the child's age or acted in reckless disregard thereof. The offense is a misdemeanor unless the actor, not being a parent or person in equivalent relation to the child, acted with knowledge that his conduct would cause serious alarm for the child's safety, or in reckless disregard of a likelihood of causing such alarm, in which case the offense is a felony of the third degree.

(2) *Custody of Committed Persons.* A person is guilty of a misdemeanor if he knowingly or recklessly takes or entices any committed person away from lawful custody when he is not privileged to do so. "Committed person" means, in addition to anyone committed under judicial warrant, any orphan, neglected or delinquent child, mentally defective or insane person, or other dependent or incompetent person entrusted to another's custody by or through a recognized social agency or otherwise by authority of law.

SECTION 212.5.   CRIMINAL COERCION

(1) *Offense Defined.* A person is guilty of criminal coercion if, with purpose unlawfully to restrict another's freedom of action to his detriment, he threatens to:

(a) commit any criminal offense; or

(b) accuse anyone of a criminal offense; or

(c) expose any secret tending to subject any person to hatred, contempt or ridicule, or to impair his credit or business repute; or

(d) take or withhold action as an official, or cause an official to take or withhold action.

It is an affirmative defense to prosecution based on paragraphs (b), (c) or (d) that the actor believed the accusation or secret to be true or the proposed official action justified and that his purpose was limited to compelling the other to behave in a way reasonably related to the circumstances which were the subject of the accusation, exposure or proposed official action, as by desisting from further misbehavior, making good a wrong done, refraining from taking any action or responsibility for which the actor believes the other disqualified.

(2) *Grading.* Criminal coercion is a misdemeanor unless the threat is to commit a felony or the actor's purpose is felonious, in which cases the offense is a felony of the third degree.

Article 213. Sexual Offenses

SECTION 213.0. DEFINITIONS

In this Article, unless a different meaning plainly is required:

(1) the definitions given in Section 210.0 apply;

(2) "Sexual intercourse" includes intercourse per os or per anum, with some penetration however slight; emission is not required;

(3) "Deviate sexual intercourse" means sexual intercourse per os or per anum between human beings who are not husband and wife, and any form of sexual intercourse with an animal.

SECTION 213.1. RAPE AND RELATED OFFENSES

(1) *Rape.* A male who has sexual intercourse with a female not his wife is guilty of rape if:

(a) he compels her to submit by force or by threat of imminent death, serious bodily injury, extreme pain or kidnapping, to be inflicted on anyone; or

(b) he has substantially impaired her power to appraise or control her conduct by administering or employing without her knowledge drugs, intoxicants or other means for the purpose of preventing resistance; or

(c) the female is unconscious; or

(d) the female is less than 10 years old.

Rape is a felony of the second degree unless (i) in the course thereof the actor inflicts serious bodily injury upon anyone, or (ii) the victim was not a voluntary social companion of the actor upon the occasion of the crime and had not previously permitted him sexual liberties, in which cases the offense is a felony of the first degree.

(2) *Gross Sexual Imposition.* A male who has sexual intercourse with a female not his wife commits a felony of the third degree if:

(a) he compels her to submit by any threat that would prevent resistance by a woman of ordinary resolution; or

(b) he knows that she suffers from a mental disease or defect which renders her incapable of appraising the nature of her conduct; or

(c) he knows that she is unaware that a sexual act is being committed upon her or that she submits because she mistakenly supposes that he is her husband.

SECTION 213.2.   DEVIATE SEXUAL INTERCOURSE BY FORCE OR IMPOSITION

(1) *By Force or Its Equivalent.* A person who engages in deviate sexual intercourse with another person, or who causes another to engage in deviate sexual intercourse, commits a felony of the second degree if:

(a) he compels the other person to participate by force or by threat of imminent death, serious bodily injury, extreme pain or kidnapping, to be inflicted on anyone; or

(b) he has substantially impaired the other person's power to appraise or control his conduct, by administering or employing without the knowledge of the other person drugs, intoxicants or other means for the purpose of preventing resistance; or

(c) the other person is unconscious; or

(d) the other person is less than 10 years old.

(2) *By Other Imposition.* A person who engages in deviate sexual intercourse with another person, or who causes another to engage in deviate sexual intercourse, commits a felony of the third degree if:

(a) he compels the other person to participate by any threat that would prevent resistance by a person of ordinary resolution; or

(b) he knows that the other person suffers from a mental disease or defect which renders him incapable of appraising the nature of his conduct; or

(c) he knows that the other person submits because he is unaware that a sexual act is being committed upon him.

SECTION 213.3.   CORRUPTION OF MINORS AND SEDUCTION

(1) *Offense Defined.* A male who has sexual intercourse with a female not his wife, or any person who engages in deviate sexual intercourse or causes another to engage in deviate sexual intercourse, is guilty of an offense if:

(a) the other person is less than [16] years old and the actor is at least [four] years older than the other person; or

(b) the other person is less than 21 years old and the actor is his guardian or otherwise responsible for general supervision of his welfare; or

(c) the other person is in custody of law or detained in a hospital or other institution and the actor has supervisory or disciplinary authority over him; or

(d) the other person is a female who is induced to participate by a promise of marriage which the actor does not mean to perform.

(2) *Grading.* An offense under paragraph (a) of Subsection (1) is a felony of the third degree. Otherwise an offense under this section is a misdemeanor.

SECTION 213.4.   SEXUAL ASSAULT

A person who has sexual contact with another not his spouse, or causes such other to have sexual conduct with him, is guilty of sexual assault, a misdemeanor, if:

(1) he knows that the contact is offensive to the other person; or

(2) he knows that the other person suffers from a mental disease or defect which renders him or her incapable of appraising the nature of his or her conduct; or

(3) he knows that the other person is unaware that a sexual act is being committed; or

(4) the other person is less than 10 years old; or

(5) he has substantially impaired the other person's power to appraise or control his or her conduct, by administering or employing without the other's knowledge drugs, intoxicants or other means for the purpose of preventing resistance; or

(6) the other person is less than [16] years old and the actor is at least [four] years older than the other person; or

(7) the other person is less than 21 years old and the actor is his guardian or otherwise responsible for general supervision of his welfare; or

(8) the other person is in custody of law or detained in a hospital or other institution and the actor has supervisory or disciplinary authority over him.

Sexual contact is any touching of the sexual or other intimate parts of the person for the purpose of arousing or gratifying sexual desire.

SECTION 213.5.   INDECENT EXPOSURE

A person commits a misdemeanor if, for the purpose of arousing or gratifying sexual desire of himself or of any person other than his spouse, he exposes his genitals under circumstances in which he knows his conduct is likely to cause affront or alarm.

SECTION 213.6.   PROVISIONS GENERALLY APPLICABLE TO ARTICLE 213

(1) *Mistake as to Age.* Whenever in this Article the criminality of conduct depends on a child's being below the age of 10, it is no defense that the actor did not know the child's age, or reasonably believed the child to be older than 10. When criminality depends on the child's being below a critical age other than 10, it is a defense for the actor to prove by a preponderance of the evidence that he reasonably believed the child to be above the critical age.

(2) *Spouse Relationships.* Whenever in this Article the definition of an offense excludes conduct with a spouse, the exclusion shall be deemed to extend to persons living as man and wife, regardless of the legal status of their relationship. The exclusion shall be inoperative as respects spouses living apart under a decree of judicial separation. Where the definition of an offense excludes conduct with a spouse or conduct by a woman, this shall not

preclude conviction of a spouse or woman as accomplice in a sexual act which he or she causes another person, not within the exclusion, to perform.

(3) *Sexually Promiscuous Complainants.* It is a defense to prosecution under Section 213.3, and paragraphs (6), (7) and (8) of Section 213.4 for the actor to prove by a preponderance of the evidence that the alleged victim had, prior to the time of the offense charged, engaged promiscuously in sexual relations with others.

(4) *Prompt Complaint.* No prosecution may be instituted or maintained under this Article unless the alleged offense was brought to the notice of public authority within [3] months of its occurrence or, where the alleged victim was less than [16] years old or otherwise incompetent to make complaint, within [3] months after a parent, guardian or other competent person specially interested in the victim learns of the offense.

(5) *Testimony of Complainants.* No person shall be convicted of any felony under this Article upon the uncorroborated testimony of the alleged victim. Corroboration may be circumstantial. In any prosecution before a jury for an offense under this Article, the jury shall be instructed to evaluate the testimony of a victim or complaining witness with special care in view of the emotional involvement of the witness and the difficulty of determining the truth with respect to alleged sexual activities carried out in private.

OFFENSES AGAINST PROPERTY
Article 220. Arson, Criminal Mischief, and Other Property Destruction

SECTION 220.1. ARSON AND RELATED OFFENSES

(1) *Arson.* A person is guilty of arson, a felony of the second degree, if he starts a fire or causes an explosion with the purpose of:

(a) destroying a building or occupied structure of another; or

(b) destroying or damaging any property, whether his own or another's, to collect insurance for such loss. It shall be an affirmative defense to prosecution under this paragraph that the actor's conduct did not recklessly endanger any building or occupied structure of another or place any other person in danger of death or bodily injury.

(2) *Reckless Burning or Exploding.* A person commits a felony of the third degree if he purposely starts a fire or causes an explosion, whether on his own property or another's, and thereby recklessly:

(a) places another person in danger of death or bodily injury; or

(b) place a building or occupied structure of another in danger of damage or destruction.

(3) *Failure to Control or Report Dangerous Fire.* A person who knows that a fire is endangering life or a substantial amount of property of another and fails to take reasonable measures to put out or control the fire, when he can do so without substantial risk to himself, or to give a prompt fire alarm, commits a misdemeanor if:

(a) he knows that he is under an official, contractual, or other legal duty to prevent or combat the fire; or

(b) the fire was started, albeit lawfully, by him or with his assent, or on property in his custody or control.

(4) *Definitions.* "Occupied structure" means any structure, vehicle or place adapted for overnight accommodation of persons, or for carrying on business therein, whether or not a person is actually present. Property is that of another, for the purposes of this section, if anyone other than the actor has a possessory or proprietary interest therein. If a building or structure is divided into separately occupied units, any unit not occupied by the actor is an occupied structure of another.

SECTION 220.2.   CAUSING OR RISKING CATASTROPHE

(1) *Causing Catastrophe.* A person who causes a catastrophe by explosion, fire, flood, avalanche, collapse of building, release of poison gas, radioactive material or other harmful or destructive force or substance, or by any other means of causing potentially widespread injury or damage, commits a felony of the second degree if he does so purposely or knowingly, or a felony of the third degree if he does so recklessly.

(2) *Risking Catastrophe.* A person is guilty of a misdemeanor if he recklessly creates a risk of catastrophe in the employment of fire, explosives or other dangerous means listed in Subsection (1).

(3) *Failure to Prevent Catastrophe.* A person who knowingly or recklessly fails to take reasonable measures to prevent or mitigate a catastrophe commits a misdemeanor if:

(a) he knows that he is under an official, contractual or other legal duty to take such measures; or

(b) he did or assented to the act causing or threatening the catastrophe.

SECTION 220.3.   CRIMINAL MISCHIEF

(1) *Offense Defined.* A person is guilty of criminal mischief if he:

(a) damages tangible property of another purposely, recklessly, or by negligence in the employment of fire, explosives, or other dangerous means listed in Section 220.2(1); or

(b) purposely or recklessly tampers with tangible property of another so as to endanger persons or property; or

(c) purposely or recklessly causes another to suffer pecuniary loss by deception or threat.

(2) *Grading.* Criminal mischief is a felony of the third degree if the actor purposely causes pecuniary loss in excess of $5,000 or a substantial interruption or impairment of public communication, transportation, supply of water, gas or power, or other public service. It is a misdemeanor if the actor purposely causes pecuniary loss in excess of $100, or a petty misdemeanor if he purposely or recklessly causes pecuniary loss in excess of $25. Otherwise criminal mischief is a violation.

Article 221. Burglary and Other Criminal Intrusion

SECTION 221.0. DEFINITIONS

In this Article, unless a different meaning plainly is required:

(1) "occupied structure" means any structure, vehicle or place adapted for overnight accommodation of persons, or for carrying on business therein, whether or not a person is actually present.

(2) "night" means the period between thirty minutes past sunset and thirty minutes before sunrise.

SECTION 221.1. BURGLARY

(1) *Burglary Defined.* A person is guilty of burglary if he enters a building or occupied structure, or separately secured or occupied portion thereof, with purpose to commit a crime therein, unless the premises are at the time open to the public or the actor is licensed or privileged to enter. It is an affirmative defense to prosecution for burglary that the building or structure was abandoned.

(2) *Grading.* Burglary is a felony of the second degree if it is perpetrated in the dwelling of another at night, or if, in the course of committing the offense, the actor:

(a) purposely, knowingly or recklessly inflicts or attempts to inflict bodily injury on anyone; or

(b) is armed with explosives or a deadly weapon.

Otherwise, burglary is a felony of the third degree. An act shall be deemed "in the course of committing" an offense if it occurs in an attempt to commit the offense or in flight after the attempt or commission.

(3) *Multiple Convictions.* A person may not be convicted both for burglary and for the offense which it was his purpose to commit after the burglarious entry or for an attempt to commit that offense, unless the additional offense constitutes a felony of the first or second degree.

SECTION 221.2. CRIMINAL TRESPASS

(1) *Buildings and Occupied Structures.* A person commits an offense if, knowing that he is not licensed or privileged to do so, he enters or surreptitiously remains in any building or occupied structure, or separately secured or occupied portion thereof. An offense under this Subsection is a misdemeanor if it is committed in a dwelling at night. Otherwise it is a petty misdemeanor.

(2) *Defiant Trespasser.* A person commits an offense if, knowing that he is not licensed or privileged to do so, he enters or remains in any place as to which notice against trespass is given by:

(a) actual communication to the actor; or

(b) posting in a manner prescribed by law or reasonably likely to come to the attention of intruders; or

(c) fencing or other enclosure manifestly designed to exclude intruders.

An offense under this Subsection constitutes a petty misdemeanor if the offender defies an order to leave personally communicated to him by the owner of the premises or other authorized person. Otherwise it is a violation.

(3) *Defenses.* It is an affirmative defense to prosecution under this Section that:

(a) a building or occupied structure involved in an offense under Subsection (1) was abandoned; or

(b) the premises were at the time open to members of the public and the actor complied with all lawful conditions imposed on access to or remaining in the premises; or

(c) the actor reasonably believed that the owner of the premises, or other person empowered to license access thereto, would have licensed him to enter or remain.

Article 222. Robbery

SECTION 222.1. ROBBERY

(1) *Robbery Defined.* A person is guilty of robbery if, in the course of committing a theft, he:

(a) inflicts serious bodily injury upon another; or

(b) threatens another with or purposely puts him in fear of immediate serious bodily injury; or

(c) commits or threatens immediately to commit any felony of the first or second degree.

An act shall be deemed "in the course of committing a theft" if it occurs in an attempt to commit theft or in flight after the attempt or commission.

(2) *Grading.* Robbery is a felony of the second degree, except that it is a felony of the first degree if in the course of committing the theft the actor attempts to kill anyone, or purposely inflicts or attempts to inflict serious bodily injury.

Article 223. Theft and Related Offenses

SECTION 223.0. DEFINITIONS

In this Article, unless a different meaning plainly is required:

(1) "deprive" means: (a) to withhold property of another permanently or for so extended a period as to appropriate a major portion of its economic value, or with intent to restore only upon payment of reward or other compensation; or (b) to dispose of the property so as to make it unlikely that the owner will recover it.

(2) "financial institution" means a bank, insurance company, credit union, building and loan association, investment trust or other organization held out to the public as a place of deposit of funds or medium of savings or collective investment.

(3) "government" means the United States, any State, county, municipality, or other political unit, or any department, agency or subdivision of

any of the foregoing, or any corporation or other association carrying out the functions of government.

(4) "movable property" means property the location of which can be changed, including things growing on, affixed to, or found in land, and documents although the rights represented thereby have no physical location. "Immovable property" is all other property.

(5) "obtain" means: (a) in relation to property, to bring about a transfer or purported transfer of a legal interest in the property, whether to the obtainer or another; or (b) in relation to labor or service, to secure performance thereof.

(6) "property" means anything of value, including real estate, tangible and intangible personal property, contract rights, choses-in-action and other interests in or claims to wealth, admission or transportation tickets, captured or domestic animals, food and drink, electric or other power.

(7) "property of another" includes property in which any person other than the actor has an interest which the actor is not privileged to infringe, regardless of the fact that the actor also has an interest in the property and regardless of the fact that the other person might be precluded from civil recovery because the property was used in an unlawful transaction or was subject to forfeiture as contraband. Property in possession of the actor shall not be deemed property of another who has only a security interest therein, even if legal title is in the creditor pursuant to a conditional sales contract or other security agreement.

SECTION 223.1.   CONSOLIDATION OF THEFT OFFENSES; GRADING; PROVISIONS APPLICABLE TO THEFT GENERALLY

(1) *Consolidation of Theft Offenses.* Conduct denominated theft in this Article constitutes a single offense. An accusation of theft may be supported by evidence that it was committed in any manner that would be theft under this Article, notwithstanding the specification of a different manner in the indictment or information, subject only to the power of the Court to ensure fair trial by granting a continuance or other appropriate relief where the conduct of the defense would be prejudiced by lack of fair notice or by surprise.

(2) *Grading of Theft Offenses.*

(a) Theft constitutes a felony of the third degree if the amount involved exceeds $500, or if the property stolen is a firearm, automobile, airplane, motorcycle, motorboat or other motor-propelled vehicle, or in the case of theft by receiving stolen property, if the receiver is in the business of buying or selling stolen property.

(b) Theft not within the preceding paragraph constitutes a misdemeanor, except that if the property was not taken from the person or by threat, or in breach of a fiduciary obligation, and the actor proves by a preponderance of the evidence that the amount involved was less than $50, the offense constitutes a petty misdemeanor.

(c) The amount involved in a theft shall be deemed to be the highest value, by any reasonable standard, of the property or services which the actor stole or attempted to steal. Amounts involved in thefts committed pursuant to one scheme or course of conduct, whether from the same person or several persons, may be aggregated in determining the grade of the offense.

(3) *Claim of Right.* It is an affirmative defense to prosecution for theft that the actor:

(a) was unaware that the property or service was that of another; or

(b) acted under an honest claim of right to the property or service involved or that he had a right to acquire or dispose of it as he did; or

(c) took property exposed for sale, intending to purchase and pay for it promptly, or reasonably believing that the owner, if present, would have consented.

(4) *Theft from Spouse.* It is no defense that theft was from the actor's spouse, except that misappropriation of household and personal effects, or other property normally accessible to both spouses, is theft only if it occurs after the parties have ceased living together.

SECTION 223.2.   THEFT BY UNLAWFUL TAKING OR DISPOSITION

(1) *Movable Property.* A person is guilty of theft if he unlawfully takes, or exercises unlawful control over, movable property of another with purpose to deprive him thereof.

(2) *Immovable property.* A person is guilty of theft if he unlawfully transfers immovable property of another or any interest therein with purpose to benefit himself or another not entitled thereto.

SECTION 223.3.   THEFT BY DECEPTION

A person is guilty of theft if he purposely obtains property of another by deception. A person deceives if he purposely:

(1) creates or reinforces a false impression, including false impressions as to law, value, intention or other state of mind; but deception as to a person's intention to perform a promise shall not be inferred from the fact alone that he did not subsequently perform the promise; or

(2) prevents another from acquiring information which would affect his judgment of a transaction; or

(3) fails to correct a false impression which the deceiver previously created or reinforced, or which the deceiver knows to be influencing another to whom he stands in a fiduciary or confidential relationship; or

(4) fails to disclose a known lien, adverse claim or other legal impediment to the enjoyment of property which he transfers or encumbers in consideration for the property obtained, whether such impediment is or is not valid, or is or is not a matter of official record.

The term "deceive" does not, however, include falsity as to matters having no pecuniary significance, or puffing by statements unlikely to deceive ordinary persons in the group addressed.

SECTION 223.4.   THEFT BY EXTORTION

A person is guilty of theft if he obtains property of another by threatening to:

(1) inflict bodily injury on anyone or commit any other criminal offense; or

(2) accuse anyone of a criminal offense; or

(3) expose any secret tending to subject any person to hatred, contempt or ridicule, or to impair his credit or business repute; or

(4) take or withhold action as an official, or cause an official to take or withhold action; or

(5) bring about or continue a strike, boycott or other collective unofficial action, if the property is not demanded or received for the benefit of the group in whose interest the actor purports to act; or

(6) testify or provide information or withhold testimony or information with respect to another's legal claim or defense; or

(7) inflict any other harm which would not benefit the actor.

It is an affirmative defense to prosecution based on paragraphs (2), (3) or (4) that the property obtained by threat of accusation, exposure, lawsuit or other invocation of official action was honestly claimed as restitution or indemnification for harm done in the circumstances to which such accusation, exposure, lawsuit or other official action relates, or as compensation for property or lawful services.

SECTION 223.5.   THEFT OF PROPERTY LOST, MISLAID, OR DELIVERED BY MISTAKE

A person who comes into control of property of another that he knows to have been lost, mislaid, or delivered under a mistake as to the nature or amount of the property or the identity of the recipient is guilty of theft if, with purpose to deprive the owner thereof, he fails to take reasonable measures to restore the property to a person entitled to have it.

SECTION 223.6.   RECEIVING STOLEN PROPERTY

(1) *Receiving.* A person is guilty of theft if he purposely receives, retains, or disposes of movable property of another knowing that it has been stolen, or believing that it has probably been stolen, unless the property is received, retained, or disposed with purpose to restore it to the owner. "Receiving" means acquiring possession, control or title, or lending on the security of the property.

(2) *Presumption of Knowledge.* The requisite knowledge or belief is presumed in the case of a dealer who:

(a) is found in possession or control of property stolen from two or more persons on separate occasions; or

(b) has received stolen property in another transaction within the year preceding the transaction charged; or

(c) being a dealer in property of the sort received, acquires it for a consideration which he knows is far below its reasonable value.

"Dealer" means a person in the business of buying or selling goods including a pawnbroker.

SECTION 223.7. THEFT OF SERVICES

(1) A person is guilty of theft if he purposely obtains services which he knows are available only for compensation, by deception or threat, or by false token or other means to avoid payment for the service. "Services" includes labor, professional services, transportation, telephone or other public service, accommodation in hotels, restaurants or elsewhere, admission to exhibitions, use of vehicles or other movable property. Where compensation for service is ordinarily paid immediately upon the rendering for such service, as is the case of hotels and restaurants, refusal to pay or absconding without payment or offer to pay gives rise to a presumption that the service was obtained by deception as to intention to pay.

(2) A person commits theft if, having control over the disposition of services of others, to which he is not entitled, he knowingly diverts such services to his own benefit or to the benefit of another not entitled thereto.

SECTION 223.8. [Omitted]

SECTION 223.9. UNAUTHORIZED USE OF AUTOMOBILES AND OTHER VEHICLES

A person commits a misdemeanor if he operates another's automobile, airplane, motorcycle, motorboat, or other motor propelled vehicle without consent of the owner. It is an affirmative defense to prosecution under this Section that the actor reasonably believed that the owner would have consented to the operation had he known of it.

Article 224. Forgery and Fraudulent Practices

SECTION 224.0. DEFINITIONS

In this Article, the definitions given in Section 223.0 apply unless a different meaning plainly is required.

SECTION 224.1. FORGERY

(1) *Definition.* A person is guilty of forgery if, with purpose to defraud or injure anyone, or with knowledge that he is facilitating a fraud or injury to be perpetrated by anyone, the actor:

(a) alters any writing of another without his authority; or

(b) makes, completes, executes, authenticates, issues or transfers any writing so that it purports to be the act of another who did not authorize that act, or to have been executed at a time or place or in a numbered sequence other than was in fact the case, or to be a copy of an original when no such original existed; or

(c) utters any writing which he knows to be forged in a manner specified in paragraphs (a) or (b).

"Writing" includes printing or any other method of recording information, money, coins, tokens, stamps, seals, credit cards, badges, trade-marks, and other symbols of value, right, privilege, or identification.

(2) *Grading.* Forgery is a felony of the second degree if the writing is or purports to be part of an issue of money, securities, postage or revenue stamps, or other instruments issued by the government, or part of an issue of stock, bonds or other instruments representing interests in or claims against any property or enterprise. Forgery is a felony of the third degree if

the writing is or purports to be a will, deed, contract, release, commercial instrument, or other document evidencing, creating, transferring, altering, terminating, or otherwise affecting legal relations. Otherwise forgery is a misdemeanor.

SECTIONS 224.2.–224.4. [*Omitted*]

SECTION 224.5. BAD CHECKS

A person who issues or passes a check or similar sight order for the payment of money, knowing that it will not be honored by the drawee, commits a misdemeanor. For the purposes of this Section as well as in any prosecutions for theft committed by means of a bad check, an issuer is presumed to know that the check or order (other than a postdated check or order) would not be paid if:

(1) the issuer had no account with the drawee at the time the check or order was issued; or

(2) payment was refused by the drawee for lack of funds, upon presentation within 30 days after issue, and the issuer failed to make good within 10 days after receiving notice of that refusal.

SECTION 224.6. CREDIT CARDS

A person commits an offense if he uses a credit card for the purpose of obtaining property or services with knowledge that:

(1) the card is stolen or forged;

(2) the card has been revoked or cancelled; or

(3) for any other reason his use of the card is unauthorized by the issuer.

It is an affirmative defense to prosecution under paragraph (3) if the actor proves by a preponderance of the evidence that he had the purpose and ability to meet all obligations to the issuer arising out of his use of the card. "Credit card" means a writing, or other evidence of an undertaking to pay for property or services delivered or rendered to or upon the order of a designated person or bearer. An offense under this Section is a felony of the third degree if the value of the property or services secured or sought to be secured by means of the credit card exceeds $500; otherwise it is a misdemeanor.

SECTIONS 224.7.–224.14. [*Omitted*]

OFFENSES AGAINST THE FAMILY
Article 230. Offenses Against the Family

SECTION 230.1. BIGAMY AND POLYGAMY

(1) *Bigamy.* A married person is guilty of bigamy, a misdemeanor, if he contracts or purports to contract another marriage, unless at the time of the subsequent marriage:

(a) the actor believes that the prior spouse is dead; or

(b) the actor and the prior spouse have been living apart for five consecutive years throughout which the prior spouse was not known by the actor to be alive; or

(c) a Court has entered a judgment purporting to terminate or annul any prior disqualifying marriage, and the actor does not know that judgment to be invalid; or

(d) the actor reasonably believes that he is legally eligible to remarry.

(2) *Polygamy.* A person is guilty of polygamy, a felony of the third degree, if he marries or cohabits with more than one spouse at a time in purported exercise of the right of plural marriage. The offense is a continuing one until all cohabitation and claim of marriage with more than one spouse terminates. This section does not apply to parties to a polygamous marriage, lawful in the country of which they are residents or nationals, while they are in transit through or temporarily visiting this State.

(3) *Other Party to Bigamous or Polygamous Marriage.* A person is guilty of bigamy or polygamy, as the case may be, if he contracts or purports to contract marriage with another knowing that the other is thereby committing bigamy or polygamy.

SECTION 230.2.   INCEST

A person is guilty of incest, a felony of the third degree, if he knowingly marries or cohabits or has sexual intercourse with an ancestor or descendant, a brother or sister of the whole or half blood [or an uncle, aunt, nephew or niece of the whole blood]. "Cohabit" means to live together under the representation or appearance of being married. The relationships referred to herein include blood relationships without regard to legitimacy, and relationship of parent and child by adoption.

SECTION 230.3.   [*Omitted*]

SECTION 230.4.   ENDANGERING WELFARE OF CHILDREN

A parent, guardian, or other person supervising the welfare of a child under 18 commits a misdemeanor if he knowingly endangers the child's welfare by violating a duty of care, protection or support.

SECTION 230.5.   PERSISTENT NON-SUPPORT

A person commits a misdemeanor if he persistently fails to provide support which he can provide and which he knows he is legally obliged to provide to a spouse, child or other dependent.

OFFENSES AGAINST PUBLIC ADMINISTRATION
Article 240. Bribery and Corrupt Influence

SECTION 240.0.   DEFINITIONS

In Articles 240–243, unless a different meaning plainly is required:

(1) "benefit" means gain or advantage, or anything regarded by the beneficiary as gain or advantage, including benefit to any other person or entity in whose welfare he is interested, but not an advantage promised generally to a group or class of voters as a consequence of public measures which a candidate engages to support or oppose;

(2) "government" includes any branch, subdivision or agency of the government of the State or any locality within it;

(3) "harm" means loss, disadvantage or injury, or anything so regarded by the person affected, including loss, disadvantage or injury to any other person or entity in whose welfare he is interested;

(4) "official proceeding" means a proceeding heard or which may be heard before any legislative, judicial, administrative or other governmental agency or official authorized to take evidence under oath, including any referee, hearing examiner, commissioner, notary or other person taking testimony or deposition in connection with any such proceeding;

(5) "party official" means a person who holds an elective or appointive post in a political party in the United States by virtue of which he directs or conducts, or participates in directing or conducting party affairs at any level of responsibility;

(6) "pecuniary benefit" is benefit in the form of money, property, commercial interests or anything else the primary significance of which is economic gain;

(7) "public servant" means any officer or employee of government, including legislators and judges, and any person participating as juror, advisor, consultant or otherwise, in performing a governmental function; but the term does not include witnesses;

(8) "administrative proceeding" means any proceeding, other than a judicial proceeding, the outcome of which is required to be based on a record or documentation prescribed by law, or in which law or regulation is particularized in application to individuals.

SECTION 240.1. BRIBERY IN OFFICIAL AND POLITICAL MATTERS

A person is guilty of bribery, a felony of the third degree, if he offers, confers or agrees to confer upon another, or solicits, accepts or agrees to accept from another:

(1) any pecuniary benefit as consideration for the recipient's decision, opinion, recommendation, vote or other exercise of discretion as a public servant, party official or voter; or

(2) any benefit as consideration for the recipient's decision, vote, recommendation or other exercise of official discretion in a judicial or administrative proceeding; or

(3) any benefit as consideration for a violation of a known legal duty as public servant or party official.

It is no defense to prosecution under this Section that a person whom the actor sought to influence was not qualified to act in the desired way whether because he had not yet assumed office, or lacked jurisdiction, or for any other reason.

SECTIONS 240.2.–240.7. [*Omitted*]

Article 241. Perjury and Other Falsification in Official Matters

SECTION 241.0. DEFINITIONS

In this Article, unless a different meaning plainly is required:

(1) the definitions give in Section 240.0 apply; and

(2) "statement" means any representation, but includes a representation of opinion, belief or other state of mind only if the representation clearly relates to state of mind apart from or in addition to any facts which are the subject of the representation.

SECTION 241.1. PERJURY

(1) *Offense Defined.* A person is guilty of perjury, a felony of the third degree, if in any official proceeding he makes a false statement under oath or equivalent affirmation, or swears or affirms the truth of a statement previously made, when the statement is material and he does not believe it to be true.

(2) *Materiality.* Falsification is material, regardless of the admissibility of the statement under rules of evidence, if it could have affected the course or outcome of the proceeding. It is no defense that the declarant mistakenly believed the falsification to be immaterial. Whether a falsification is material in a given factual situation is a question of law.

(3) *Irregularities No Defense.* It is not a defense to prosecution under this Section that the oath or affirmation was administered or taken in an irregular manner or that the declarant was not competent to make the statement. A document purporting to be made upon oath or affirmation at any time when the actor presents it as being so verified shall be deemed to have been duly sworn or affirmed.

(4) *Retraction.* No person shall be guilty of an offense under this Section if he retracted the falsification in the course of the proceeding in which it was made before it became manifest that the falsification was or would be exposed and before the falsification substantially affected the proceeding.

(5) *Inconsistent Statements.* When the defendant made inconsistent statements under oath or equivalent affirmation, both having been made within the period of the statute of limitations, the prosecution may proceed by setting forth the inconsistent statements in a single count alleging in the alternative that one or the other was false and not believed by the defendant. In such case it shall not be necessary for the prosecution to prove which statement was false but only that one or the other was false and not believed by the defendant to be true.

(6) *Corroboration.* No person shall be convicted of an offense under this Section where proof of falsity rests solely upon contradiction by testimony of a single person other than the defendant.

SECTIONS 241.2.–241.9. [*Omitted*]

Article 242. Obstructing Governmental Operations; Escapes

SECTIONS 242.0.–242.1. [*Omitted*]

SECTION 242.2. RESISTING ARREST OR OTHER LAW ENFORCEMENT

A person commits a misdemeanor if, for the purpose of preventing a public servant from effecting a lawful arrest or discharging any other duty, the person creates a substantial risk of bodily injury to the public servant or anyone else, or employs means justifying or requiring substantial force to overcome the resistance.

SECTION 242.3. HINDERING APPREHENSION OR PROSECUTION

A person commits an offense if, with purpose to hinder the apprehension, prosecution, conviction or punishment of another for crime, he:

(1) harbors or conceals the other; or

(2) provides or aids in providing a weapon, transportation, disguise or other means of avoiding apprehension or effecting escape; or

(3) conceals or destroys evidence of the crime, or tampers with a witness, informant, document or other source of information, regardless of its admissibility in evidence; or

(4) warns the other of impending discovery or apprehension, except that this paragraph does not apply to a warning given in connection with an effort to bring another into compliance with law; or

(5) volunteers false information to a law enforcement officer.

The offense is a felony of the third degree if the conduct which the actor knows has been charged or is liable to be charged against the person aided would constitute a felony of the first or second degree. Otherwise it is a misdemeanor.

SECTIONS 242.4.–242.5. [*Omitted*]

SECTION 242.6. ESCAPE

(1) *Escape.* A person commits an offense if he unlawfully removes himself from official detention or fails to return to official detention following temporary leave granted for a specific purpose or limited period. "Official detention" means arrest, detention in any facility for custody of persons under charge or conviction of crime or alleged or found to be delinquent, detention for extradition or deportation, or any other detention for law enforcement purposes; but "official detention" does not include supervision of probation or parole, or constraint incidental to release on bail.

(2) *Permitting or Facilitating Escape.* A public servant concerned in detention commits an offense if he knowingly or recklessly permits an escape. Any person who knowingly causes or facilitates an escape commits an offense.

(3) *Effect of Legal Irregularity in Detention.* Irregularity in bringing about or maintaining detention, or lack of jurisdiction of the committing or detaining authority, shall not be a defense to prosecution under this Section if the escape is from a prison or other custodial facility or from detention pursuant to commitment by official proceedings. In the case of other detention, irregularity or lack of jurisdiction shall be a defense only if:

(a) the escape involved no substantial risk of harm to the person or property of anyone other than the detainee; or

(b) the detaining authority did not act in good faith under color of law.

(4) *Grading of Offenses.* An offense under this Section is a felony of the third degree where:

(a) the actor was under arrest for or detained on a charge of felony or following conviction of crime; or

(b) the actor employs force, threat, deadly weapon or other dangerous instrumentality to effect the escape; or

(c) a public servant concerned in detention of persons convicted of crime purposely facilitates or permits an escape from a detention facility.

Otherwise an offense under this section is a misdemeanor.

SECTIONS 242.7.–242.8. *[Omitted]*

Article 243. Abuse of Office [*Omitted*]
OFFENSES AGAINST PUBLIC ORDER AND DECENCY
Article 250. Riot, Disorderly Conduct, and Related Offenses

SECTION 250.1. Riot; Failure to Disperse

(1) *Riot.* A person is guilty of riot, a felony of the third degree, if he participates with [two] or more others in a course of disorderly conduct:

(a) with the purpose to commit or facilitate the commission of a felony or misdemeanor;

(b) with purpose to prevent or coerce official action; or

(c) when the actor or any other participant to the knowledge of the actor uses or plans to use a firearm or other deadly weapon.

(2) *Failure of Disorderly Persons to Disperse upon Official Order.* Where [three] or more persons are participating in a course of disorderly conduct likely to cause substantial harm or serious inconvenience, annoyance or alarm, a peace officer or other public servant engaged in executing or enforcing the law may order the participants and others in the immediate vicinity to disperse. A person who refuses or knowingly fails to obey such order commits a misdemeanor.

SECTION 250.2. DISORDERLY CONDUCT

(1) *Offense Defined.* A person is guilty of disorderly conduct if, with purpose to cause public inconvenience, annoyance or alarm, or recklessly creating a risk thereof, he:

(a) engages in fighting or threatening, or in violent or tumultuous behavior; or

(b) makes unreasonable noise or offensively coarse utterance, gesture or display, or addresses abusive language to any person present; or

(c) creates a hazardous or physically offensive condition by any act which serves no legitimate purpose of the actor.

"Public" means affecting or likely to affect persons in a place to which the public or a substantial group has access; among the places included are highways, transport facilities, schools, prisons, apartment houses, places of business or amusement, or any neighborhood.

(2) *Grading.* An offense under this section is a petty misdemeanor if the actor's purpose is to cause substantial harm or serious inconvenience, or if he persists in disorderly conduct after reasonable warning or request to desist. Otherwise disorderly conduct is a violation.

SECTIONS 250.3.–250.4. [*Omitted*]

SECTION 250.5. PUBLIC DRUNKENNESS; DRUG INCAPACITATION

A person is guilty of an offense if he appears in any public place manifestly under the influence of alcohol, narcotics or other drug, not therapeutically administered, to the degree that he may endanger himself or other persons or property, or annoy persons in his vicinity. An offense under this Section constitutes a petty misdemeanor if the actor has been convicted hereunder twice before within a period of one year. Otherwise the offense constitutes a violation.

SECTION 250.6. LOITERING OR PROWLING

A person commits a violation if he loiters or prowls in a place, at a time, or in a manner not usual for law-abiding individuals under circumstances that warrant alarm for the safety of persons or property in the vicinity. Among the circumstances which may be considered in determining whether such alarm is warranted is the fact that the actor takes flight upon appearance of a peace officer, refuses to identify himself, or manifestly endeavors to conceal himself or any object. Unless flight by the actor or other circumstance makes it impracticable, a peace officer shall prior to any arrest for an offense under this Section afford the actor an opportunity to dispel any alarm which would otherwise be warranted, by requesting him to identify himself and explain his presence and conduct. No person shall be convicted of an offense under this Section if the peace officer did not comply with the preceding sentence, or if it appears at trial that the explanation given by the actor was true and, if believed by the peace officer at the time, would have dispelled the alarm.

SECTIONS 250.7.–250.12. [*Omitted*]

Article 251. Public Indecency

SECTION 251.1. OPEN LEWDNESS

A person commits a petty misdemeanor if he does any lewd act which he knows is likely to be observed by others who would be affronted or alarmed.

SECTION 251.2. PROSTITUTION AND RELATED OFFENSES

(1) *Prostitution.* A person is guilty of prostitution, a petty misdemeanor, if he or she:

(a) is an inmate of a house of prostitution or otherwise engages in sexual activity as a business; or

(b) loiters in or within view of any public place for the purpose of being hired to engage in sexual activity.

"Sexual activity" includes homosexual and other deviate sexual relations. A "house of prostitution" is any place where prostitution or promotion of prostitution is regularly carried on by one person under the control, management or supervision of another. An "inmate" is a person who engages in prostitution in or through the agency of a house of prostitution. "Public place" means any place to which the public or any substantial group thereof has access.

(2) *Promoting Prostitution.* A person who knowingly promotes prostitution of another commits a misdemeanor or felony as provided in Subsection (3). The following acts shall, without limitation of the foregoing, constitute promoting prostitution:

(a) owning, controlling, managing, supervising or otherwise keeping, alone or in association with others, a house of prostitution or a prostitution business; or

(b) procuring an inmate for a house of prostitution or a place in a house of prostitution for one who would be an inmate; or

(c) encouraging, inducing, or otherwise purposely causing another to become or remain a prostitute; or

(d) soliciting a person to patronize a prostitute; or

(e) procuring a prostitute for a patron; or

(f) transporting a person into or within this state with purpose to promote that person's engaging in prostitution, or procuring or paying for transportation with that purpose; or

(g) leasing or otherwise permitting a place controlled by the actor, alone or in association with others, to be regularly used for prostitution or the promotion of prostitution, or failure to make reasonable effort to abate such use by ejecting the tenant, notifying law enforcement authorities, or other legally available means; or

(h) soliciting, receiving, or agreeing to receive any benefit for doing or agreeing to do anything forbidden by this Subsection.

(3) *Grading of Offenses Under Subsection (2).* An offense under Subsection (2) constitutes a felony of the third degree if:

(a) the offense falls within paragraph (a), (b) or (c) of Subsection (2); or

(b) the actor compels another to engage in or promote prostitution; or

(c) the actor promotes prostitution of a child under 16, whether or not he is aware of the child's age; or

(d) the actor promotes prostitution of his wife, child, ward or any person for whose care, protection or support he is responsible.

Otherwise the offense is a misdemeanor.

(4) *Presumption From Living off Prostitutes.* A person, other than the prostitute or the prostitute's minor child or other legal dependent incapable

of self-support, who is supported in whole or substantial part by the proceeds of prostitution is presumed to be knowingly promoting prostitution in violation of Subsection (2).

(5) *Patronizing Prostitutes.* A person commits a violation if he hires a prostitute to engage in sexual activity with him, or if he enters or remains in a house of prostitution for the purpose of engaging in sexual activity.

(6) *Evidence.* On the issue whether a place is a house of prostitution the following shall be admissible evidence: its general repute; the repute of the persons who reside in or frequent the place; the frequency, timing and duration of visits by non-residents. Testimony of a person against his spouse shall be admissible to prove offenses under this Section.

SECTION 251.3.–251.4.   [*Omitted*]

PART III. TREATMENT AND CORRECTION [*Omitted*]
PART IV. ORGANIZATION OF CORRECTION [*Omitted*]

THE PATRIOT ACT

A major change in criminal procedure was ushered in by the Patriot Act. Provisions of this Act are discussed, as appropriate, at various points in this supplement. Reprinted below is the United States Department of Justice's summary of the Act and its impact on the law.

Field Guidance on New Authorities (Redacted) Enacted in the 2001 Anti–Terrorism Legislation

Section 202. Authority to Intercept Voice Communications in Computer Hacking Investigations

Previous law: Under previous law, investigators could not obtain a wiretap order to intercept *wire* communications (those involving the human voice) for violations of the Computer Fraud and Abuse Act (18 U.S.C. § 1030). For example, in several investigations, hackers have stolen teleconferencing services from a telephone company and used this mode of communication to plan and execute hacking attacks.

Amendment: Section 202 amends 18 U.S.C. § 2516(1)—the subsection that lists those crimes for which investigators may obtain a wiretap order for wire communications—by adding felony violations of 18 U.S.C. § 1030 to the list of predicate offenses.[1] This provision will sunset December 31, 2005.

Section 209. Obtaining Voice-mail and Other Stored Voice Communications

Previous law: Under previous law, the Electronic Communications Privacy Act ("ECPA"), 18 U.S.C. § 2703 *et seq.,* governed law enforcement access to stored electronic communications (such as e-mail), but not stored wire communications (such as voice-mail). Instead, the wiretap statute governed such access because the definition of "wire communication" (18 U.S.C. § 2510(1)) included stored communications, arguably requiring law enforcement to use a wiretap order (rather than a search warrant) to obtain unopened voice communications. Thus, law

---

1. This amendment does not affect applications to intercept *electronic* communications in hacking investigations. As before, investigators may base an application to intercept electronic communications on any federal felony criminal violation. 18 U.S.C. § 2516(3). . . .

129

enforcement authorities used a wiretap order to obtain voice communications stored with a third party provider but could use a search warrant if that same information were stored on an answering machine inside a criminal's home.

Regulating stored wire communications through section 2510(1) created large and unnecessary burdens for criminal investigations. Stored voice communications possess few of the sensitivities associated with the real-time interception of telephones, making the extremely burdensome process of obtaining a wiretap order unreasonable.

Moreover, in large part, the statutory framework envisions a world in which technology-mediated voice communications (such as telephone calls) are conceptually distinct from non-voice communications (such as faxes, pager messages, and e-mail). To the limited extent that Congress acknowledged that data and voice might co-exist in a single transaction, it did not anticipate the convergence of these two kinds of communications typical of today's telecommunications networks. With the advent of MIME—Multipurpose Internet Mail Extensions—and similar features, an e-mail may include one or more "attachments" consisting of any type of data, including voice recordings. As a result, a law enforcement officer seeking to obtain a suspect's unopened e-mail from an ISP by means of a search warrant (as required under 18 U.S.C. § 2703(a)) had no way of knowing whether the inbox messages include voice attachments (*i.e.*, wire communications) which could not be compelled using a search warrant.

Amendment: Section 209 of the Act alters the way in which the wiretap statute and ECPA apply to stored voice communications. The amendments delete "electronic storage" of wire communications from the definition of "wire communication" in section 2510 and insert language in section 2703 to ensure that stored wire communications are covered under the same rules as stored electronic communications. Thus, law enforcement can now obtain such communications using the procedures set out in section 2703 (such as a search warrant), rather than those in the wiretap statute (such as a wiretap order).

This provision will sunset December 31, 2005.

Section 210.   Scope of Subpoenas for Electronic Evidence

Previous law: Subsection 2703(c) allows the government to use a subpoena to compel a limited class of information, such as the customer's name, address, length of service, and means of payment. Prior to the amendments in Section 210 of the Act, however, the list of records that investigators could obtain with a subpoena did not include certain records (such as credit card number or other form of payment for the communication service) relevant to determining a customer's true identity. In many cases, users register with Internet service providers using false names. In order to hold these individuals responsible for criminal acts committed online, the method of payment is an essential means of determining true identity.

Moreover, many of the definitions in section 2703(c) were technology-specific, relating primarily to telephone communications. For example, the list included "local and long distance telephone toll billing records," but did not include parallel terms for communications on computer networks, such as "records of session times and durations." Similarly, the previous list allowed the government to use a subpoena to obtain the customer's "telephone number or other subscriber number or identity," but did not define what that phrase meant in the context of Internet communications.

Amendment: Amendments to section 2703(c) update and expand the narrow list of records that law enforcement authorities may obtain with a subpoena. The new subsection 2703(c)(2) includes "records of session times and durations," as well as "any temporarily assigned network address." In the Internet context, such records include the Internet Protocol (IP) address assigned by the provider to the customer or subscriber for a particular session, as well as the remote IP address from which a customer connects to the provider. Obtaining such records will make the process of identifying computer criminals and tracing their Internet communications faster and easier. Note that these changes do not apply to voice messages in the possession of the user, such as the answering machine tape in a person's home. Those types of records remain outside of the statute.

Moreover, the amendments clarify that investigators may use a subpoena to obtain the "means and source of payment" that a customer uses to pay for his or her account with a communications provider, "including any credit card or bank account number." 18 U.S.C. § 2703(c)(2)(F). While generally helpful, this information will prove particularly valuable in identifying the users of Internet services where a company does not verify its users' biographical information. (This section is not subject to the sunset provision in section 224 of the Act).

Section 211. Clarifying the Scope of the Cable Act

Previous law: The law contains two different sets of rules regarding privacy protection of communications and their disclosure to law enforcement: one governing cable service (the "Cable Act") (47 U.S.C. § 551), and the other applying to the use of telephone service and Internet access (the wiretap statute, 18 U.S.C. § 2510 et seq.; ECPA, 18 U.S.C. § 2701 et seq.; and the pen register and trap and trace statute (the "pen/trap" statute), 18 U.S.C. § 3121 et seq.).

Prior to the amendments in Section 211 of the Act, the Cable Act set out an extremely restrictive system of rules governing law enforcement access to most records possessed by a cable company. For example, the Cable Act did not allow the use of subpoenas or even search warrants to obtain such records. Instead, the cable company had to provide prior notice to the customer (even if he or she were the target of the investigation), and the government had to allow the customer to appear in court with an attorney and then justify to the court the investigative need to obtain the records. The court could then order disclosure of the records only if it found by "clear and convincing evidence"—a standard greater than probable cause or even a preponderance of the evidence—that the subscriber was "reasonably suspected" of engaging in criminal activity. This procedure was completely unworkable for virtually any criminal investigation.

The legal regime created by the Cable Act caused grave difficulties in criminal investigations because today, unlike in 1984 when Congress passed the Cable Act, many cable companies offer not only traditional cable programming services but also Internet access and telephone service. In recent years, some cable companies have refused to accept subpoenas and court orders pursuant to the pen/trap statute and ECPA, noting the seeming inconsistency of these statutes with the Cable Act's harsh restrictions. See In re Application of United States, 36 F.Supp.2d 430 (D. Mass. Feb. 9, 1999) (noting apparent statutory conflict and ultimately granting application for order under 18 U.S.C. 2703(d) for records from cable company providing Internet service). Treating identical records differently depending on the technology used to access the Internet made little sense. Moreover, these complications at times delayed or ended important investigations.

Amendment: Section 211 of the Act amends title 47, section 551(c)(2)(D), to clarify that ECPA, the wiretap statute, and the trap and trace statute govern disclosures by cable companies that relate to the provision of communication services—such as telephone and Internet services.

The amendment preserves, however, the Cable Act's primacy with respect to records revealing what ordinary cable television programing a customer chooses to purchase, such as particular premium channels or "pay per view" shows. Thus, in a case where a customer receives both Internet access and conventional cable television service from a single cable provider, a government entity can use legal process under ECPA to compel the provider to disclose only those customer records relating to Internet service. (This section is not subject to the sunset provision in Section 224 of the Act).

Section 212. Emergency Disclosures by Communications Providers

Previous law: Previous law relating to voluntary disclosures by communication service providers was inadequate in two respects. *First,* it contained no special provision allowing providers to disclose customer records or communications in emergencies. If, for example, an Internet service provider ("ISP") independently learned that one of its customers was part of a conspiracy to commit an imminent terrorist attack, prompt disclosure of the account information to law enforcement could save lives. Since providing this information did not fall within one of the statutory exceptions, however, an ISP making such a disclosure could be sued civilly.

Second, prior to the Act, the law did not expressly permit a provider to voluntarily disclose *non-content* records (such as a subscriber's login records) to law enforcement for purposes of self-protection, even though providers could disclose the content of communications for this reason. See 18 U.S.C. § 2702(b)(5), 2703(c)(1)(B). Yet the right to disclose the contended of communications necessarily implies the less intrusive ability to disclose non-content records.

Cf. United States v. Auler, 539 F.2d 642, 646 n.9 (7th Cir.1976) (phone company's authority to monitor and disclose conversations to protect against fraud necessarily implies right to commit lesser invasion of using, and disclosing fruits of, pen register device) (citing United States v. Freeman, 524 F.2d 337, 341 (7th Cir.1975)). Moreover, as a practical matter, providers must have the right to disclose to law enforcement the facts surrounding attacks on their systems. For example, when an ISP's customer hacks into the ISP's network, gains complete control over an e-mail server, and reads or modifies the e-mail of other customers, the provider must have the legal ability to report the complete details of the crime to law enforcement.

Amendment: Section 212 corrects both of these inadequacies in previous law. Section 212 amends subsection 2702(b)(6) to permit, but not require, a service provider to disclose to law enforcement either content or non-content customer records in emergencies involving an immediate risk of death or serious physical injury to any person. This voluntary disclosure, however, does not create an affirmative obligation to review customer communications in search of such imminent dangers.

The amendments in Section 212 of the Act also change ECPA to allow providers to disclose information to protect their rights and property. It accomplishes this change by two related sets of amendments. First, amendments to sections 2702 and 2703 of title 18 simplify the treatment of voluntary disclosures by providers by moving all such provisions to 2702. Thus, section 2702 now regulates all permissive disclosures (of content and non-content records alike), while section 2703 covers only compulsory disclosures by providers. Second, an amendment to new subsection 2702(c)(3) clarifies that service providers *do* have the statutory authority to disclose non-content records to protect their rights and property. All of these changes will sunset December 31, 2005.

Section 213. Authority for Delaying Notice of the Execution of a Warrant

Prior law governing the delayed provision of notice that a warrant had been executed was a mix of inconsistent rules, practices, and court decisions varying widely from jurisdiction to jurisdiction across the country. The lack of uniformity hindered the investigation of terrorism cases and other nationwide investigations.

Section 213 resolved this problem by amending 18 U.S.C. § 3103a to create a uniform statutory standard authorizing courts to delay the provision of required notice if the court finds "reasonable cause" to believe that providing immediate notification of the execution of the warrant may have an adverse result as defined by 18 U.S.C. § 2705 (including endangering the life or physical safety of an individual, flight from prosecution, evidence tampering, witness intimidation, or otherwise seriously jeopardizing an investigation or unduly delaying a trial).

The section provides for the giving of notice within a "reasonable period" of a warrant's execution, which period can be further extended by a court for good cause.

This section is primarily designed to authorize delayed notice of *searches*, rather than delayed notice of *seizures*: the provision requires that any warrant issued under it must prohibit the seizure of any tangible property, any wire or electronic communication, or, except as expressly provided in chapter 121, any stored wire or electronic information, unless the court finds "reasonable necessity" for the seizure.

The "reasonable cause" standard adopted by the provision is in accord with prevailing caselaw for delayed notice of warrants. *See United States v. Villegas*, 899 F.2d 1324, 1337 (2d Cir.1990) (government must show "good reason" for delayed notice of warrants). It is also in accord with the standards for exceptions to the general requirements that agents knock and announce themselves before entering and that warrants be executed during the daytime. *See Richards v. Wisconsin*, 520 U.S. 385 (1997) (no-knock entry to execute warrant is justified when the police have "reasonable suspicion" that knocking and announcing their presence would be dangerous or futile or would inhibit the effective investigation); Fed.R.Crim.P. 41(c)(1) ("The warrant shall be served in the daytime unless the issuing authority, by appropriate provision of the warrants, and for reasonable cause shown, authorizes its execution at times other than daytime.").

The requirement of notice within a "reasonable period" is a flexible standard to meet the circumstances of the case. *Villegas*, 899 F.2d at 1337 ("What constitutes a reasonable time will depend on the circumstances of each individual case"). Analogy to other statutes suggest that the period of delay could be substantial if circumstances warrant. *See* 18 U.S.C. § 2518(8)(d) (notice of a wiretap may be delayed for "a reasonable time" but not more than 90 days after the termination of the wiretap); *cf. United States v. Allie*, 978 F.2d 1401, 1405 (5th Cir.1992) (suggesting that 60 days is a "reasonable period" for purposes of detaining a material witness under 18 U.S.C. § 3144). Caselaw regarding a "reasonable" period for delayed notice of warrants is still developing. The Second Circuit has interpreted it to ordinarily mean a seven-day initial delay, although subject to additional extensions. *Villegas*, 899 F.2d at 1337. The Ninth Circuit, although relying on the argument that the Constitution itself required prompt notice (*but see United States v. Pangburn*, 983 F.2d 449, 454–455 (2d Cir.1993); *Simons*, 206 F.3d 392, 403 (4th Cir.2000) (45–day delay in notice of execution of warrant does not render search unconstitutional)), also has held that delays ordinarily should not exceed seven days. *United States v. Freitas*, 800 F.2d 1451,

1456 (9th Cir.1986) ("Such time should not exceed seven days except upon a strong showing of necessity."). Other courts have suggested that a "reasonable period" could be significantly longer. *Cf. Simons*, 206 F.3d 392, 403 (45–day delay in notice of execution of search warrant did not render search unconstitutional).

The "reasonable necessity" standard for seizing items during the search is not well developed in the caselaw. The Second Circuit and other courts have equated the phrase "reasonable necessity" with "good reason" in the context of delayed notice. *Villegas*, 899 F.2d at 1337; *United States v. Ludwig*, 902 F.Supp. 121, 126 (W.D.Tex.1995); *accord United States v. Ibarra*, 725 F.Supp. 1195, 1200 (D.Wyo.1989) ("reasonable necessity" to impound a vehicle).

In the weeks ahead, the Department may be providing additional guidance with respect to the use of this delayed notice provision. The Department expects that delayed notice will continue to be an infrequent exception to the general rule that notice of the execution of a warrant will be provided promptly.

Section 216. Pen Register and Trap and Trace Statute

The pen register and trap and trace statute (the "pen/trap" statute) governs the prospective collection of non-content traffic information associated with communications, such as the phone numbers dialed by a particular telephone. Section 216 updates the pen/trap statute in three important ways: (1) the amendments clarify that law enforcement may use pen/trap orders to trace communications on the Internet and other computer networks; (2) pen/trap orders issued by federal courts now have nationwide effect; and (3) law enforcement authorities must file a special report with the court whenever they use a pen/trap order to install their own monitoring device (such as the FBI's DCS1000) on computers belonging to a public provider. The following sections discuss these provisions in greater detail. (This section is not subject to the sunset provision in Section 224 of the Act).

Using pen/trap orders to trace communications on computer networks

Previous law: When Congress enacted the pen/trap statute in 1986, it could not anticipate the dramatic expansion in electronic communications that would occur in the following fifteen years. Thus, the statute contained certain language that appeared to apply to telephone communications and that did not unambiguously encompass communications over computer networks. Although numerous courts across the country have applied the pen/trap statute to communications on computer networks, no federal district or appellate court has explicitly ruled on its propriety. Moreover, certain private litigants have challenged the application of the pen/trap statute to such electronic communications based on the statute's telephone-specific language.

Amendment: Section 216 of the Act amends sections 3121, 3123, 3124, and 3127 of title 18 to clarify that the pen/trap statute applies to a broad variety of communications technologies. For example, the statute defined "pen register" as "a device which records or decodes electronic or other impulses which identify the *numbers dialed* or otherwise transmitted on the *telephone line* to which such device is *attached*." 18 U.S.C. § 3127(3) (emphasis supplied). References to the target "line," for example, are revised to encompass a "line or other facility."

Such a facility might include, for example, a cellular telephone number; a specific cellular telephone identified by its electronic serial number; an Internet user account or e-mail address; or an Internet Protocol address, port number, or similar computer network address or range of addresses. In addition, because the statute takes into account a wide variety of such facilities, amendments to section 3123(b)(1)(C) now allow applicants for pen/trap orders to submit a description of the communications to be traced using any of these or other identifiers.

Moreover, the amendments clarify that orders for the installation of pen register and trap and trace devices may obtain any non-content information—all "dialing, routing, addressing, and signaling information"—utilized in the processing and transmitting of wire and electronic communications. Such information includes IP addresses and port numbers, as well as the "To" and "From" information contained in an e-mail header. Pen/trap orders cannot, however, authorize the interception of the content of a communication, such as words in the "subject line" or the body of an e-mail. Agents and prosecutors with questions about whether a particular type of information constitutes content should contact the Office of Enforcement Operations in the telephone context (202–514–6809) or the Computer Crime and Intellectual Property Section in the computer context (202–514–1026).

Further, because the pen register or trap and trace "device" often cannot be physically "attached" to the target facility, Section 216 makes two other related changes. First, in recognition of the fact that such functions are commonly performed today by software instead of physical mechanisms, the amended statute allows the pen register or trap and trace device to be "attached or applied" to the target facility. Likewise, Section 216 revises the definitions of "pen register" and "trap and trace device" in section 3127 to include an intangible "process" (such as a software routine) which collects the same information as a physical device.

Nationwide effect of pen/trap orders

Previous law: Under previous law, a court could only authorize the installation of a pen/trap device "within the jurisdiction of the court." Because of deregulation in the telecommunications industry, however, a single communication may be carried by many providers. For example, a telephone call may be carried by a competitive local exchange carrier, which passes it to a local Bell Operating Company, which passes it to a long distance carrier, which hands it to a local exchange carrier elsewhere in the U.S., which in turn may finally hand it to a cellular carrier. If these carriers do not pass source information with each call, identifying that source may require compelling information from a string of providers located throughout the country—each requiring a separate order.

Moreover, since, under previous law, a court could only authorize the installation of a pen/trap device within its own jurisdiction, when one provider indicated that the source of a communication was a different carrier in another district, a second order in the new district became necessary. This order had to be acquired by a supporting prosecutor in the new district from a local federal judge—neither of whom had any other interest in the case. Indeed, in one case investigators needed three separate orders to trace a hacker's communications. This duplicative process of obtaining a separate order for each link in the communications chain has delayed or—given the difficulty of real-time tracing—completely thwarted important investigations.

Amendment: Section 216 of the Act divides section 3123 of title 18 into two separate provisions. New subsection (a)(1) gives federal courts the authority to compel assistance from any provider of communication services in the United States whose assistance is appropriate to effectuate the order.

For example, a federal prosecutor may obtain an order to trace calls made to a telephone within the prosecutor's local district. The order applies not only to the local carrier serving that line, but also to other providers (such as long-distance carriers and regional carriers in other parts of the country) through whom calls are placed to the target telephone. In some circumstances, the investigators may have to serve the order on the first carrier in the chain and receive from that carrier information identifying the communication's path to convey to the next carrier in the chain. The investigator would then serve the same court order on the next carrier, including the additional relevant connection information learned from the first carrier; the second carrier would then provide the connection information in its possession for the communication. The investigator would repeat this process until the order has been served on the originating carrier who is able to identify the source of the communication.

When prosecutors apply for a pen/trap order using this procedure, they generally will not know the name of the second or subsequent providers in the chain of communication covered by the order. Thus, the application and order will not necessarily name these providers. The amendments to section 3123 therefore specify that, if a provider requests it, law enforcement must provide a "written or electronic certification" that the order applies to that provider.

The amendments in Section 216 of the Act also empower courts to authorize the installation and use of pen/trap devices in other districts. Thus, for example, if a terrorism or other criminal investigation based in

Virginia uncovers a conspirator using a phone or an Internet account in New York, the Virginia court can compel communications providers in New York to assist investigators in collecting information under a Virginia pen/trap order.

Consistent with the change above, Section 216 of the Act modifies section 3123(b)(1)(C) of title 18 to eliminate the requirement that federal pen/trap orders specify their geographic limits. However, because the new law gives nationwide effect for federal pen/trap orders, an amendment to section 3127(2)(A) imposes a "nexus" requirement: the issuing court must have jurisdiction over the particular crime under investigation.

Reports for use of law enforcement pen/trap devices on computer networks

Section 216 of the Act also contains an additional requirement for the use of pen/trap devices in a narrow class of cases. Generally, when law enforcement serves a pen/trap order on a communication service provider that provides Internet access or other computing services to the public, the provider itself should be able to collect the needed information and provide it to law enforcement. In certain rare cases, however, the provider may be unable to carry out the court order, necessitating installation of a device (such as Etherpeek or the FBI's DCS1000) to collect the information. In these infrequent cases, the amendments in section 216 require the law enforcement agency to provide the following information to the court under seal within thirty days: (1) the identity of the officers who installed or accessed the device; (2) the date and time the device was installed, accessed, and uninstalled; (3) the configuration of the device at installation and any modifications to that configuration; and (4) the information collected by the device. 18 U.S.C. § 3123(a)(3).

Section 217. Intercepting the Communications of Computer Trespassers

Prior law: Although the wiretap statute allows computer owners to monitor the activity on their machines to protect their rights and property, until Section 217 of the Act was enacted it was unclear whether computer owners could obtain the assistance of law enforcement in conducting such monitoring. This lack of clarity prevented law enforcement from assisting victims to take the natural and reasonable steps in their own defense that would be entirely legal in the physical world. In the physical world, burglary victims may invite the police into their homes to help them catch burglars in the act of committing their crimes. The wiretap statute should not block investigators from responding to similar requests in the computer context simply because the means of committing the burglary happen to fall within the definition of a "wire or electronic communication" according to the wiretap statute. Indeed, because providers often lack the expertise, equipment, or financial resources required to monitor attacks themselves they commonly have no effective way to exercise their rights to protect themselves from unauthorized attackers. This anomaly in the law created, as one commentator has noted, a "bizarre result," in which a "computer hacker's undeserved statutory privacy right trumps the legitimate privacy rights of the hacker's victims." Orin S. Kerr, *Are We Overprotecting Code? Thoughts on First–Generation Internet Law*, 57 Wash. & Lee L. Rev. 1287, 1300 (2000).

Amendment: To correct this problem, the amendments in Section 217 of the Act allow victims of computer attacks to authorize persons "acting under color of law" to monitor trespassers on their computer systems. Under new section 2511(2)(i), law enforcement may intercept the communications of a computer trespasser transmitted to, through, or from a protected computer. Before monitoring can occur, however, four requirements must be met. First, section 2511(2)(i)(I) requires that the owner or operator of the protected computer must authorize the interception of the trespasser's communications. Second, section 2511(2)(i)(II) requires that the person who intercepts the communication be lawfully engaged in an ongoing investigation. Both criminal and intelligence investigations qualify, but the authority to intercept ceases at the conclusion of the investigation.

Third, section 2511(2)(i)(III) requires that the person acting under color of law have reasonable grounds to believe that the contents of the communication to be intercepted will be relevant to the ongoing investigation. Fourth, section 2511(2)(i)(IV) requires that investigators intercept only the communications sent or received by trespassers. Thus, this section would only apply where the configuration of the computer system allows the interception of communications to and from the trespasser, and not the interception of non-consenting users authorized to use the computer.

Finally, section 217 of the Act amends section 2510 of title 18 to create a definition of "computer trespasser." Such trespassers include any person who accesses a protected computer (as defined in section 1030 of title 18) without authorization. In addition, the definition explicitly excludes any person "known by the owner or operator of the protected computer to have an existing contractual relationship with the owner or operator for access to all or part of the computer." 18 U.S.C. § 2510(21). For example, certain Internet service providers do not allow their customers to send bulk unsolicited e-mails (or "spam"). Customers who send spam would be in violation of the provider's terms of service, but would not qualify as trespassers—both because they are authorized users and because they have an existing contractual relationship with the provider. These provisions will sunset December 31, 2005.

Section 219. Single–Jurisdiction Search Warrants for Terrorism

Under prior law, Rule 41(a) of the Federal Rules of Criminal Procedure required that a search warrant be obtained within a district for searches within that district. The only exception was for cases in which property or a person within the district might leave the district prior to execution of the warrant. The rule created unnecessary delays and burdens for the government in the investigation of terrorist activities and networks that spanned a number of districts, since warrants must be separately obtained in each district.

Section 219 resolves that problem by providing that, in domestic or international terrorism cases, a search warrant may be issued by a magistrate judge in any district in which activities related to the terrorism have occurred for a search of property or persons located within or outside of the district.

Section 220.   Nationwide Search Warrants for E-mail

Previous law: Section 2703(a) requires the government to use a search warrant to compel a provider to disclose unopened e-mail less than six months old. Because Rule 41 of the Federal Rules of Criminal Procedure requires that the "property" to be obtained be "within the district" of the issuing court, however, some courts have declined to issue section 2703(a) warrants for e-mail located in other districts. Unfortunately, this refusal has placed an enormous administrative burden on those districts in which major ISPs are located, such as the Eastern District of Virginia and the Northern District of California, even though these districts may have no relationship with the criminal acts under investigation. In addition, requiring investigators to obtain warrants in distant jurisdictions has slowed time-sensitive investigations.

Amendment: Section 220 of the Act amends section 2703(a) of title 18 (and parallel provisions elsewhere in section 2703) to allow investigators to use section 2703(a) warrants to compel records outside of the district in which the court is located, just as they use federal grand jury subpoenas and orders under section 2703(d). This 4 Section 1030 defines a protected computer as any computer used in interstate or foreign commerce, as well as most computers used by financial institutions or the U.S. Government. Thus, almost any computer connected to the Internet qualifies as a "protected computer" change enables courts with jurisdiction over investigations to compel evidence directly, without requiring the intervention of agents, prosecutors, and judges in the districts where major ISPs are located. This provision will sunset December 31, 2005.

Section 315.   Inclusion of Foreign Corruption Offenses as Money Laundering Crimes

Until now, the only foreign crimes listed as predicates for money laundering under 18 U.S.C. §§ 1956 and 1957 were drug trafficking, bank fraud, and certain crimes of violence including murder, kidnaping, robbery, extortion and use of explosives. *See* 18 U.S.C. § 1956(c)(7)(B). Section 315 expands the list to include any crime of violence, bribery of a public official or misappropriation of public funds, smuggling munitions or technology with military applications, and any "offense with respect to which the United States would be obligated by multilateral treaty" to extradite or prosecute the offender.

By adding these offenses to the definition of "specified unlawful activity," Congress makes it possible to prosecute any person who conducts a financial transaction in the United States involving the proceeds of such offense with the requisite specific intent (or with no such intent if, as provided in section 1957, more than $10,000 is involved). Moreover, under section 1956(a)(2)(A), it will be an offense to send any money from any source into or out of the United States with the intent to promote one of the foreign offenses.

Section 316. Anti–Terrorist Forfeiture Protection

This section provides certain procedural protections to owners of property confiscated under the International Emergency Economic Powers Act (IEEPA), 50 U.S.C. § 1702 et seq., as assets of suspected international terrorists. The provision allows the owner of such property to interpose the defense that the property is not subject to confiscation under IEEPA and the "innocent owner" defense of 18 U.S.C. § 983(c).

Finally, this section also exempts confiscations from the requirements of the Civil Asset Forfeiture Reform Act of 2000 (CAFRA).

Section 317. Long-arm Jurisdiction Over Foreign Money Launderers

Section 1956(b) creates a civil cause of action by the government against any person who commits a money laundering offense. It is an alternative to a criminal prosecution under section 1956(a) that is sometimes used when the offender is a corporation (including a bank) against whom a criminal prosecution is of less importance than a finding of liability and the imposition of a monetary penalty.

One defect in prior section 1956(b) was that it created a cause of action only for violations of section 1956(a). As amended by section 317, section 1956(b) now permits the government to base its case on a violation of section 1957, which in many instances will be easier for the government to prove.

Second, under prior law there was some question whether the government could bring a section 1956(b) lawsuit against a foreign person, including a foreign bank, that committed a money laundering offense but could not be found in the United States. For example, if employees of a Mexican bank conducted financial transactions that constituted a violation of section 1956(a), and the government wanted to file a lawsuit against the Mexican bank under section 1956(b), there was uncertainty whether the bank would be subject to the jurisdiction of a U.S. court if it had no physical presence in the United States. As amended, section 1956(b) now provides that the court has jurisdiction if the money laundering offense occurred in part in the United States, or the foreign bank has a correspondent account in the United States.

Third, section 1956(b) was amended to permit a court to take jurisdiction over an action brought by the government to enforce a forfeiture judgment based on a violation of section 1956. Section 317 provides that if property is ordered forfeited under section 982(a)(1), based on a violation of section 1956, and the government files a lawsuit against a foreign person who has converted that forfeited property to his own use instead of turning it over to the government, the district court will have jurisdiction over the foreign person. What the amendment does is to eliminate any uncertainty over what circumstances will permit a court to exercise long-arm jurisdiction in such cases.

Finally, section 317 amends section 1956(b) to authorize a court to enter a restraining order to ensure "that any bank account or other property held by the defendant in the United States is available to satisfy a judgment under this section." The court is also authorized to appoint, at the request of the Attorney General, a receiver to manage assets in three categories of cases: 1) where assets are subject to a civil penalty under section 1956(b); 2) where assets are subject to any civil or criminal forfeiture under sections 981 or 982; and 3) where assets are subject to a restitution order in a section 1956 or 1957 criminal case. This authority—both to enter restraining orders and to appoint receivers—appears to be limited, however, to cases in which the court is exercising its long-arm authority over a foreign person.

Section 318. Laundering Money Through a Foreign Bank

18 U.S.C. § 1956 prohibits conducting a transaction involving a financial institution if the transaction involves criminally derived property. Similarly, section 1957 creates an offense relating to the deposit, withdrawal, transfer or exchange of criminally derived funds "by, to or through a financial institution." Both statutes employ the definition of "financial institution" found in 31 U.S.C. § 5312. See 18 U.S.C. § 1956(c)(6); 18 U.S.C. § 1957(f).

Under prior law, the definition of "financial institution" did not explicitly include foreign banks. Such banks arguably were within the meaning of "commercial bank" or other terms in the statute, but there was some confusion over whether the government could rely on section 5312 to prosecute an offense under either section 1956 or 1957 involving a transaction through a foreign bank, even if the offense occurred in part in the United States. Section 318 ends the confusion by explicitly including foreign banks within the definition of "financial institution" in section 1956(c)(6).

Section 319. Forfeiture of Funds in United States Interbank Accounts

It is quite common for foreign criminals to deposit money derived from crimes committed in the United States into foreign bank accounts. This is often done by depositing the money directly into the correspondent account that a foreign bank maintains at another bank in the United States. When the government tries to seize and forfeit the money in the correspondent account, however, the foreign bank, which is considered the owner of the funds in its correspondent account, is able to assert an innocent owner defense under 18 U.S.C. § 983(d). In Section 319, Congress has addressed this problem by creating a new provision codified as 18 U.S.C. § 981(k).

Section 981(k)(1) provides that if funds are deposited into an account in a foreign bank, and that foreign bank has a correspondent account in the United States, "the funds deposited into the [foreign bank] shall be deemed to have been deposited into the correspondent account in the United States," and the government may seize, arrest or restrain the funds in the correspondent account "up to the value of the funds deposited" into the foreign bank. Moreover, section 981(k)(2) provides that when a forfeiture action is brought against those funds, "the government shall not be required to establish that such funds are directly traceable to the funds [that were deposited into the foreign bank], nor shall it be necessary for the government to rely on the application of Section 984." Thus, if a drug dealer deposits funds into a foreign bank that has a correspondent account in the United States, the government can now seize and bring a forfeiture action against an equivalent sum of money in the correspondent account, regardless of whether the money in the correspondent account is traceable to the foreign deposit, and without having to be concerned with the application of the fungible property provisions of 18 U.S.C. § 984.

Section 981(k)(3) and (4) provide that for purposes of the application of the innocent owner defense in section 983(d), the "owner" of the funds is the person who deposited the funds into the foreign bank, not the foreign bank or intermediary institution that may have been involved in the transfer of the funds. As explained in the legislative history, "[u]nder this arrangement, if funds traceable to criminal activity are deposited into a foreign bank, the government may bring a forfeiture action against funds in that bank's correspondent account, and only the initial depositor, and not the intermediary bank, would have standing to contest it." *See* H.Rep. 107–250. The only exception to this rule applies when the government's theory of forfeiture is that the foreign bank was itself the wrongdoer (thus subjecting the money in its correspondent account to civil forfeiture), or when the foreign depositor had already withdrawn his money from the foreign bank before the money in the correspondent account was restrained, seized or arrested.

This provision will greatly facilitate the ability of federal prosecutors to forfeit funds that domestic criminals seek to insulate from forfeiture by depositing them in foreign banks and then hiding behind the banks' innocent owner defenses, even though the funds are safely maintained in a correspondent account in the United States.

In another part of section 319, Congress has given law enforcement a potent new investigative tool by creating a mechanism for serving a subpoena for bank records on a foreign bank. New 31 U.S.C. § 5318(k)(3) provides that the Attorney General or the Secretary of the

Treasury may serve "a summons or subpoena" on any foreign bank that has a correspondent account in the United States, and request records relating to that correspondent account or any "records maintained outside of the United States relating to the deposit of funds into the foreign bank." *See* H.Rep. 107–250 ("Under this provision, a foreign bank that maintains a correspondent account in the United States must have a representative in the United States who will accept service of a subpoena for any records of any transaction with the foreign bank that occurs overseas."). Thus, if the government wished to obtain records maintained by the foreign bank in its offices overseas, it would no longer be necessary to seek those records pursuant to a mutual legal assistance treaty or other procedure that is dependent upon the cooperation of a foreign government.

Rather, the government could proceed by serving a summons or subpoena, issued by the Department of Justice or the Department of the Treasury, on the person the foreign bank is required to designate to "accept service of legal process" in the United States.

Section 5318(k)(3) provides a sanction for a foreign bank's failure to comply with the "summons or subpoena." Upon notification by either the Secretary of the Treasury or the Attorney General that a foreign bank has failed to comply with a summons or subpoena issued under the new statute, a U.S. bank that maintains a correspondent account for the foreign bank must close that account or face civil penalties of up to $10,000 per day "until the correspondent relationship is terminated."

Finally, section 319 gives the courts explicit authority to order the repatriation of assets in criminal cases. While numerous courts have directed criminal defendants to repatriate assets to the United States for the purpose of forfeiture as part of a pre-trial restraining order, this provision establishes clear statutory authority for that practice.

Section 319 amends 21 U.S.C. § 853(e) to include a new paragraph explicitly authorizing a court to order a defendant to repatriate any property subject to forfeiture to the United States, and to deposit it with the Marshals Service, the Secretary of the Treasury, or in the registry of the court. Moreover, the same section amends the substitute asset provision in 21 U.S.C. § 853(p) to provide that in addition to ordering the forfeiture of substitute assets, the court may order a defendant who has placed his forfeitable property beyond the jurisdiction of the court to "return the property to the jurisdiction of the court so that the property may be seized and forfeited." Section 853(e)(4) also includes a provision giving the court the authority to sanction a defendant who fails to comply with a repatriation order by increasing his sentence under obstruction of justice provisions of the sentencing guidelines or by holding the defendant in contempt of court.

Section 320. Proceeds of Foreign Crimes

Under 18 U.S.C. § 981(a)(1)(C), as amended by CAFRA, any proceeds of any offense listed in the definition of "specified unlawful activity" are subject to civil forfeiture. Thus, Congress automatically created authority to forfeit the proceeds of the expanded list of foreign crimes merely by including them in section 1956(c)(7)(B).

However, section 320 also amends 18 U.S.C. § 981(a)(1)(B) to authorize the forfeiture of both the proceeds of, *and any property used to facilitate,* any offense listed in section 1956(c)(7)(B), if the offense would be a felony if committed within the jurisdiction of the United States.

Section 322. Corporation Represented by a Fugitive

One of the key provisions in CAFRA was the reinstatement of the fugitive disentitlement doctrine. As codified at 28 U.S.C. § 2466, the doctrine provides that a person who is a fugitive in a criminal case cannot contest the forfeiture of his property in a related forfeiture case unless he surrenders to face the criminal charges. It has become apparent, however, that this provision contains a loophole: while the fugitive himself may not be able to file a claim, a corporation claiming to be the true owner of the property may do so, even if the corporation is owned by the fugitive, or the fugitive files the claim on the corporation's behalf. While the government could in some cases defeat this ploy by showing that the corporation was not the true owner of the property or that the corporation was the *alter ego* of the defendant, the loophole impaired the effective application of section 2466.

In section 322, Congress closed this gap by providing that the fugitive disentitlement doctrine applies to claims filed by corporations "if any majority shareholder, or individual filing the claim on behalf of the corporation" is otherwise disqualified from contesting the forfeiture by section 2466. As explained in the legislative history, "[t]he amendment clarifies that a natural person who is a fugitive may not circumvent this provision by filing, or having another person file, a claim on behalf of a corporation that the fugitive controls." H.Rep. 107–250.

Section 323. Enforcement of Foreign Judgments

CAFRA gave the federal courts authority to enforce foreign forfeiture judgments.

Under 28 U.S.C. § 2467, a judgment of forfeiture of property located in the United States that is issued by a foreign court can be certified by the Attorney General and presented to a federal district court to be registered and enforced. This statute contained two major deficiencies: first, it provided no mechanism for preserving the property while the foreign forfeiture action was pending in the foreign court; and second, it applied only to a narrow range of foreign offenses such as drug trafficking and bank fraud.

Section 323 corrects both of these problems. First, it inserts new language in section 2467(d)(3) authorizing a district court to "preserve the availability of property subject to a foreign forfeiture or confiscation judgment" by issuing a civil forfeiture restraining order pursuant to 18 U.S.C. § 983(j). The order may be issued "at any time before or after" the government receives a final judgment of forfeiture from the foreign court. The new statute provides that no person may contest the issuance of the restraining order "on any ground that is the subject of parallel litigation involving the same property that is pending in a foreign court." This provision avoids the "two bites at the apple" problem that often arises when the United States asks a foreign country to restrain property in that jurisdiction that is subject to forfeiture in a case pending in the United States. Almost invariably, the foreign court that restrains the property will allow potential claimants to object to the restraining order on grounds (such as an innocent owner defense) that could also be raised in the forfeiture proceeding underway in the U.S. This gives the foreign claimant the advantage of being able to attack the forfeiture twice on the same grounds: if he is unsuccessful in persuading the foreign court to vacate the restraining order, he may file a claim in the United States and assert the same defense all over again. (While the amendment to section 2467 can do nothing to prevent foreign courts from continuing to give their citizens two bites at the apple, the change to the federal statute will provide an example for other countries to follow in reforming their own laws.)

Second, to rectify the narrow application of section 2467, Congress amended section 2467(a)(2)(A) to provide that federal courts may enforce a foreign forfeiture order based on "any violation of foreign law that would constitute a violation of an offense for which property could be forfeited under Federal law if the offense were committed in the United States."

Section 371. Bulk Cash Smuggling Into or Out of the United States

In *United States v. Bajakajian,* 524 U.S. 321 (1998), the Supreme Court held that forfeiture of 100 percent of the unreported currency in a CMIR case would be "grossly disproportional to the gravity of the offense," unless the currency was involved in some other criminal activity. In so holding, the Court ruled that the unreported currency is not the *corpus delicti* of the crime. This contrasts, the Court said, with the various anti-smuggling statutes which authorize the forfeiture of 100 percent of the items concealed from the Customs Service or imported in violation of the Customs laws.

Section 371 makes currency smuggling a criminal offense, thus elevating the seriousness of smuggling currency into or out of the United States to the same level as the smuggling of firearms, jewels or counterfeit merchandise. As codified at 31 U.S.C. § 5332(a), the new statute makes it an offense for any person, with the intent to evade a currency reporting requirement under section 5316, to conceal more than $10,000 in currency in any fashion, and to transport, or attempt to transport, such currency into or out of the United States. Section 5332(b) provides for criminal forfeiture of the property involved in the offense, including a personal money judgment if the directly forfeitable property cannot be found and the defendant does not have sufficient substitute assets to satisfy the forfeiture judgment. Section 5332(c) authorizes civil forfeiture for the same offense.

In anticipation of legal attacks suggesting that the new statute is nothing more than a recodification of the existing penalties for violating the CMIR requirement, and that forfeiture of 100 percent of the smuggled currency would still violate the Eighth Amendment, Congress made findings emphasizing the seriousness of currency smuggling and the importance of authorizing confiscation of the smuggled money. In particular, the "findings" state that the intentional transportation of currency into or out of the United States "in a manner designed to circumvent the mandatory reporting [requirements] is the equivalent of, and creates the same harm as, smuggling goods." Moreover, the findings state that "only the confiscation of smuggled bulk cash can effectively break the cycle of criminal activity of which the laundering of bulk cash is a critical part." The findings conclude that "in cases where the only criminal violation under current law is a reporting offense, the law does not adequately provide for the confiscation of smuggled currency."

"In contrast," Congress found, "if the smuggling of bulk cash were itself an offense, the cash could be confiscated as the *corpus delicti* of the smuggling offense."

The House Report on this provision specifies that "[t]he civil forfeiture provision would apply to conduct occurring before the effective date of the act."

Section 372. Forfeiture in Currency Reporting Cases

Section 372 contains a seemingly minor amendment that strikes the references to 31 U.S.C. sections 5313, 5316 and 5324 from sections 981(a)(1)(A) and 982(a)(1), respectively, and places the authority to forfeit the property involved in those offenses in 31 U.S.C. § 5317(c). Sections 5313, 5316 and 5324 are the provisions requiring the filing of CTR and CMIR reports, and prohibiting the structuring of transactions to evade the reporting requirements.

Sections 981(a)(1)(A) and 982(a)(1) do not provide for the forfeiture of property involved in a conspiracy to commit any of the enumerated currency reporting offenses.

Thus, under the prior law, the government could forfeit property involved in a structuring offense under 31 U.S.C. sections 5324(a)(3), but not property involved only in a conspiracy to commit that offense in violation of the general conspiracy statute, 18 U.S.C. section 371. In the revised version of section 5317(c), however, Congress has provided for the forfeiture of all property, real or personal, involved in a violation of sections 5313, 5316 or 5324, "or any conspiracy to commit such offense."

Section 373. Illegal Money Transmitting Businesses

When it was enacted in 1992, 18 U.S.C. § 1960 made it a federal offense to conduct a money transmitting business without a State license. While in the past this statute has been of limited use to federal law enforcement, section 373's amendments to section 1960 are likely to make the statute a much more effective tool against money laundering.

Under the prior law, the government had to prove that the defendant knew that his money transmitting business was "intentionally operated without an appropriate [State] money transmitting license" or that it did not comply with the registration requirements of 31 U.S.C. § 5330. Arguably, this required the government to prove that the defendant knew of the State licensing requirements or federal registration requirements and knew that his business did not comply with them; it may also have required proof that the defendant knew that operating a business in such circumstances was illegal. Section 373 eliminated this ambiguity by clearly converting section 1960 into a "general intent" crime, making it illegal to conduct any unlicenced money transmitting business, "whether or not the defendant knew that the operation was required to be licensed" or that operation without a license was a criminal offense. Section 373 also makes it an offense for anyone to conduct a money transmitting business that fails to comply with the provisions of section 5330 (or the regulations that the Department of the Treasury is to promulgate within the next few months). *See* H.Rep. 107–250.

Most importantly, section 373 expands the scope of section 1960 to include any business, licensed or unlicenced, that involves the movement of funds that the defendant knows were derived from a criminal offense, or are intended to be used "to promote or support unlawful activity." Thus, under this new provision, a person operating a money transmitting business could be prosecuted for conducting transactions that the defendant knows involve drug proceeds, or that he knows involve funds that someone is planning to use to commit an unlawful act. Moreover, as explained in the House Report, "[i]t would not be necessary for the government to show that the business was a storefront or other formal business open to walk-in trade. To the contrary, it would be sufficient to show that the defendant offered his services as a money transmitter to another."

It is already an offense under sections 1956 and 1957, of course, for any person to conduct a financial transaction involving criminally derived property. But section 1957 has a $10,000 threshold requirement, and section 1956 requires proof of specific intent either to promote another offense or to conceal or disguise the criminal proceeds. New section 1960 contains neither of these requirements if the property is criminal proceeds, or alternatively, if there is proof that the purpose of the financial transaction was to commit another offense, it does not require proof that the transmitted funds were tainted by an prior misconduct. Thus, in cases where the defendant is a money transmitting business, section 1960 may prove more potent than either section 1956 or 1957 as a tool of the prosecution.

Finally, the changes to section 1960 include an amendment to 18 U.S.C. § 981(a)(1)(A) authorizing civil forfeiture of all property involved in the section 1960 violation.

Section 503. DNA Identification of Terrorists and Other Violent Offenders

Under prior law, the statutory provisions governing the collection of DNA samples from convicted federal offenders (42 U.S.C. § 14135a(d)) have been restrictive and, in particular, have not included persons convicted for the crimes that are most likely to be committed by terrorists. DNA samples could not be collected even from persons federally convicted of terrorist murders in many circumstances.

Section 503 addressed that deficiency, and generally strengthened the collection of DNA samples from federal offenders, by extending sample collection to all federal offenders convicted of the types of offenses that are likely to be committed by terrorists (as set forth in 18 U.S.C. § 2332b(g)(5)(B)) or any crime of violence (as defined in 18 U.S.C. § 16).

Section 801. Terrorist Attacks and Other Acts of Violence Against Mass Transportation Systems

Section 801 created a new offense codified at 18 U.S.C. § 1993, prohibiting various violent offenses against mass transportation systems, vehicles, facilities, or passengers. The provision prohibits disabling or wrecking a mass transportation vehicle; placing a biological agent or destructive substance or device in a mass transportation vehicle with intent to endanger safety or with reckless disregard for human life; setting fire to or placing a biological agent or destructive substance or device in a mass transportation facility knowing or having reason to know that the activity is likely to disable or wreck a mass transportation vehicle; disabling mass transportation signaling systems; interfering with personnel with intent to endanger safety or with reckless disregard for human life; use of a dangerous weapon with intent to cause death or serious bodily injury to a person on the property of a mass transportation provider; conveying false information about any such offense; and attempt and conspiracy. The provision carries a maximum sentence of 20 years imprisonment, or life imprisonment if the crime results in death.

Section 802. Definition of Domestic Terrorism

Section 802 added to 18 U.S.C. § 2331 a new definition of "domestic terrorism," corresponding to the existing definition of "international terrorism." The term is defined to mean activities occurring primarily within the territorial jurisdiction of the United States involving acts dangerous to human life that are a violation of the criminal laws of the United States or any state and appear to be intended to intimidate or coerce a civilian population, influence the policy of a government by intimidation or coercion, or affect the conduct of a government by mass destruction, assassination, or kidnaping. The provision also makes a minor conforming change in the definition of "international terrorism."

The definition is used in other provisions of the Act, including the provision allowing nationwide service of search warrants in cases of international or domestic terrorism.

Section 803.   Prohibition Against Harboring Terrorists

Section 803 created a new offense codified at 18 U.S.C. § 2339 that prohibits harboring or concealing persons who have committed or are about to commit a variety of terrorist offenses, including destruction of aircraft or aircraft facilities, use of nuclear materials or chemical or biological weapons, use of weapons of mass destruction, arson or bombing of government property, destruction of energy facilities, sabotage of nuclear facilities, or aircraft piracy. The harboring offense of prior law prohibited only the harboring of spies (see 18 U.S.C. § 792); there was no comparable terrorism provision, though the harboring of terrorists creates a risk to national security readily comparable to that posed by harboring spies.

Section 804.   Jurisdiction Over Crimes Committed at U.S. Facilities Abroad

Section 804 explicitly extended the special maritime and territorial jurisdiction of the United States to U.S. diplomatic and consular premises and related private residences overseas for offenses committed by or against a U.S. national. When offenses are committed by or against a U.S. national abroad at such U.S. facilities, the country in which the offense occurs may have little interest in prosecuting the case. Unless the United States is able to prosecute such offenders, these crimes may go unpunished.

Section 804 clarified inconsistent prior caselaw to establish that the United States may prosecute offenses committed in its missions abroad, by or against its nationals. The provision explicitly exempts offenses committed by members or employees of the U.S. armed forces and persons accompanying the armed forces, who are covered under a provision of existing law, 18 U.S.C. § 3261(a).

Section 805.   Material Support for Terrorism

18 U.S.C. § 2339A prohibits providing material support or resources to terrorists.

The prior definition of "material support or resources" was generally not broad enough to encompass expert advice and assistance—for example, advice provided by a civil engineer on destroying a building, or advice by a biochemist on making a biological agent more lethal. Section 805 amends 18 U.S.C. § 2339A to include expert advice and assistance, making the offense applicable to experts who provide advice or assistance knowing or intending that it is to be used in preparing for or carrying out terrorism crimes. Section 805 also eliminates language in § 2339A restricting its application to material support provided within the United States, and adds to the list of underlying terrorism crimes for which provision of material support is barred. Other provisions in the section provide that material support offenses can be prosecuted in any district in which the underlying offense was committed, and make it clear that prohibited material support includes all types of monetary instruments.

Section 806. Assets of Terrorist Organizations

Prior law did not specifically provide authority for the confiscation of terrorist assets. Instead, forfeiture was authorized only in narrow circumstances for the proceeds of murder, arson, and some terrorism offenses, or for laundering the proceeds of such offenses. However, most terrorism offenses do not yield "proceeds," and available forfeiture laws required detailed tracing that is quite difficult for accounts coming through the banks of countries used by many terrorists.

Section 806 increases the government's ability to strike at terrorist organizations' economic base by permitting the forfeiture of their property regardless of the source of the property, and regardless of whether the property has actually been used to commit a terrorism offense. This is similar in concept to the forfeiture now available under RICO.

In parity with the drug forfeiture laws, the section also authorizes the forfeiture of property used or intended to be used to facilitate a terrorist act, regardless of its source.

Section 806 amends 18 U.S.C. § 981(a)(1) to include a new subparagraph (G) which makes the following property subject to civil forfeiture:

"(G) All assets, foreign or domestic—

"(i) of any individual, entity or organization engaged in planning or perpetrating any act of domestic terrorism or international terrorism (as defined in section 2331) against the United States, citizens or residents of the United States, or their property, and all assets, foreign or domestic, affording any person a source of influence over any such entity or organization;

"(ii) acquired or maintained by any person with the intent and for the purpose of supporting, planning, conducting, or concealing an act of domestic terrorism or international terrorism (as defined in section 2331) against the United States, citizens or residents of the United States, or their property; or

"(iii) derived from, involved in, or used or intended to be used to commit any act of domestic terrorism or international terrorism (as defined in section 2331) against the United States, citizens or residents of the United States, or their property".

Prosecutors are encouraged to check with AFMLS before commencing any civil forfeiture action based on section 981(a)(1)(G) so that we may coordinate application of the new law.

Section 807. Technical Clarification Relating to Provision of Material Support to Terrorism

The Trade Sanctions Reform and Export Enhancement Act of 2000, Title IX of Public Law 106–387, creates exceptions in the nation's Trade

Sanctions Programs for food and agricultural products. Section 807 makes clear that the Trade Sanctions Reform and Export Enhancement Act of 2000 does not limit 18 U.S.C. §§ 2339A or 2339B. In other words, the exceptions to trade sanctions for these items does not prevent criminal liability for the provision of these items to support terrorist activity or to foreign terrorist organizations as described in 2339A and 2339B. This is not a change from existing law, but rather serves to foreclose any possible misunderstanding or argument that the Act in some manner trumps or limits the prohibition on providing material support or resources to terrorism.

Section 808. Definition of Federal Crime of Terrorism

Section 808 added several offenses, including a number of aircraft violence crimes and certain computer crimes, to the list of predicate offenses in the definition of "Federal crime of terrorism" that appears in 18 U.S.C. § 2332b(g)(5). That term is defined as any of a comprehensive list of offenses likely to be committed by terrorists (set forth in § 2332b(g)(5)(B)) if calculated to influence or affect the conduct of government by intimidation or coercion, or to retaliate against government conduct. The list of predicate crimes in § 2332b(g)(5)(B) is used elsewhere in the Act to define the scope of other provisions, including a longer statute of limitations (section 809), lengthened periods of supervised release (section 812), and additional crimes that are now RICO predicates (section 813).

Because of Congressional concerns about overbreadth, this section removes some crimes from prior § 2332b(g)(5)(B) (primarily offenses involving assault and less grave property crimes). To fully preserve the Attorney General's primary investigatory authority over these offenses, section 808 includes a conforming amendment to § 2332b(f) which explicitly adds these offenses to that provision.

Section 809. No Statute of Limitations for Certain Terrorism Offenses

Most non-capital federal offenses are subject to a five-year statute of limitations; under prior law, many terrorism offenses were subject to an eight-year statute of limitations under 18 U.S.C. § 3286. Section 809 expands the list of offenses subject to the eight-year limitation period to include all offenses listed in § 2332b(g)(5)(B), unless otherwise subject to a longer limitation period. In addition, section 809 provides that any offense listed in § 2332b(g)(5)(B) may be prosecuted without limitation of time if the offense resulted in, or created a foreseeable risk of, death or serious bodily injury to a person other than the defendant. This will make it possible to prosecute the perpetrators of such terrorist acts whenever they are identified and apprehended.

The section expressly provides that it is applicable to offenses committed before the date of enactment of the statute, as well as those committed thereafter. This retroactivity provision ensures that the section's limitation period reforms will apply, for example, to the prosecution of crimes committed in connection with the September 11, 2001 terrorist attacks. The constitutionality of such retroactive applications of changes in statutes of limitations is well settled. *See, e.g., United States v. Grimes*, 142 F.3d 1342, 1350–51 (11th Cir.1998); *People v. Frazer*, 982 P.2d 180 (Cal.1999).

Section 810. Alternative Maximum Penalties for Terrorism Offenses

Section 810 amended existing statutes prescribing punishment levels for crimes likely to be committed by terrorists that previously were subject to inadequate maximum penalties. This section provides for enhanced maximum penalties for arson offenses under 18 U.S.C. § 81, destruction of an energy facility under § 1366, material support to terrorists under § 2339A, material support to designated foreign terrorist organizations under § 2339B, destruction of national-defense materials under § 2155(a), sabotage of nuclear facilities or fuel under 42 U.S.C. § 2284, carrying weapons aboard aircraft with reckless disregard for human life under 49 U.S.C. § 46505(c), and damaging or destroying an interstate gas or hazardous liquid pipeline facility under 49 U.S.C. § 60123(b).

Section 811. Penalties for Terrorist Conspiracies

While many terrorism offenses contain specific provisions punishing conspiracies with the same maximum penalties as substantive offenses, under prior law, some did not.

If no specific conspiracy provisions existed, the alternative was proceeding under the general conspiracy provision (18 U.S.C. § 371), which carries a maximum penalty of five years even if the object of the conspiracy is a serious crime carrying a far higher maximum penalty. Section 811 amended several criminal statutes to provide adequate conspiracy penalties by authorizing maximum penalties equal to the completed offense.

Section 811 created enhanced conspiracy penalties for arson under 18 U.S.C. § 81, killings in federal facilities under § 930(c), injuring or destroying communications lines or systems under § 1362, injuring or destroying buildings or property within the special maritime and territorial jurisdiction of the United States under § 1363, wrecking trains under § 1992, material support to terrorists under § 2339A, torture under § 2340A, sabotage of nuclear facilities or fuel under 42 U.S.C. § 2284, interference with flight crew members and attendants under 49 U.S.C. § 46504, carrying weapons aboard aircraft under 49 U.S.C. § 46505, and damaging or destroying an interstate gas or hazardous liquid pipeline facility under 49 U.S.C. § 60123(b).

Section 812. Post–Release Supervision of Terrorists

Prior federal law (18 U.S.C. § 3583(b)) generally capped the maximum period of post-imprisonment supervision for released felons at 3 or

5 years. Thus, for a released but unreformed terrorist, there was no means of tracking the person or imposing conditions to prevent renewed involvement in terrorist activities beyond a period of a few years. The drug laws (21 U.S.C. § 841) mandate longer supervision periods for persons convicted of certain drug trafficking crimes, and specify no upper limit on the duration of supervision, but there was nothing comparable for terrorism offenses.

Section 812 added a new subsection to 18 U.S.C. § 3583 to authorize longer supervision periods, including potentially lifetime supervision, for persons convicted of certain terrorism crimes. This permits appropriate tracking and oversight following release of offenders whose involvement with terrorism may reflect lifelong ideological commitments. The covered class of crimes is the crimes listed in 18 U.S.C. § 2332b(g)(5)(B), where the commission of the offense resulted in, or created a foreseeable risk of, death or serious injury to another person.

Section 813. Inclusion of Acts of Terrorism as Racketeering Activity

Under prior law, the list of predicate federal offenses for RICO, appearing in 18 U.S.C. § 1961(1), did not include the offenses which are most likely to be committed by terrorists. Section 813 added the crimes listed in § 2332b(g)(5)(B) to the list of RICO predicates, which will make it possible to use RICO more readily in the prosecution of terrorist organizations.

Section 814. Deterrence and Prevention of Cyberterrorism

Section 814 makes a number of changes to improve 18 U.S.C. § 1030, the Computer Fraud and Abuse Act. This section increases penalties for hackers who damage protected computers (from a maximum of 10 years to a maximum of 20 years); clarifies the *mens rea* required for such offenses to make explicit that a hacker need only intend damage, not a particular *type* of damage; adds a new offense for damaging computers used for national security or criminal justice; expands the coverage of the statute to include computers in foreign countries so long as there is an effect on U.S. interstate or foreign commerce; counts state convictions as "prior offenses" for purpose of recidivist sentencing enhancements; and allows losses to several computers from a hacker's course of conduct to be aggregated for purposes of meeting the $5,000 jurisdictional threshold.

The following discussion analyzes these and other provisions in more detail.

Section 1030(c)—Raising the maximum penalty for hackers that damage protected computers and eliminating mandatory minimums

Previous law: Under previous law, first-time offenders who violate section 1030(a)(5) could be punished by no more than five years' imprisonment, while repeat offenders could receive up to ten years. Certain offenders, however, can cause such severe damage to protected computers that this five-year maximum did not adequately take into account the seriousness of their crimes. For example, David Smith pled guilty to violating section 1030(a)(5) for releasing the "Melissa" virus that damaged thousands of computers across the Internet. Although Smith agreed, as part of his plea, that his conduct caused over $80,000,000 worth of loss (the maximum dollar figure contained in the Sentencing Guidelines), experts estimate that the real loss was as much as ten times that amount.

In addition, previous law set a mandatory sentencing guidelines minimum of six months imprisonment for any violation of section 1030(a)(5), as well as for violations of section 1030(a)(4) (accessing a protected computer with the intent to defraud).

Amendment: Section 814 of the Act raises the maximum penalty for violations for damaging a protected computer to ten years for first offenders, and twenty years for repeat offenders. 18 U.S.C. § 1030(c)(4). Congress chose, however, to eliminate all mandatory minimum guidelines sentencing for section 1030 violations.

Subsection 1030(c)(2)(C) and (e)(8)—Hackers need only intend to cause damage, not a particular consequence or degree of damage

Previous law: Under previous law, in order to violate subsections (a)(5)(A), an offender had to "intentionally [cause] damage without authorization." Section 1030 defined "damage" as impairment to the integrity or availability of data, a program, a system, or information that (1) caused loss of at least $5,000; (2) modified or impairs medical treatment; (3) caused physical injury; or (4) threatened public health or safety.

The question repeatedly arose, however, whether an offender must *intend* the $5,000 loss or other special harm, or whether a violation occurs if the person only intends to damage the computer, *that in fact* ends up causing the $5,000 loss or harming the individuals. It appears that Congress never intended that the language contained in the definition of "damage" would create additional elements of proof of the actor's mental state. Moreover, in most cases, it would be almost impossible to prove this additional intent.

Amendment: Section 814 of the Act restructures the statute to make clear that an individual need only intend to damage the computer or the information on it, and not a specific dollar amount of loss or other special harm. The amendments move these jurisdictional requirements to 1030(a)(5)(B), explicitly making them elements of the offense, and define "damage" to mean "*any* impairment to the integrity or availability of data, a program, a system or information." 18 U.S.C. § 1030(e)(8) (emphasis supplied).

Under this clarified structure, in order for the government to prove a violation of 1030(a)(5), it must show that the actor caused damage to a protected computer (with one of the listed mental states), and that the actor's conduct caused either loss exceeding $5,000, impairment of medical records, harm to a person, or threat to public safety. 18 U.S.C. § 1030(a)(5)(B).

Section 1030(c)—Aggregating the damage caused by a hacker's entire course of conduct

Previous law: Previous law was unclear about whether the government could aggregate the loss resulting from damage an individual caused to different protected computers in seeking to meet the jurisdictional threshold of $5,000 in loss. For example, an individual could unlawfully access five computers on a network on ten different dates—as part of a related course of conduct—but cause only $1,000 loss to each computer during each intrusion. If previous law were interpreted not to allow aggregation, then that person would not have committed a federal crime at all since he or she had not caused over $5,000 to any particular computer.

Amendment: Under the amendments in Section 814 of the Act, the government may now aggregate "loss resulting from a related course of conduct affecting one or more other protected computers" that occurs within a one year period in proving the $5,000 jurisdictional threshold for damaging a protected computer. 18 U.S.C. § 1030(a)(5)(B)(i).

Section 1030(c)(2)(C)—New offense for damaging computers used for national security and criminal justice

Previous law: Section 1030 previously had no special provision that would enhance punishment for hackers who damage computers used in furtherance of the administration of justice, national defense, or national security. Thus, federal investigators and prosecutors did not have jurisdiction over efforts to damage criminal justice and military computers where the attack did not cause over $5,000 loss (or meet one of the other special requirements). Yet these systems serve critical functions and merit felony prosecutions even where the damage is relatively slight. Indeed, attacks on computers used in the national defense that occur during periods of active military engagement are particularly serious—even if they do not cause extensive damage or disrupt the war-fighting capabilities of the military—because they divert time and attention away from the military's proper objectives. Similarly, disruption of court computer systems and data could seriously impair the integrity of the criminal justice system.

Amendment: Amendments in Section 814 of the Act create section 1030(a)(5)(B)(v) to solve this inadequacy. Under this provision, a hacker violates federal law by damaging a computer "used by or for a government entity in furtherance of the administration of justice, national defense, or national security," even if that damage does not result in provable loss over $5,000.

Subsection 1030(e)(2)—expanding the definition of "protected computer" to include computers in foreign countries

Previous law: Before the amendments in Section 814 of the Act, section 1030 of title 18 defined "protected computer" as a computer used by the federal government or a financial institution, or one "which is used in interstate or foreign commerce." 18 U.S.C. § 1030(e)(2). The definition did not explicitly include computers outside the United States.

Because of the interdependency and availability of global computer networks, hackers from within the United States are increasingly targeting systems located entirely outside of this country. The statute did not explicitly allow for prosecution of such hackers. In addition, individuals in foreign countries frequently route communications through the United States, even as they hack from one foreign country to another. In such cases, their hope may be that the lack of any U.S. victim would either prevent or discourage U.S. law enforcement agencies from assisting in any foreign investigation or prosecution.

Amendment: Section 814 of the Act amends the definition of "protected computer" to make clear that this term includes computers outside of the United States so long as they affect "interstate or foreign commerce or communication of the United States." 18 U.S.C. § 1030(e)(2)(B). By clarifying the fact that a domestic offense exists, the United States can now use speedier domestic procedures to join in international hacker investigations. As these crimes often involve investigators and victims in more than one country, fostering international law enforcement cooperation is essential.

In addition, the amendment creates the option, where appropriate, of prosecuting such criminals in the United States. Since the U.S. is urging other countries to ensure that they can vindicate the interests of U.S. victims for computer crimes that originate in their nations, this provision will allow the U.S. to provide reciprocal coverage.

Subsection 1030(e)(10)—counting state convictions as "prior offenses"

Previous law: Under previous law, the court at sentencing could, of course, consider the offender's prior convictions for State computer crime offenses. State convictions, however, did not trigger the recidivist sentencing provisions of section 1030, which double the maximum penalties available under the statute.

Amendment: Section 814 of the Act alters the definition of "conviction" so that it includes convictions for serious computer hacking crimes under State law—*i.e.*, State felonies where an element of the offense is "unauthorized access, or exceeding authorized access, to a computer." 18 U.S.C. § 1030(e)(10).

Subsection 1030(e)(11)—Definition of "loss"

Previous law: Calculating "loss" is important where the government seeks to prove that an individual caused over $5,000 loss in order to meet the jurisdictional requirements found in 1030(a)(5)(B)(i). Yet prior to the amendments in Section 814 of the Act, section 1030 of title 18 had no definition of "loss." The only court to address the scope of the definition of loss adopted an inclusive reading of what costs the government may include. In United States v. Middleton, 231 F.3d 1207, 1210–11 (9th Cir.2000), the court held that the definition of loss includes a wide range of harms typically suffered by the victims of computer crimes, including costs of responding to the offense, conducting a damage assessment, restoring the system and data to their condition prior to the offense, and any lost revenue or costs incurred because of interruption of service.

Amendments: Amendments in Section 814 codify the appropriately broad definition of loss adopted in Middleton. 18 U.S.C. § 1030(e)(11).

Section 815. Additional Defense to Civil Actions Relating to Preserving Records in Response to government Requests

Section 815 added to an existing defense to a cause for damages for violations of the Electronic Communications Privacy Act, Chapter 121 of Title 18. Under prior law it was a defense to such a cause of action to rely in good faith on a court warrant or order, a grand jury subpoena, a legislative authorization, or a statutory authorization. This amendment makes clear that the "statutory authorization" defense includes good-faith reliance on a government request to preserve evidence under 18 U.S.C. § 2703(f).

Section 816. Development and Support of Cybersecurity Forensic Capabilities

Section 816 requires the Attorney General to establish such regional computer forensic laboratories as he considers appropriate, and to provide support for existing computer forensic laboratories, to enable them to provide certain forensic and training capabilities. The provision also authorizes the spending of money to support those laboratories.

Section 817. Expansion of the Biological Weapons Statute

Section 817 expanded the coverage of existing restrictions on the possession and use of biological agents and toxins. Prior law prohibited the possession, development, acquisition, etc., of biological agents or toxins "for use as a weapon." 18 U.S.C. § 175.

Section 817 amended the definition of "for use as a weapon" to include all situations in which it can be proven that the defendant had any purpose other than a prophylactic, protective, bona fide research, or other peaceful purpose. This enhances the government's ability to prosecute suspected terrorists in possession of biological agents or toxins, and conforms the scope of the criminal offense in 18 U.S.C. § 175 more closely to the related forfeiture provision in 18 U.S.C. § 176.

Moreover, the section added a subsection to 18 U.S.C. § 175 which defines an additional offense of possessing a biological agent or toxin of a type or in a quantity that, under the circumstances, is not reasonably justified by a prophylactic, protective, bona fide research, or other peaceful purpose. Finally, this section also enacts a new statute, 18 U.S.C. § 175b, which generally makes it an offense for certain restricted persons (including felons, persons indicted for felonies, fugitives, drug users, illegal aliens, mentally impaired persons, aliens from certain terrorist states, and persons dishonorably discharged from the U.S. armed services) to possess a biological agent or toxin listed as a "select agent" by the Secretary of Health and Human Services.

* * *

Section 1004. Venue in Money Laundering Cases

In *United States v. Cabrales*, 524 U.S. 1 (1998), the Supreme Court held that a money laundering prosecution may be brought in any district where the financial or monetary transaction takes place, but not in the district where the specified unlawful activity took place, if the financial or monetary transaction occurred wholly in another district. The court suggested, however, that the situation might be different if the defendant had transported the funds from the district where the underlying crime occurred to the district where the financial or monetary transaction was conducted. In that case, the court said, the money laundering offense might be considered a continuing offense. Several courts of appeals have ruled that venue is appropriate in the district where the specified unlawful activity occurred in that situation. *See United States v. Angotti,* 105 F.3d 539 (9th Cir.1997); *United States v. Abuhouran,* 1996 WL 451368 (E.D. Pa. 1996); *United States v. Beddow,* 957 F.2d 1330 (6th Cir.1992).

Section 1004 codifies the suggestion made in *Cabrales,* making it clear that a substantive money laundering prosecution may be brought in the district where the underlying specified unlawful activity took place if the defendant participated in the movement of the criminal proceeds from that district to the district where the financial or monetary transaction occurred. It also makes clear that the transfer of funds from one district to another, such as a wire transfer of drug proceeds is a single, continuing offense, so that any defendant who conducts any part of the transfer can be prosecuted in any district in which any part of the transfer takes place. This addresses an interpretation of the current statute in *United States v. Stewart,* 256 F.3d 231 (4th Cir.2001), which held that a defendant who received drug proceeds that were transferred by wire from Virginia to California could be prosecuted only in California, because the wire transfer comprised two separate transactions: a deposit in Virginia and a withdrawal in California. Under the amendment, the defendant in that case could be prosecuted in either Virginia or California because the wire transfer would constitute a single, continuing offense in which the defendant had participated.

Finally, the amendment codifies the present rule that venue for attempts and conspiracies is not limited to the district where the completed offense would have occurred, but will lie in any district where an overt act was committed.

Section 1006. Inadmissibility of Aliens Engaged in Money Laundering

Section 1006 provides for inadmissibility of any individual whom a consular officer has reason to believe has or is engaged in certain money laundering offenses, or any criminal activity in a foreign country that would constitute such an offense if committed in the United States, regardless of whether a judgment of conviction has been entered or avoided due to flight, corruption, etc. This section treats money launderers under the same standard applicable to drug traffickers and will make our ability to exclude aliens involved in such activities less dependent upon our ability to draw inferences about a person's intent to do something illicit in the United States. Money laundering offenses are, in general, related to underlying crimes involving moral turpitude that are already grounds for exclusion under the Immigration and Nationality Act.

Section 1011. Crimes Against Charitable Americans

Section 1011, entitled the "Crimes Against Charitable Americans Act of 2001" responds to fraudulent charity scams that arose in the wake of the September 11 terrorist attack. Section 1011 has three principal provisions. First, it amends the Telemarketing and Consumer Fraud and Abuse Protection Act (15 U.S.C. § 6101 et seq.) by adding three new substantive provisions that expand the authority of the Federal Trade Commission (FTC) over telemarketing fraud and abuse. Second, it amends 18 U.S.C. § 917, which prohibits falsely impersonating a member or agent of the American National Red Cross for the purpose of soliciting, collecting, or receiving money or material. It increases the maximum term of imprisonment from one to five years, making section 917 a felony (and thereby increasing the maximum fine to $250,000).

Third, section 1011 amends the definition of "telemarketing" in the Senior Citizens Against Marketing Scams Act of 1994, 18 U.S.C. § 2325, to include a plan, program, promotion, or campaign that is conducted to induce a charitable contribution, donation, or gift of money or any other thing of value, by use of interstate telephone calls.

See 18 U.S.C. § 2325(1). This makes clear that participants in a scheme that fraudulently solicits charitable contributions or donations, even if they do not require the prospective victim to purchase other goods or services, may be subject to enhanced penalties for telemarketing fraud under 18 U.S.C. § 2326 and mandatory restitution under 18 U.S.C. § 2327.

†